22.95
T

D0209033

WHAT IS AN ANIMAL?

ONE WORLD ARCHAEOLOGY
Series Editor: P. J. Ucko

WHAT IS AN ANIMAL?

Edited by Tim Ingold

Department of Social Anthropology, University of Manchester

London and New York

First published by Unwin Hyman Ltd in 1988

First published in paperback 1994
by Routledge
11 New Fetter Lane, London EC4P 4EE

Simultaneously published in the USA and Canada
by Routledge
29 West 35th Street, New York, NY 10001

© 1988, 1994 Tim Ingold and contributors

Typeset in 10 on 11 point Bembo by Book Ens, Saffron Walden, Essex

Printed and bound in Great Britain at the University Press, Cambridge

All rights reserved. No part of this book may be reprinted or reproduced or
utilized in any form or by any electronic, mechanical, or other means, now
known or hereafter invented, including photocopying and recording, or in any
information storage or retrieval system, without permission in writing from
the publishers.

British Library Cataloguing in Publication Data
A catalogue record for this book is available from the British Library

Library of Congress Cataloging in Publication Data
    What is an animal?
    One world archaeology series: 1 – CIP foreword.
    Bibliography: p.
    Includes index.
    1. Man – Animal nature – Congresses.   2. Human behaviour – congresses.
3. Animal behaviour – congresses.
I. Ingold, Tim
GN280.7.W43   1987   128   87–29005

ISBN 0–415–09556–5

List of contributors

Stephen R. L. Clark, Department of Philosophy, University of Liverpool, UK.

Jennie Coy, Faunal Remains Unit, Department of Archaeology, University of Southampton, UK.

Brian Goodwin, Department of Biology, The Open University, Milton Keynes, UK.

Tim Ingold, Department of Social Anthropology, University of Manchester, UK.

Mary Midgley, formerly Department of Philosophy, University of Newcastle upon Tyne, UK.

Balaji Mundkur, Department of Molecular and Cell Biology, University of Connecticut, USA.

Edward S. Reed, Department of Humanities and Communications, Drexel University, Pennsylvania, USA.

Thomas A. Sebeok, Research Center for Language and Semiotic Studies, Indiana University, USA.

Nancy M. Tanner, Clark Kerr Hall, University of California, Santa Cruz, USA.

Richard L. Tapper, Department of Anthropology and Sociology, School of Oriental and African Studies, University of London, UK.

This book derives from discussions on the theme of 'Cultural Attitudes to Animals, including Birds, Fish and Invertebrates', organized by T. Ingold and M. Maltby, which took place at the World Archaeological Congress, September 1986.

Foreword

This book is one of a major series of more than 20 volumes resulting from the World Archaeological Congress held in Southampton, England, in September 1986. The series reflects the enormous academic impact of the Congress, which was attended by 850 people from more than 70 countries, and attracted many additional contributions from others who were unable to attend in person.

The *One World Archaeology* series is the result of a determined and highly successful attempt to bring together for the first time not only archaeologists and anthropologists from many different parts of the world, as well as academics from a host of contingent disciplines, but also non-academics from a wide range of cultural backgrounds, who could lend their own expertise to the discussions at the Congress. Many of the latter, accustomed to being treated as the 'subjects' of archaeological and anthropological observation, had never before been admitted as equal participants in the discussion of their own (cultural) past or present, with their own particularly vital contribution to make towards global, cross-cultural understanding.

The Congress therefore really addressed world archaeology in its widest sense. Central to a world archaeological approach is the investigation not only of how people lived in the past but also of how, and why, changes took place resulting in the forms of society and culture which exist today. Contrary to popular belief, and the archaeology of some 20 years ago, world archaeology is much more than the mere recording of specific historical events, embracing as it does the study of social and cultural change in its entirety. All the books in the *One World Archaeology* series are the result of meetings and discussions which took place within a context that encouraged a feeling of self-criticism and humility in the participants about their own interpretations and concepts of the past. Many participants experienced a new self-awareness, as well as a degree of awe about past and present human endeavours, all of which is reflected in this unique series.

The Congress was organized around major themes. Several of these themes were based on the discussion of full-length papers which had been circulated some months previously to all who had indicated a special interest in them. Other sessions, including some dealing with areas of specialization defined by period or geographical region, were based on oral addresses, or a combination of pre-circulated papers and lectures. In all cases, the entire sessions were recorded on cassette, and all contributors were presented with the recordings of the discussion of their papers. A major part of the thinking behind the Congress was that a meeting of many hundreds of participants that did not leave behind a published record of its academic discussions would be little more than an exercise in tourism.

Thus, from the very beginning of the detailed planning for the World Archaeological Congress, in 1982, the intention was to produce post-Congress books containing a selection only of the contributions, revised in the light of discussions during the sessions themselves as well as during subsequent consultations with the academic editors appointed for each book. From the outset, contributors to the Congress knew that if their papers were selected for publication, they would have only a few months to revise them according to editorial specifications, and that they would become authors in an important academic volume scheduled to appear within a reasonable period following the Southampton meeting.

The speed in publishing the series reflects the intense planning which took place before the Congress. Not only were all contributors aware of the subsequent production schedules, but also session organizers were already planning their books before and during the Congress. The editors were entitled to commission additional chapters for their books when they felt that there were significant gaps in the coverage of a topic during the Congress, or where discussion at the Congress indicated a need for additional contributions.

One of the main themes of the Congress was devoted to 'Cultural Attitudes to Animals, including Birds, Fish and Invertebrates'. The theme was based on discussion of precirculated full-length papers, covering four and a half days, and was under the overall control of Dr Tim Ingold, Senior Lecturer in the Department of Social Anthropology, University of Manchester, and Mark Maltby, Research Fellow in the Faunal Remains Unit of the Department of Archaeology, University of Southampton. The choice of this topic for a major theme arose from a desire to explore, from an interdisciplinary perspective, the many facets of the varying relationships that have developed between humans and animals, as these are reflected by the historical diversity of cultural traditions.

Discussions during the Congress were grouped around four main headings, each of which has led to the publication of a book. The first, organized by Tim Ingold, was concerned with 'What is an Animal?', leading to this book of the same title. The second subtheme, on 'The Appropriation, Domination and Exploitation of Animals', lasted for over a day and a half and was under the control of Juliet Clutton-Brock, editor of the volume *The walking larder: Patterns of domestication, pastoralism, and predation*. A day was devoted to discussion of the 'Semantics of Animal Symbolism' and the co-ordinator, Roy Willis, is also the editor of the resulting book on *Signifying animals: Human meaning in the natural world*. Howard Morphy was in charge of the fourth sub-theme on 'Learning from Art about the Cultural Relationships between Humans and Animals', and has edited the volume on *Animals into art*.

The overall theme took as its starting point the assumption that there is no *one* human attitude consistently maintained towards a particular species of animal, and that similar human sentiments have been attached to a huge variety of different animals at different times and in different places. It set out to investigate the similarities and differences in practices and beliefs connected with animals, inluding birds, fish and invertebrates, across both time and space.

Prior to this century, in the West, animal behaviour was usually portrayed and interpreted in terms of a contrast with human behaviour. Darwin was not alone in his frequent adoption of an anthropocentric perspective in formulating questions and in presenting hypotheses and interpretations. It has often been claimed that people of non-western cultures generally view animals quite differently.

Another aim of the Congress theme was to explore such contrasts and to suggest some of the factors underlying both anthropomorphic and anthropocentric perceptions of animals which are currently prevalent at least in Western society.

Ecological, psychological, cultural, and utilitarian considerations are all involved in peoples' attitudes to, and treatment of, other species. These factors were considered not only from a wide, interdisciplinary point of view but also, as befits a world archaeological context, especially in an historical perspective, giving due emphasis to their changes over time.

For example, in the West when those of us who live in towns and cities think of dogs and cats we usually think of them as companions, although dogs are also, in other contexts, considered essential for herding, guarding, and hunting other animals. In ancient Egypt, cats were often shown in artwork as pets, but they were possibly also used to hunt and catch birds. In many present-day cultures across the world people think of quite different animals, such as cattle and pigs, as friends or companions. On the other hand, the hyaena is normally considered by the layman today to be wild and untrainable, yet an ancient Egyptian representation appears to show one being handled. Once we move beyond the normal level of trying to ascertain from any excavation simply what animals were eaten or used for transportation, we are bound to look again at the nature of the relationships and interactions between human groups and the animals in their environments. Another aim of this theme, therefore, was to investigate how different people think, and thought, about different classes of animals, to discover the principles of classification involved, and to show how these principles constituted logical systems of belief and action. The presence of so many Congress participants from the so-called Third and Fourth Worlds made it possible to embrace a truly cross-cultural perspective on these issues.

One point of interest lies in the investigation, on a world-wide basis, of the reasons why particular animals have been domesticated by humans –whether for food, such as meat or milk, or for other reasons, such as for ritual purposes.

Contributors to the theme on 'Cultural Attitudes to Animals' adopted a variety of perspectives for looking at the complex ways that past and present humans have interrelated with beings they classify as animals. Some of these perspectives were predominantly economic and ecological, others were symbolic, concerned with the classification of both the physical and the social environment, and still others were primarily philosophical or theological. All these different perspectives are required for a full interpretation of the artworks of the past, which in their representations of humans and animals reveal some of the foci and inspirations of cultural attitudes to animals.

In focusing on the nature of the varying relationships that can develop between humans and animals, one is led inevitably to the question: what actually is an animal or a human? By asking such a question, archaeologists and others are forced to become aware of their own individual and cultural preconceptions, and to pay attention to a set of problems concerning attitudes.

In this book Tim Ingold and his contributors set out to show what the distinction drawn (if drawn at all) between human and animal in any society, of whatever period and in whatever part of the world, reveals about the characteristics of the social humans who together form that particular culture. Contrary to the normal assumption, the borderline between humans and animals, or more specifically between humans and birds, fish or invertebrates, is anything but obvious, clear and immutable.

As a striking example of this, we may recall that the first explorers of foreign lands sometimes classed their human inhabitants alongside apes, whereas others assumed monkeys and apes to be humans. This book discusses how humans have attempted to decide what to recognize as human or animal, or as animals of particular kinds such as fish, birds or invertebrates.

What is an animal? reveals that our Western European classification of human versus non-human, derived from Judeo-Christian and Classical traditions, does not conform to those of many past cultures. This realization of the essentially subjective nature of arguments about what features should come together to constitute a human being has profound implications. Few of us who live in cities in the West, or for that matter our children, have any direct contact with animals other than certain variants of cats and dogs. Our conceptual stereotypes of humans and animals derive largely from television, nature films, and books. This book is a striking demonstration of the complexity of human attempts to define the human, and is in itself a concrete example of how human endeavour differs from the works of other animals.

What is an animal? is particularly fitting as the first book in the *One World Archaeology* series. It is a demonstration of the breadth of concern of modern archaeology and the essentially interdisciplinary nature of archaeological and anthropological investigation and interpretation.

P. J. Ucko
Southampton

Contents

When I carefully consider the curious habits of dogs
I am compelled to conclude
That man is the superior animal.

When I consider the curious habits of man
I confess, my friend, I am puzzled.

Ezra Pound

Reprinted by permission of Faber and Faber Ltd
from *Collected shorter poems* by Ezra Pound

Preface

Apart from the chapter by Tapper, who chaired this session of the Congress, all of the chapters in this book are more- or less-heavily revised versions of papers originally prepared for the Congress itself and precirculated to participants. The chapters by Coy and Mundkur were presented in two subsequent sessions, on 'The Appropriation, Domination and Exploitation of Animals' and 'The Semantics of Animal Symbolism', respectively, but were considered to be more suited to this book. Unfortunately, neither Reed nor Clark was able to attend the Congress, and their contributions were discussed in their absence. Clark wishes it to be known that he did not attend because of his objection to the decision of the Congress to exclude South African and Namibian participants.

T. Ingold

Preface to the paperback edition

My brief, in writing this preface, is to report on developments concerning the theme of the volume since its original publication, and to place it within the context of current thinking in archaeology and anthropology. The first objective is not easily achieved within a limited compass. Since the volume is, by nature, interdisciplinary, and since the issues with which it deals are so general and fundamental, a report of the kind called for would entail reviewing five years of work in fields as diverse as biology, philosophy, psychology and semiotics, not to mention archaeology and anthropology. Moreover, to the basic question 'What is an animal?', we cannot claim to be any closer to a final answer – but this is because the question is not one of the kind that admits such an answer. The purpose of asking it is that it forces us to be more explicit about the assumptions that we carry into the search for answers to other, more limited questions, of a kind more amenable to empirical investigation. Many of these questions, concerning – say – the zoological characteristics of this or that animal species, lie beyond the scope of anthropological and archaeological inquiry. But there are three kinds of questions, in particular, that are central to the concerns of these disciplines. The first have to do with the specific capacities of human beings and their establishment in the course of evolution; the second bear on the history of relations between human beings and other animals, and the third concern the range of ideas that people have held, in different times and places, about the kinds of beings that animals are. In what follows I shall take a brief look at these questions in the light of recent developments in archaeology and anthropology.

Perhaps the central problem in the study of human evolution has been to account for the origins of what is called the 'capacity for culture'. Current investigations have tended to converge on the position that this capacity, with its foundations in language and self-awareness, emerged much more recently than previously thought – around 40 thousand years ago, at the end point rather than during the initial stages of the process of hominization. It is marked by a series of features without precedent in the archaeological record: regionally specific tool traditions, highly structured camp sites, exotic trade goods, art and ornamentation, ritualistic burials, and so on. The people responsible for these features are said to have been anatomically and behaviourally 'modern' humans, *Homo sapiens sapiens*, 'like us'. That is, they were endowed with all the capacities, of language, intelligence and technical proficiency, that contemporary humans possess today. They did not, of course, live in cities, ride bicycles or write scientific monographs – not, however, because of any constitutional incapability, but because the historical processes that established the possibility of such activities had yet to run their course. Thus the histories of science and technology, for example, belong to the progressive realization of an innate capacity, not to its evolution. Upper Palaeolithic hunter-gatherers are placed accordingly at the point of intersection of two continua: the one evolutionary, leading from ancestral pongid and hominid forms to 'modern' humans; the other historical, leading from technologically and organizationally 'simple' forms of society to advanced industrial civilization.

In order to reconcile the process whereby apes became human with that whereby humans became scientists, it is necessary to suppose that at some point – by an event or chain of events without parallel in the entire history of life – our ancestors crossed a threshold to culture, and in so doing launched themselves onto an entirely new plane of existence, ideational rather than physical. This supposition, however, is deeply problematic. For one thing, it goes against the premise of evolutionary continuity, to the effect that the human is just another species of nature. Yet scientists, at least, have to place themselves above the natural world, in order to be in a position to imagine the rest of humanity to be immersed within it. Their claim that human beings differ in degree and not kind from other animals derives its very authority from a historical process – the advance of science – that differs in kind, not degree, from the process of evolution. For another thing, a definition of humanity in terms of the achievement of culture sits uneasily with the genealogical principle whereby taxa are normally defined in modern (i.e. post-Darwinian) biology. According to this principle, there is no way in which the descendants of present-day chimpanzees or whales could become human beings. Yet who is to say that they will not, at some future time, develop symbolic and linguistic competences of their own – that is, if they have not done so already? Would they not then be non-human human animals?

Indeed, we are forever being challenged by the results of research on ape language, which now seem to show that chimpanzees reared in a human environment with speaking caregivers are capable of the spontaneous acquisition of linguistic syntax and semantics of a complexity equivalent to that used by small children. Chimpanzees reared under 'natural' conditions, however, do not learn to speak. The question that we need to ask ourselves is this: in what way, if at all, does the 'wild' chimpanzee's failure to speak differ from the failure of Upper Palaeolithic hunter-gatherers to read and write? How can we justify the attribution of the former to innate incapacity, when the latter is attributed to unfulfilled historical conditions? A comparable challenge is presented by evidence showing that while humans of an *anatomically* modern form appeared at least 130 thousand years ago, it took another 90 thousand years before any signs appeared of modern human *behaviour*. I believe that the only way to meet challenges of this kind is by radically rethinking the concept of 'capacity'. For people are no more born with the capacity to speak than they are with the capacity to read and write. Such capacities *develop* in the early life of each individual, and they will only do so if the appropriate conditions are present not only internally, in the composition of the genome, but also in the surrounding environment. Thus capacities are properties not of the genotype, but of the total developmental system constituted by a nexus of reactants both internal (including genes) and external to the organism.

It follows that it is pointless to ask whether chimpanzees, modern humans or pre-human hominids 'have' or 'had' language, culture or whatever, as though these capacities were programmed into them from the start. Or, more generally, if capacities are to be attributed to an animal, then the environment must form part of the specification of what that animal is, along with other components of the developmental system through which it comes into being. And since animals, in their practical activities, can modify the environmental conditions of development for successor generations, developmental systems – and the capacities specified therein – can go on evolving with or without any corresponding change in the genotype. In this respect the evolution of supposedly 'acquired' capacities, such as reading and writing or riding a bicycle, is no different from that of supposedly 'innate' capacities, such as speech or bipedal locomotion. By taking the animal-in-its-environment as our point of departure, we can dispense with the dichotomies between biology and culture, and between evolution and history, that up to now have been the source of so much trouble in anthropological thinking. We might even begin to be able to break down the intellectual barriers that currently divide biological anthropology from the social and cultural branches of the discipline. But this task cannot be achieved so long as the structure of contemporary evolutionary theory is retained intact. Short of having one theory for humans and another for every other life-form, the only alternative is to devise a theory of evolution that can accommodate genotypic change within a more comprehensive account of the transformation by organisms, in the contexts of their mutual relations, of their respective conditions of development. As human beings, specifically, make their own history, so animals in general are the causes and consequences of their own evolution.

Let me now turn to my second theme, which concerns the history of relations between human beings and other animals. Once again, we find the contradiction between the human as a species of animal and humanity as a condition *opposed* to animality playing havoc with anthropological and archaeological thinking. I should like to draw attention to three areas in which this is particularly apparent.

The first has to do with the application of so-called 'optimal foraging theory'. This theory aims to model the interactions between human hunter-gatherers and their prey on the expectation that the former will adopt strategies of procurement that will maximize their rate of energy gain. The theory itself comes from biology – or more precisely from studies of animal behaviour conducted within the framework of evolutionary ecology – and is premised on the assumption that energetically optimal strategies will generally be advantageous in terms of reproductive fitness, and will therefore tend to become established through natural selection. What happens, then, when the theory is applied to human behaviour? Suppose that its predictions are reasonably borne out in practice (as indeed they often are): what has been shown? That hunter-gatherers unthinkingly follow procurement strategies that have already been devised for them by natural selection working, if not on genetic traits, then on some cultural analogue of these, likewise transmitted to offspring through the reproduction of their carriers? Or that hunter-gatherers are just as capable as optimal foraging theorists of working out what is in their best interests, and acting accordingly? On the one hand, as beings whose lives are still supposedly encompassed, like those of non-human animals, within the world of nature, human hunter-gatherers are considered peculiarly apt as targets for an approach originally designed to show how animals, presumed to lack the faculty of reason, nevertheless come up with strategies that would appear highly rational, had they worked them out for themselves. On the other hand, as human beings, hunter-gatherers should be as well endowed with reason as are Western scientists and economists. And so, optimal foraging theorists contrive to have it both ways, claiming thereby to have achieved a miraculous synthesis between neo-Darwinian biology and neo-classical microeconomics! In the figure of the primitive hunter-gatherer are combined the selective principles of nature and reason, on whose separation the practice of science depends.

   The second area concerns the transformations in the relations between humans and animals in the movement from hunting to pastoralism or other forms of animal husbandry. The received vocabulary for characterizing human activities towards their environmental resources offers just two general terms: collection (or foraging) and production. Collection, common to human hunter-gatherers and non-human foragers, is envisaged as an *interaction* in nature; production, common to human agriculturalists and pastoralists, is seen as a planned *intervention* in nature. In order to be in a position to intervene, producers must have achieved that mastery or control over the world of nature that hunter-gatherers are supposed to lack, and that is commonly denoted by the concept of domestication. Thus the difference between collection and production corresponds to that between the opposed views of humanity outlined above: as a species of animal and as a state of transcendence over animality. When, however, we turn to look at the ways in which hunters and pastoralists *actually* relate to animals, as opposed to the ways in which these relations are constructed in Western discourse on humanity and animality, we find that neither of the terms on offer provides an adequate characterization. Hunting cannot be reduced to predation as it is modelled in animal ecology – the mere behavioural execution of a precalculated foraging strategy, mechanically triggered by given environmental stimuli. It is rather a mode of skilled and attentive engagement with non-human animals which, since they are also possessed of powers of agency, are likewise attending to the hunter. Similarly with pastoralism, the herdsman's control over his animals is premised on the assumption that the latter, like human slaves, are sentient beings with the capacity to act and suffer. No *absolute* boundary, then, separates the domain of human involvement with non-human animals from the domain of their involvement with one another. True, the quality of this involvement differs profoundly as between hunting and pastoral societies – a difference that I have elsewhere characterized in terms of a contrast between *trust* and *domination*. But the contrast applies equally to relations both with humans and with non-humans. Far from marking the outer limits of the social world, the border between the human and the non-human delineates a particular region within it.

The third area concerns the principles of conservation. These principles, as formulated by Western science, are firmly rooted in the doctrine of the human transcendence of nature. Indeed it is often inferred that merely by virtue of their presence in an environment, human beings – at least of the 'civilized' variety – are bound to alter it from its 'natural' state. We consequently tend to think that the only environments that persist in a genuinely pristine condition are those remaining beyond the bounds of human civilization. Likewise, the wild animal that lives an authentically natural life is one untainted by human contact (a view, incidentally, that has stymied research on domestic animals: once in the service of man, it seems, an animal is no longer a proper object of scientific inquiry). Scientific conservation works, accordingly, by sealing off portions of the environment and their animal inhabitants, and by restricting intervention so as to exclude any possibility of direct participation. However, many areas designated for conservation are also home to indigenous peoples – most often to hunter-gatherers who are not thought to have altered the environment to any significant extent. For conservationists, their presence can be a source of acute embarrassment, since there is no way of accommodating them within schemes of scientific conservation *except as parts of the wildlife*. Yet again, we find a double standard being applied for humanity: one for the scientist as conserver of nature, the other for the hunter-gatherer as a species of nature conserved. But hunter-gatherers, too, regard themselves as the conservers of their environments, entrusted with the responsibility for 'looking after' it. Not for them, however, the detached, hands-off approach of the scientist. On the contrary, they see themselves as caring for the plants and animals in the environment with the same close and affectionate involvement that they bring to caring for other people. Hence they find no contradiction between conservation and participation.

This brings me to my final theme – that of cultural variation in peoples' ideas about what kinds of beings animals are. Such variation is abundantly documented in ethnographic accounts. The key question, however, is: what is the relation between these ideas and the ontological assumptions that anthropologists have brought to the task of documentation? The latter are epitomized in the formula 'nature is culturally constructed'. In this formula, nature appears in two guises: as a biophysical reality 'out there' with an existence quite independent of people's minds; and as it is given form and meaning within one or another system of collective mental representations. Conventionally, the former – 'really natural nature' – is taken to be the object of inquiry for natural science, leaving the latter – 'culturally perceived nature' – as the object of interest for anthropology. And by the same token, natural scientists study real animals, whereas cultural anthropologists study 'animals of the mind'. But there is a paradox here. For in the Western mind, animals (with the possible exception of pets) are creatures of nature, excluded in consequence from direct participation in the world of human society and its relationships. For many if not most non-Western peoples, by contrast, both human beings and non-human animals participate in the *same* world of persons. Yet the Western ontology, with its separation of humanity and nature, is implicit in the very project that sets up these Western and non-Western views as objects for comparison in the first place. It is thus an illusion to suppose that they can be compared on level terms.

To the non-Western claim that animals are, or can be, persons, the usual anthropological response is to observe that, of course, this is not *really* so – the people are merely allowing themselves to be deceived by their liberal (and, to them, unrecognized as such) use of anthropomorphic metaphor. Thus the animal world is said to be culturally constructed in the image of human society. By this device, the challenge that the non-Western claim presents to Western ontology is conveniently neutralized: it can be treated as 'just another' cultural construction of reality, alternative to the Western one. What happens if, on the contrary, we treat this claim with the seriousness it deserves, by starting out from the ontological premise that non-human animals do indeed participate in the same world as ourselves?

We might commence from an observation with which both Western and non-Western thinkers would surely agree: that what human beings and non-human animals have in common is that they are *alive*. In Western biology, however, life tends to be understood as the reaction of organisms, bound by their separate natures, to the given conditions of their respective environments. Thus every organism must be specified, with regard to its essential nature, *prior* to its entry into the life process – a specification which, in modern biology, is attributed to the genome. With this view of life, personal powers – of awareness, agency and intentionality – can form no part of the organism *as such*, but must necessarily be 'added on' as capacities not of body but of mind, capacities that Western thought has traditionally reserved for humans. Even today, now that the possibility of non-human animal awareness has arisen as a legitimate topic of scientific speculation, the basic dualism of body and mind is retained – for the question is phrased as one about the existence of animal *minds*.

If we listen to what non-Western peoples (and indeed certain Western philosophers critical of mainstream thought) are telling us, we can begin to grasp a quite different view of life: not as the revelation of pre-specified forms but as the process wherein forms are generated. Every living being, as it is caught up in this process and carries it forward, arises as an undivided centre of awareness and agency – an enfoldment, at some particular nexus, of the generative potential of a total field of relations. Thus personhood, far from being 'added on' to the animal, is implicated in the very condition of being alive. Animals are not just *like* persons, they *are* persons. As organism-persons and fellow participants in the life process, human beings and non-human animals are ontologically equivalent. It follows that it is no more anthropomorphic to liken the animal to the human than it is zoomorphic to liken the human to the animal. The object of such comparisons, whether drawn in one direction or the other, is not to establish figurative parallels across domains – of humanity and animality – that are fundamentally distinct, but rather to reveal the underlying level on which humans and non-human animals share the *same* existential status, as living beings or persons. In other words, the use of metaphor should be understood as a way of drawing attention to real relational unities rather than of figuratively papering over dualities.

It has become almost commonplace in recent anthropology to expose the artificiality of the nature/culture dichotomy as a particular product of the Western tradition of thought and science. Over and over again, it has been shown that people from other backgrounds do not make this distinction. Yet anthropologists continue to cling to it as the foundation upon which they are able to distinguish their comparative project from that of natural science. Thus, whereas scientists compare species in nature, of which the human is but one, anthropologists compare peoples' *views* of natural species, of which the 'Western scientific' is but one. I believe, however, that an anthropologically informed critique of Western science, taken to its logical conclusion, requires a much more radical step. We need to make a fresh start in understanding ourselves and other animals, for which the point of departure is the inescapable fact of their mutual involvement, as centres of perception and action, in a continuous life process. For it is only from a position of such involvement, not from a platform above the world, that human beings are able to launch their imaginative speculations about what that world – including its animal inhabitants – is like.

Tim Ingold
Manchester, January 1993

1 Introduction

TIM INGOLD

All human societies, past and present, have coexisted with populations of animals of one or many species. Throughout history, people have variously killed and eaten animals, or on rarer occasions been killed and eaten by them; incorporated animals into their social groups, whether as domestic familiars or captive slaves; and drawn upon their observations of animal morphology and behaviour in the construction of their own designs for living. People's ideas about animals, and attitudes towards them, are correspondingly every bit as variable as their ways of relating to one another, in both cases reflecting that astonishing diversity of cultural tradition that is widely thought to be the hallmark of humanity. Yet, in the recognition of this diversity, we are immediately presented with an awkward paradox. How can we reach a comparative understanding of human cultural attitudes towards animals if the very conception of what an animal might be, and by implication of what it means to be human, is itself culturally relative? Does not the anthropological project of cross-cultural comparison rest upon an implicit assumption of human uniqueness *vis-à-vis* other animals that is fundamentally anthropocentric? Moreover if we follow the promptings of modern evolutionary theory in recognizing the essential continuity between human and non-human animals, does this not entail the adoption of an ethnocentrically 'Western' conception of human nature? Is it possible, even in theory, simultaneously to transcend the limitations of *both* anthropocentrism and ethnocentrism?

With dilemmas such as these in mind, the programme for the major theme of the World Archaeological Congress on 'Cultural Attitudes to Animals' was prefaced by a session in which contributors were invited to address the key question 'What is an animal?'. Each contributor was asked to tackle the question from his or her personal or disciplinary point of view, and I made a deliberate attempt to include perspectives from as wide a range of disciplines as possible, including social and cultural anthropology, archaeology, biology, psychology, philosophy and semiotics. It came as no surprise that my question spawned answers of very different kinds, and that they disagreed on many fundamental points of principle. Perhaps more surprising was the degree of passion aroused in the course of the discussion, which seemed to confirm two points on which I think all the contributors would agree: first, that there is a strong emotional undercurrent to our ideas about animality; and, secondly, that to subject these ideas to critical scrutiny is to expose highly sensitive and largely unexplored aspects of the understanding of our own humanity.

The limits of the animate

Of course, the question 'What is an animal?' can itself be construed in any number of ways, all of which are concerned with problems surrounding the definition of boundaries, whether between humans and non-human animals, animals and plants, or living and non-living. The last of these boundaries is the most inclusive, for it rests upon the criterion of animacy, on the very distinction between animate and inanimate objects. This is a central theme in two of the contributions to this volume: those by Reed and Goodwin. Reed argues that the distinctive property of animate beings lies in their capacity for autonomous movement – that is, movement is what animals do, rather than the mechanical resultant of what is done to them. This leads him to ask what one animal can afford to another in its environment that an inanimate object cannot. He shows that, besides being autonomous agents which can 'act back' or literally interact, all animate objects have the property of undergoing growth and that, unlike machines, their activity is never perfectly repetitive. For Goodwin these dynamic properties of organisms represent the starting point from which he attempts to resolve the problem of the generation of form in biology, a problem that until now has proved resistant to approaches couched in terms of a conventional, reductionist paradigm inspired by the Cartesian view of the animal as a complex automaton. Adopting a logic of process, he shows that the stability of form is not given by the interaction of its elementary constituents, but is actively 'held in place' by a movement of intention: thus, change is primitive, persistence is derived. In Goodwin's words 'it is not composition that determines organismic form and transformation, but dynamic organization'. From this he concludes that the animal is not an automaton but 'a centre of immanent, self-generating or creative power', one locus in the continuous unfolding or modulation of a total field of relations. But to take this philosophy of process to its ultimate conclusion is to dissolve the very boundaries of the animate, to recognize that in a certain sense the entire world is an organism, and its unfolding an organic process.

Rather less inclusively, the question 'What is an animal?' is one of macrotaxonomy – of distinguishing animals from the other major classes of life forms such as plants, fungi and bacteria. This is one sense in which the question is taken up by Sebeok. He begins with a characterization of the fundamental properties of living systems, which link two processes: one of energy conversion, the other an exchange of information. All organisms receive signs from their environments, transmuting them into outputs consisting of further signs, but this sign-process – or *semiosis* – may be radically different for animals from what it is (say) for plants. The varieties of semiosis, raising fascinating questions (to which I shall return) concerning the ways in which organisms of different kinds engage in the construction of their own environments, provide one basis for their possible taxonomic distinction. Sebeok reviews semiotic and other 'scientific' macrotaxonomic criteria by which animals may be distinguished from other forms. There are, of course, many alternative criteria, and hence there can be multiple taxonomies, whose number is immeasurably increased if we accord equivalent value (and validity, on their own terms) to the 'folk' taxonomies of other cultures, based as they often are on a profound practical and theoretical knowledge of the natural world. Just as a deeper understanding of a myth, following the advice of Lévi-Strauss (1985), may be obtained from the simultaneous reading of its many versions, so perhaps we can come closer to discovering the meaning of the 'animal' by treating each taxonomy as one of a set, each providing a partial answer to a problem whose complete solution requires a reading of the entire set as a structured totality.

Animality and humanity

Although our question touches on the properties of both life and the major classes of organisms, it is more popularly construed, narrowly and reflexively, as a question about *ourselves*. Every attribute that it is claimed we uniquely have, the animal is consequently supposed to lack; thus, the generic concept of 'animal' is negatively constituted by the sum of these deficiencies. But as Clark observes in his contribution to this book, whatever attributes might popularly be selected as the distinguishing marks of humanity (and these vary from one culture to another), we shall find some creatures born of man and woman who – for whatever reason – fail to qualify (see also Hull 1984, p. 35). One controversial attribute, which I discuss later but which will serve for now as an example, is the faculty of language. There are some individuals of human descent who lack this faculty. To date, no animal of any other species has conclusively been shown to possess it, though many claims to this effect have been made. But this does not mean that one may never be found, nor does it rule out the possibility that a linguistic capacity fully equal to our own might, in future times, evolve quite independently in some other line of descent, without its bearers thereby joining the human species.

Supposing that humanity were defined as *Homo loquens*, a natural kind including all animals with language and speech, we would have to admit the possibility both of individuals of human parentage 'dropping out' of humankind, and of individuals of non-human parentage 'coming in'. But if by humanity we mean the biological species *Homo sapiens*, the former would unequivocally belong and the latter would not. Comparing 'folk' and 'scientific' taxonomies, Clark shows that biological species (our own included) are *not* natural kinds. That is, the individuals of a species are linked by their genealogical connection, as actual co-descendants of a common ancestor or as potential co-ancestors of a common descendant. Given the variability and unpredictability of the similarities and differences between individual human beings and organisms of other species, it follows that if the boundaries of the moral community are defined sufficiently widely to embrace all human beings and their future descendants, then by the same token they must embrace the non-human animals with which humans share a common ancestry. This at once calls into question even the best-intentioned attempts to validate our moral and political ideals by appeal to a common, species-specific humanity, and has considerable implications with regard to our responsibilities towards non-human animals. For it inevitably blurs those comfortable distinctions by which we order our lives: between domestication and slavery, hunting and homicide, and carnivory and cannibalism.

As Midgley points out, in her discussion of the history of the terms 'animal' and 'beast', the former term is now commonly employed in two contradictory senses: one benign and inclusive of humanity, the other negative and exclusive, denoting all that is considered inhuman or anti-human. Tapper remarks on the same phenomenon, noting how this ambivalence in the conception of animals, as both akin to us yet alien in their ways, makes them peculiarly apposite as models or exemplars in the process of socialization, or the intergenerational transmission of culture and morality. Coy also observes the inconsistency, in recent Western literature on animal welfare, between treating animals as 'dumb beasts' that are worthy of protection, and attributing to them the full gamut of human feelings. These contradictions stem, to a large degree, from our propensity to switch back and forth between two quite different approaches to the definition of animality: as a domain or 'kingdom', including humans; and as a state or condition, opposed to humanity (see Fig. 1.1). In the context of the first approach, humankind is identified with the biological taxon *Homo sapiens*, one of an immense number of animal species inhabiting the Earth, connected synchronically in a complex web

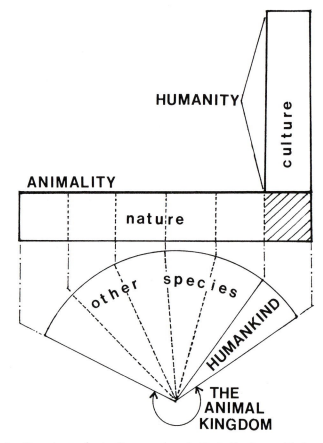

Figure 1.1   Two views of animality: as a domain (including humankind) and as a condition (excluding humanity). The shaded area represents human nature, or 'human animality'.

of ecological interdependencies, and diachronically in the all-encompassing genealogy of phylogenetic evolution. Quite clearly the process of 'becoming human', which Tanner charts in her chapter, although it entailed a unique sequence of morphological and behavioural innovations, was not a movement out of animality but an extension of its frontiers. In this sense, modern humans are no less 'animal' than Australopithecines or chimpanzees.

Yet, following the second approach, the concept of animality has been employed to characterize a state of being otherwise known as 'natural', in which actions are impelled by innate emotional drives that are undisciplined by reason or responsibility. In this guise it has been extended to describe the imagined condition of human beings 'in the raw', untouched by the values and mores of culture or civilization. 'Becoming human', then, is tantamount to the process of enculturation which virtually all children of our species undergo in their passage to maturity and which – according to an earlier anthropology – the entire species is destined to undergo in its uneven passage towards civilization. This view of emergent humanity – as an overcoming of, rather than an extension of, intrinsic animality – lay behind the attempts of many 19th-century anthropologists to reconstruct 'human nature' as a universal baseline for all subsequent social and cultural evolution. It continues to inform much of the more popular sociobiological speculation on the same theme, which usually takes the form of a search for the prototypes of human behavioural responses in the innate repertoire of other species. The approach is exemplified in this book by Mundkur, though in substance his contribution is in a different class altogether, since it is backed by a formidable, discipline-spanning erudition and a colossal weight of empirical documentation of the kind that most human sociobiology so conspicuously lacks.

Mundkur is concerned to uncover the primordial foundations of what he calls 'religiosity', defined as 'a state of mind incited by belief in forces perceived as supernatural'. This state of mind, he argues, is embedded in the emotion of fear which is demonstrably wired-in to the sensory systems of at least all higher vertebrates, and which has clear adaptive functions that would have promoted its establishment under pressures of natural selection. What appears, in the history of religions, as an almost capricious diversity of belief and practice, is in fact this base religiosity refracted in countless ways through the cultural traditions that have been superimposed upon it. It is rather significant that Mundkur presents his project as an enquiry into 'human animality', an enquiry that calls for mechanistic explanations couched in terms of the 'harder' biological sciences – genetics, biochemistry and neurophysiology. Of course, this kind of enquiry is anathema to many social and cultural anthropologists for whom, as Tapper notes, 'human nature *is* cultural diversity'. From their perspective the essence of humanity is constituted, *in opposition* to animality, by a 'capacity for culture' whose historical and contemporary manifestations make up the subject of study for the range of disciplines collectively known as the 'humanities'. Paradoxically, the sociobiological quest for the rudiments of human nature turns out to be an attempt to discover what is *inhuman* in man – to characterize the human being stripped of humanity, revealing an animal residue.

Thus, although as members of a particular species human beings unquestionably belong to the animal kingdom, they are also seen to embody two contrary conditions, to which Western thought has attached the labels of animality and humanity (Fig. 1.1). Of these the latter points to the status of the particular human being as a person, an agent endowed with intentions and purposes, motivated in his or her actions by social values and a moral conscience. The conceptual ambiguity is no accident; it reflects a widely held belief that (with the exception of quasi-human animals such as pets) personhood as a state of being is open only to individuals of the species *Homo sapiens*, both the moral condition and the biological taxon being conflated under the single rubric of 'humanity'. According to this belief, whereas humans can behave in a way that is considered 'inhuman' or 'bestial' if they allow themselves to be unduly swayed by primordial passions (particularly the nastier ones), animals of other species can *only* act 'as if continually in a passion', and therefore – like human infants – they are in no way responsible or accountable for what they do (Shotter 1984, p. 42). It follows that although we may, following Mundkur's example, launch an enquiry into human animality, *there can be no enquiry into the humanity of non-human animals.* That is, acts which, if performed by humans, we would have no hesitation in regarding as intentionally motivated and culturally designed would, if performed by animals, have to be explained as the automatic output of an innate, genetically determined neural mechanism.

Intentionality and language

Midgley has trenchantly exposed the double standards inherent in this view. Why, she asks, should intentionality be excluded from the scientific conception of the animal, even though it seems self-evident to practical people who have actually worked with such animals as dogs, elephants or chimpanzees that their actions have an intentional component, just as the intentionality of our own actions is self-evident to us? Her answer is that the science of animal behaviour has been deluded by a kind of 'species solipsism', a sceptical pretence of ignorance about the content of animals' conscious states. In their attempts to account for the often very complex and variable performances of other species, in a way that does not transgress the conventional bounds of animality, scientists have been forced either to simplify their descriptions of what the animals do by omitting troublesome detail, or to propose the most tortuous and convoluted mechanisms for generating the observed patterns. Yet the normal, scientifically approved principle of explanatory parsimony, if consistently applied, would favour much more economical accounts couched in terms of the animals' abilities to make their own adjustments of means to ends through a process of rational deliberation.

The view that non-human animals may be regarded as self-conscious subjects with thoughts and feelings of their own is still something of a heresy in ethological and psychological circles. It has been vigorously championed in recent years by Griffin (1984), of whose work Midgley is a strong advocate. Griffin's ideas on the question of animal awareness are also discussed in this book by Coy and by Ingold. Coy admits some scepticism, but is prepared to accept the notion that non-human animals engage in conscious thinking at least as a working hypothesis, and in order to redress the heavy Cartesian bias in favour of the view that they do not. There is, after all, no *a priori* reason why the latter should be accorded more credibility than the former. Moreover, the kinds of selective pressures that might have promoted the development of conscious awareness in humans should have been equally at work on other species with which humans have had close and lasting contacts. Coy suggests that these pressures would have lain in the adaptive advantages for the individual of one species conferred by the ability to predict the likely actions of individuals of the same or another species – whether predators, competitors or prey. Thus, to the extent that the human hunter benefits from forecasting the reactions of the deer, so the deer benefits from being able to predict the hunter's prediction, and to confound it by exercising autonomous powers of intentional action. So every increment in the development of awareness on one side of the interspecific relationship would increase the pressure for further development on the other, and vice versa.

Where Midgley is an advocate and Coy a sceptic, Ingold is strongly critical of Griffin's arguments. His criticisms hinge on the controversial issue of whether non-human animals are endowed with the faculty of language, an issue that is also touched upon briefly by Tanner. Her point is that the claim 'humans alone have language' can only be sustained by arbitrarily selecting, as definitive of language, those design features apparently peculiar to human communication: the employment of words and syntax. Yet, in common with other animals, humans communicate by means of an extensive repertoire of non-verbal signs. By what right do we privilege verbal communication among human beings over non-verbal communication among other animals? If it were true that language is no more than a species-specific mechanism of communication, in that sense comparable with other, equally distinctive mechanisms employed by other species, then there would be some force in this objection. However, there are strong arguments against the common presumption that the primary function of language is one of communication. These counterarguments have been put particularly by Chomsky (1980), whose ideas are briefly reviewed by Goodwin in this book, and by Sebeok (1986). They hold that language is first and foremost an instrument of cognition, or a modelling device that enables its possessors to construct, in the imagination, possible future worlds, alternative scenarios and plans for action. As such, language does not lie on an evolutionary continuum with non-verbal communication; moreover, the forms of the latter, far from being gradually displaced and superseded by speech in the process of our 'becoming human', have themselves expanded to assume a volume and complexity unmatched elsewhere in the animal kingdom.

Adopting the premise that there is more to language than speech, Ingold argues in the same vein that language is not just a tool for broadcasting ideas that are somehow preformed in the mind of the speaking subject, and which would otherwise remain private and hidden from view. On the contrary, he holds that it is the very instrument of their generation. Equipped with this facility, human beings are able to design worlds *in advance* of their practical implementation, which is also to say that they can author a truly 'artificial' environment. This is the crux of Ingold's objections to the picture of the animal conveyed by Griffin. For according to Griffin the animal thinks things out in advance but, lacking language, it cannot communicate its thoughts – at least to a human 'participant observer'. Ingold, by contrast, maintains that although animals are constantly in communication with one another, lacking language the substance of their communication has no ideational content, consisting of instructions rather than propositions. In other words, they do not converse. For this reason ethological attempts to enter into the worlds of other species cannot be likened to the anthropologists' linguistically mediated participation with the people of other cultures.

Animals and automata

Opposition to the legacy of Cartesian thinking in Western science is a theme that links many of the contributions to this book; Mundkur alone rallies to its defence in arguing for a starkly mechanistic account of animality. However, this opposition takes radically different forms. One of these holds that Descartes was wrong in attributing a capacity for creative thought only to human beings, and in treating the rest of the animal kingdom as an assortment of clockwork. This is Midgley's view, and again it accords with Griffin's position. It asserts that humans and other animals differ in degree rather than kind – not, however, through a reductionist appeal to 'human animality', but through a reverse accreditation of powers of reason and intellect, conventionally reserved for humans, to non-human animals. Ingold documents how an almost identical view was put forward a century ago by Lewis Henry Morgan, himself one of the founders of modern anthropology. Yet Morgan was a convinced rationalist, who had no doubts about the complementary separation of mental and bodily states, and who believed that to act purposively is first to consider the alternatives and then to execute the chosen plan. Similarly, when Griffin attributes consciousness to animals it takes the form of a capacity for rational deliberation and reflexive self-awareness, and his notion of intentional action presupposes that every doing is preceded by a thinking. That is, the animal, insofar as it is conscious and aware, holds before its mind images of desired future states, chooses among the means to achieve them, and acts accordingly.

Yet, as Ingold points out, it is rather ironic that – as a condition of being considered conscious – the animal should be supposed always to think before it acts, when we know very well that much of what we ourselves do, quite consciously and intentionally, is not so premeditated. While accepting the Cartesian premise that thinking in the sense of the construction of prior intentions, being dependent upon language, is a uniquely human capacity, Ingold rejects the view that such planning is a condition for the intentionality of action. Thus, 'the question of animal *consciousness* ... must ... be separated from that of animal *thinking*'. The animal that does not premeditate and plan is not therefore an automaton, but a conscious agent and patient who acts, feels and suffers, just as we do. Like us, it is responsible for its actions, having caused them to happen, even though it lacks our human ability to render an account of its performance, whether beforehand as a plan or retrospectively as a report. This view requires us to adopt a view of consciousness and creativity quite different from that entailed in Cartesian rationalism, and accepted equally by critics of Descartes who would attribute rationality to animals. Consciousness is no longer to be seen as a *capacity* to generate thoughts, but as a process or *movement*, of which thoughts are an inessential by-product (Ingold 1986, p. 210). This process is none other than the self-creation of the acting subject.

It is at this point that Ingold's argument converges with the critique of Cartesian biology offered by Goodwin, and both are independently inspired by Whitehead's philosophy of organism. Animals, as Goodwin writes, 'are both cause and effect of themselves, pure self-sustaining activity'. In this, not in their possession of the faculty of reason, they are the very opposite of machines. Here the charge against Descartes is not so much that he drew the boundary between the mental and the organic at the interface between human beings and other animals, but rather that he drew such a boundary at all, as though organisms were *opposed* to minds as matter to spirit, or as machines to their designers. Dualisms of this kind, once implanted into the scientific imagination, tend to proliferate in every branch of enquiry, and it is precisely the legacy of dualistic thinking in biology, manifested in such well-worn oppositions as genotype–phenotype and organism–environment, that Goodwin is out to refute. The implication of his argument is that mind (or consciousness) and organism, far from standing in counterpoint as contrary substances (ideal and material), are both *processes* in the real world, aspects of that overall movement of becoming throughout nature in its entirety to which Whitehead (1929, p. 314) referred as a 'creative advance into novelty'.

Anthropocentrism and human uniqueness

If we accept that animals other than human beings may be conscious, intentional agents, then we have also to ascribe to them personal as well as natural powers. That is, we are forced to recognize that they embody attributes of personhood which in the West are popularly identified with the condition of 'humanity'. As Clark puts it, 'other creatures than the biologically human might be persons', a view that might seem strange to us, but which for people of many non-Western cultures is more like a statement of the obvious (Hallowell 1960). However, Tapper warns that in any investigation of 'animal humanity' we surely run the risk of rebounding from an objectionable Cartesian anthropocentrism which restricted personhood to human beings, to an equally objectionable anthropomorphism (or, worse still, 'ethnomorphism') which simply transplants into animal minds the thoughts and feelings we recognize in ourselves, laden as they are with cultural as well as species-specific bias. The risk is doubtless a real one, and Tapper has some sharp words of criticism for moral philosophers such as Midgley who, in his view, fail to address the anthropological problem of translation, imputing similarities with other minds when the real problem is to understand their differences. However, anthropomorphism is not an inevitable consequence of treating animals as persons. To understand elephants (say), we do not have to pretend that they are 'just like humans', let alone that they are just like 20th-century, Western, middle-class humans. But we may have to apply some of the interpretative methods common to the humanities and classically reserved for the study of human culture and history. To suggest that such methods may be equally appropriate for understanding the lives and times of non-human animals is merely the obverse of Mundkur's thesis: that approaches from the 'harder' natural sciences are needed to explain the psychobiological bases of both human and non-human animal behaviour. In short, the disciplinary division between the humanities and the sciences can no longer be aligned with, but actually cross-cuts, the division in their subject matter between the worlds of human beings and of other animals.

It is not, of course, anthropocentric to assert that the human species is unique, for uniqueness is a property that all species – as historical entities (Hull 1984) – have in common. Indeed, it is arguably far more anthropocentric to base estimations of other species on the measure to which they can perform as we do, which is why claims of the type 'chimpanzees (or dolphins, elephants, parrots, or whatever) can do it too' have always had such popular appeal. As Coy rightly stresses: 'other species are *different*', they are not to be regarded as failed – or at best partially successful – attempts at humanity; and our respect for (say) chimpanzees should no more be conditional upon their ability to use language than should our respect for the natives of another culture be conditional upon their ability to read and write. To defeat anthropocentrism we must stop interpreting statements about the disabilities of other species as assertions of their inferiority. It may be true that human beings are distinguished by a level of internal cognitive complexity unmatched elsewhere in the animal kingdom, yet precisely *because* of the freedom from environmental constraint this confers, it is counterbalanced by an equivalent simplicity in the field of their external social and ecological relations. Thus, for all their cognitive abilities, the social organization of hunters and gatherers is pretty rudimentary compared with that of many non-human animals. Real complexity in human societies is contingent upon the emergence of power differentials, and upon the systematic repression of personal autonomy. This is what gives rise to the impersonal vocabularies of hierarchical dominance and control, and Tanner is quite correct to emphasize their utter inappropriateness for describing the intimate relationships of small primate or human hunter–gatherer groups.

Culture and the human construction of animality

Anthropology has classically staked its claim for human uniqueness upon the concept of culture although, as Ingold documents, anthropologists have never been able to agree upon a satisfactory definition of what culture is. The criteria adopted to locate the essence of humanity in the domain of culture have either been too broad or too narrow, depending on whether culture is identified with a learning-transmitted tradition or with the symbolic organization of experience. Traditional transmission by observational learning is widespread in the animal kingdom, and does not presuppose a capacity for symbolic thought; conversely, much but by no means all of the learned behaviour of humans is grounded in a symbolic matrix. But whatever may turn out to be distinctively human in culture, it did not appear in one momentous step. Tanner shows that the 'capacity for culture' of modern humans, underwriting the present diversity of their designs for living, was the outcome of a long chain of small evolutionary steps. The creatures who activated the intermediate steps were not half-finished humans, lumbered with a system not yet fully operational, but fully formed hominids with a system that worked *for them*. To understand the evolution of culture, we have to place every increment of change within the context of the system in which it arose, showing what the innovation afforded for the people who were using it. However, Tanner thinks that there was an identifiable 'first step' towards culture. Redressing the androcentric bias of the classic scenario of human evolution, whose hero was 'man the hunter', she argues that it was females who took that step, when they began to gather plant food with tools.

Cultural anthropologists have tended to adopt a strangely ambivalent attitude towards non-human animals. They rightly point out that the idea of man's control over animality (including both his own and that of women) is part and parcel of a more inclusive ideology of the human mastery, or appropriation of nature whose roots lie deep in the traditions of Western thought. They correctly observe that people of other cultures do not share this view of human superiority, or of nature, placing themselves on a level with – or even subordinate to – non-human kinds. Like Tapper in this book, they are reluctant to enter into debate on the Great Question: 'What is human nature?', preferring to stand further back and examine in what social and cultural contexts such a question might come to be asked. 'Humanity' and 'animality', they say, are – like the concept of nature itself – cultural constructs, and as such their definitions are widely variable and historically contingent. Yet behind such assertions there does lie a certain view of human beings as the *constructors* of their respective environments, imposing their symbolically constituted designs upon a world 'out there' that they confront initially as so much raw material, devoid of form and meaning, and which may be bent to any social purpose whatever. Thus, the anthropological view of culture appears, after all, to rest upon the idea of the human symbolic appropriation of nature – whether animate or inanimate – and hence on an assumption (which Sahlins craftily misconstrues as a 'discovery') that 'the creation of meaning is the distinguishing and constituting quality of all men – the "human essence" of an older discourse' (Sahlins 1976, p. 102). Perhaps anthropologists can avoid asking the Great Question because they already claim to have an answer, one that simultaneously relativizes the question itself. If humans everywhere and at all times have engaged in the activity of world-making, perhaps the difference

between Western and other cultures is that the world-view of the former incor-
porates the idea of man as maker, or *Homo faber*, whereas those of the latter
incorporate a denial of human authorship.

This difference has a critical bearing on the classic anthropological problem of
totemism, for a premise of totemic belief and cult is that it was the animals who
made the world for man, who originally laid down the order and design of human
social existence, and who are ultimately responsible for its continuation. The
Western cult of conservation precisely inverts this premise, proclaiming that
from now on it shall be man who determines the conditions of life for animals
(even those still technically wild shall be 'managed'), and who shoulders the responsibility for their survival or extinction. Yet from the relativizing perspective
of the anthropologist, the animals that occupy the cultic worlds of totemists and
conservationists alike are creations of the human imagination. Concluding his
enquiry into totemic thought, Tapper remarks that it does not matter whether
there are in reality any animals about that might be isomorphic with these conceptions: 'there are always animals about, even if they exist only as *images in the
mind*'. Similarly, for the Western television viewer, observing the antics of a
strange and exotic animal on his screen, he might as well be watching a work of
science fiction as a nature documentary. So what is the relationship between these
'animals in the mind' and those that actually surround us? Do we see the latter
only by interposing the former between them and ourselves? Do animals exist for
us as meaningful entities only insofar as each may be thought to manifest or
exemplify an ideal type constituted within the set of symbolic values making up
the 'folk taxonomy' specific to our culture? Or do we perceive animals directly,
by virtue of their immersion in an environment that is largely ours as well, regardless of the images that we may hold of them, or of whether we hold such
images at all?

Reed, in his contribution to this book, argues powerfully for the latter view. In
so doing he launches a frontal attack on the idea that all meaning is man-made,
challenging anthropology on its most fundamental premise. Thus, where Tapper
maintains that 'the animal' is a culturally constructed category, Reed holds –
quite to the contrary – that animacy is an inherent characteristic of environmental
objects with the power of autonomous movement, quite independently of the
symbolic interpretation that human subjects of one culture or another might
place upon them. Because of their distinctive properties of transformational
growth and non-repetitive motion, we *see* animals as such, irrespective of how we
might come to describe and classify them; moreover, there are good experimental grounds for believing that most mammals and birds – which lack the human
penchant for symbolic classification – directly perceive animate objects and
actions in much the same way. To argue, as anthropologists often do, that all
meaning in the world is 'endowed' upon it by the cultural imagination of thinking subjects is to imply that the 'reality' which is thus endowed is – in itself –
totally disorganized and unstructured, mere substance or, as in the physicists'
view, unbounded space filled with quanta of matter and energy. This, Reed
argues, is tantamount to the dissolution of the environment in which we live, an
environment that consists in reality of structured surfaces and configurations of

places, and of both animate and inanimate objects with their inherent properties. Because of these properties environmental objects, including animals, *afford* certain things to the subject, and *hinder* (negatively afford) other things. Thus, nature is not infinitely malleable; in relating to our environments we do not so much impose our own meanings onto things, as discover the significance, for ourselves, of the meanings those things already have.

The environment of animals

The concept of affordances, on which Reed bases his entire argument, is derived from the ecological psychology of Gibson (1979). It is worth comparing Gibson's view of the environmental niche, as a set of affordances, with the notion of *Umwelt*, first introduced by Jakob von Uexküll, and discussed in this book by Sebeok (see Uexküll 1982 [1940]). For Uexküll the *Umwelt* of an animal, conventionally translated as its 'subjective universe', is the environment as constituted within that animal's life project. Central to his approach was the idea that the animal, far from fitting into a given corner of the world (a niche), actually fits the world to itself, by ascribing functional meanings to the objects it encounters, and thereby integrating them into a coherent system of its own. These meanings, he insisted, were not given in the objects themselves, but were *acquired* by those objects by virtue of their having entered into a relationship with an animal subject. Thus, the stone acquires a 'missile-quality' for the angry human who would hurl it at his adversary, or an 'anvil-quality' for the thrush which would use it to smash snail-shells. One important corollary of this view is that human beings are not alone in constructing their environments. Rather, as I have already suggested, their distinctiveness may lie in the extent to which, with the aid of the modelling device of language, they can author their own projects of construction, matching their surroundings to an internal conceptual design.

Gibson's concept of affordance corresponds closely to Uexküll's concept of quality: both refer to the properties of an object that render it apt for the project of a subject. Thus, Gibson would include throwing and smashing in the catalogue of affordances of the stone – although, of course, missile and anvil describe only two of numerous possibilities. However, there is a crucial contrast: affordances are not acquired by environmental objects, but are said to exist as invariant properties of the objects themselves, quite independently of their being put to use by a subject. From this it follows that, whereas for Uexküll every animal is enclosed within its own subjective world, a kind of 'reality-bubble' accessible only to itself, for Gibson different animals can live in a *shared* environment, and moreover can share their perceptions of what it affords. Therefore, as Reed argues, perception need not be a private matter at all: indeed, he concludes that sociality has its foundations in an awareness of shared perceptions, in the direct mutuality or intersubjective involvement that comes from living in a common environment. Here again he challenges conventional anthropological wisdom, according to which social life depends on an objectification of the experience of private subjects, initially closed to one another, within public, symbolically encoded systems of collective representations.

Human–animal relations

I conclude by turning to one more theme that reappears in a number of the contributions to this book: that of the relations between human beings and other animals. I began by remarking on the powerful emotional influences that appear to condition our own (human) attitudes to animals, and this point is central to the arguments of both Midgley and Mundkur. 'The notion of "an animal" ', Midgley writes, 'is a deeply and incurably emotive one', and she sets out to show how our everyday feelings have coloured, in a largely unacknowledged way, what are supposed to be intellectually unbiased, 'scientific' discussions of the species barrier. Recognizing the emotive load that attaches to this barrier forces us to reconsider our own moral responsibilities towards non-human animals. Although she identifies the main emotion involved as one of fear, she does not attempt to explain how it arose, nor is it clear whether we are to regard it as a human universal or as a peculiarly Western affliction born of an ideological propensity to equate animality with the darker side of human nature and the threat that it apparently poses to cherished values of reason and civilization. Mundkur agrees that human attitudes to animals are embedded in fear, but goes further in attempting to account for its origin within a scenario of organic evolution. One of his more remarkable observations is the fact that people often have intense fears of dangerous animals that they would be very unlikely ever to encounter, an observation that seems to confirm the status of such fears as human universals whose roots lie far back in the evolutionary past of the primate order. The major puzzle for the kind of analysis he offers is to show how fearful emotions that originated within the context of predator–prey interactions should be generalized from their specific objects and displaced to the gentlest and most inoffensive of animals, which could not possibly cause humans any physical harm. It may make adaptive sense to fear tigers or venomous snakes, . . . but butterflies?

The diversity of kinds of relationship or association that can exist between humans and animals is a subject common to the contributions of Sebeok, Coy and Tapper. Considering a wide range of types of human–animal encounter – from predation and parasitism to partnership, taming and training – Sebeok is concerned with the way in which the form of the encounter (understood as an exchange of signs) can influence the conception of what 'counts' as an animal for humans, or the way in which the animal itself becomes a sign – 'a chunk of concentrated information' – in human social interaction. Coy neatly turns the tables on the usual tendency to consider human–animal relations only from the human point of view. The central theme of her contribution is the mutual empathy that can develop when such relations become close and intense, an empathy that allows each party to 'read the mind' of the other, and hence – at least to some extent – to predict its actions. Not only humans but also non-human animals, Coy suggests, might have sufficient levels of awareness to be able to impute motivations both to individual conspecifics and to animals of other species – including humans. An ability on the part of the animal to predict human behaviour may make it difficult to hunt, but could significantly ease the process of its domestication. She concludes that it is most important for us to understand those domestic species with which we have the closest links, as they are most likely to reveal the attitudes of animals towards people. However, this conclusion might be qualified by Sebeok's observation that the human training of animals can take two opposed forms, one of which (*apprentissage*) is an entirely impersonal type of behavioural conditioning, the other (*dressage*) depending on a relation of utmost intimacy between trainer and trainee. Whereas in the latter the mutual involvement of human and animal reaches its maximum, it is reduced to a bare minimum in the former.

Tapper's contribution is also concerned with variation in human familiarity with animals, and he shares with Coy an interest in the ways in which animals figure in popular literature, especially as models for use in teaching and socialization. In an ingenious revision of the classic Marxian paradigm, Tapper extends the concept of social relations of production across the species barrier, and examines the parallel range of forms of 'human–animal relations of production'. Thus, in a hunting economy, where prey are construed as fellow persons, 'communal' human–animal relations prevail. Under early domestication, in which animals are tamed as part-members of human households, these give way to 'slavery'. The development of pastoralism, where animals are herded without being necessarily tame, leads to more contractual human–animal relations akin to those of feudalism. With modern factory farming, relations of production are further depersonalized, assuming an exploitative form characteristic of capitalism. These different kinds of human–animal relations could perhaps be understood in terms of a double movement: from without to within the human household and, simultaneously, from the personal to the impersonal. Thus, the animal moves from being a strange person to a familiar thing, through various intermediate stages. Tapper attempts to show that to each stage there corresponds a specific usage of animal metaphor, and therefore that it is possible to ground ideas about human nature and the relation of humanity to animality in fundamental economic imperatives, albeit conditioned by historically contingent features of the socio-political environment.

I have endeavoured, in this introductory chapter, to present some idea of the diversity and the richness of the contributions that follow, and more importantly, to bring out the principal connections between them. There are, of course, many more points of contact besides those I have reviewed here. I do not believe that the question of 'What is an animal?' can be resolved by a unitary theoretical or conceptual paradigm. It has, rather, been my purpose to show that every such paradigm has some view of animality already deeply embedded, and often only dimly recognized, within its most fundamental assumptions. Therefore, our question is not one that can even be asked, let alone answered, within the axiomatic framework constituting any particular system of thought. It is only through a concerted effort, by scholars representing many disciplines and intellectual traditions, that we can begin to unpack the multiple and many-layered meanings of 'the animal'. This book represents a step in that direction, and what links the contributions of its ten authors is not a theory, but a question.

References

Chomsky, N. 1980. *Rules and representations.* New York: Columbia University Press.

Gibson, J. J. 1979. *The ecological approach to visual perception.* Boston: Houghton Mifflin.

Griffin, D. R. 1984. *Animal thinking.* Cambridge, Massachusetts: Harvard University Press.

Hallowell, A. I. 1960. Ojibwa ontology, behavior and world view. In *Culture in history: essays in honor of Paul Radin*, S. Diamond (ed.), 19–52. New York: Columbia University Press.

Hull, D. L. 1984. Historical entities and historical narratives. In *Minds, machines and evolution: philosophical studies*, C. Hookway (ed.), 17–42. Cambridge: Cambridge University Press.

Ingold, T. 1986. *Evolution and social life.* Cambridge: Cambridge University Press.

Lévi-Strauss, C. 1985. *La potière jalouse.* Paris: Plon.

Sahlins, M. D. 1976. *Culture and practical reason.* Chicago: University of Chicago Press.

Sebeok, T. A. 1986. *I think I am a verb.* New York: Plenum Press.

Shotter, J. 1984. *Social accountability and selfhood.* Oxford: Blackwell.

Uexküll, J. von 1982 [1940]. The theory of meaning [transl. by B. Stone & H. Weiner from *Bedeutungslehre*, T. von Uexküll (ed.)]. *Semiotica* **42**, 1–87.

Whitehead, A. N. 1929. *Process and reality.* Cambridge: Cambridge University Press.

2 Is humanity a natural kind?

STEPHEN R. L. CLARK

Preface

The idea that humanity is a natural kind is implicit in a good deal of modern moral and political practice, and in anthropological and archaeological inquiry. I argue in the first section that biological species are not natural kinds, and in the second section that we therefore cannot rely upon the claim that 'humankind is all one species' to validate our political or anthropological assumptions. The third section suggests that two possibilities are open to us. Either we must acknowledge that we are individual organisms having largely unpredictable similarities with or differences from other creatures, that we cannot take it for granted that all tool-makers or all artists will also have other familiar 'human' or 'personal' characteristics, and that there is no essential or puzzling difference between (say) 'domestication' and 'slavery'. Alternatively, we must insist that the natural kind of 'persons' is a Platonic Form, and not to be identified with the biological taxon of 'human beings'.

Folk taxonomy and scientific taxa

There was a time for most of us when adult male humans and teddy bears were all teddies, and 'ka' signified any furry quadruped. As we learnt our mother-tongues we also learnt a folk taxonomy which lives in us still: English speakers have no usual doubts that there are weeds, flowers, dogs, trees, fish, animals and birds and creepy-crawlies, mushrooms, toadstools, germs – and, of course, human beings. Greater learning will reveal to us that there are many kinds of tree or mushroom, but we remain happily confident that the larger generic kinds are real. Naively, we may believe that all (say) weeds are alike in having perceptible properties which together amount to weediness: properties which are the necessary and sufficient conditions of being a weed. If something looks just like a weed, it is one. Greater sophistication may suggest first that there is no set of properties such that all weeds have them, and that the most we can expect is that all weeds resemble each other, but not necessarily by virtue of their all having a particular property. It further suggests that what makes them all weeds may not be something directly perceptible. Maybe they are weeds because they compete with our food-crops – because 'we' no longer eat Good King Henry, it is a weed. Even then it will take an effort to remember that calling something a weed tells us very little about its own being, and to sympathize with linguistic communities for which our weeds are useful herbs, or which have no single slot for the class we so characterize.

Of course, no-one seriously supposes that weeds constitute a natural kind, that the failure to count something as a weed, or a germ, amounts to scientific ignorance or moral error, though even Linnaeus included such orders as 'beasts of burden (*iumenta*)' in his taxonomy (Oldroyd 1980, p. 15). We are more convinced of the reality of trees and fish, even if we modify our account of them:

> **Fish**, sb.: I.1. In popular language, any animal living exclusively in the water; primarily denoting vertebrate animals provided with fins and destitute of limbs; but extended to include various cetaceans, crustaceans, molluscs, etc. In modern scientific language (to which popular usage now tends to approximate) restricted to a class of vertebrate animals, provided with gills throughout life, and cold-blooded; the limbs, if present, being modified into fins, and supplemented by unpaired median fins (*Compact Oxford English Dictionary* 1971, I, p. 1008).

Yet more exact analysis will show that even the second, more restricted usage (*pace* Quine 1969, p. 21) is too large. *Chrondichthyes, osteichthyes* and *agnatha* are all 'fish', but constitute distinct taxonomic groups whose members resemble each other through convergent evolution – as do dolphins and ichthyosaurs. Similarly, it turns out that daisies, cacti and oak trees are all angiosperms, related more closely than any are to pine trees (gymnosperms). 'Tree' is not a scientific taxon (see Dupre 1981). This is not simply to say that daisies and oak trees have more similarities than do pines and oaks: for most ordinary purposes they do not. 'By primitive standards the marsupial mouse is more similar to the ordinary mouse than to the kangaroo; by theoretical standards the reverse is true' (Quine 1969, p. 15) – but calling kangaroos and marsupial mice 'more similar' is not quite the point. Their similarities are not more extensive, but more significant: they are signs of common ancestry.

The differences between folk taxonomy (the discriminations learnt with our mother-tongue) and scientific taxonomy go deeper still. A creature lying on a fishmonger's slab, gutted and gill-less, is no less a fish because it has no gills, fins or guts, and is not in the water. We call it a fish because it would, in nature, have these things: without them, if it were still living, it would be maimed. If it had never had them it would be diseased or deformed. In folk taxonomy things are almost perfect exemplars of their class, by their possession of those features which they would 'in nature' be expected to have, apart from accidental defect or disaster. Seals, by Aristotle's guess, are deformed quadrupeds. The modern scientific taxon, by contrast, has no perfect type: there is not, nor could there be, a perfect osteichthys by comparison with which one could measure the failure of all other osteichthyes. The folk taxon includes all those creatures that have, or would have, a sufficient number of the taxon's defining characteristics, and each such taxon bears along with it the image of a perfect type. The scientific taxon consists of historically, genealogically related individuals which do not necessarily resemble each other much more than they do other unrelated individuals: such a taxon has no perfect type, no criteria of deformity. 'Typical forms' may be invoked, largely for heuristic and mnemonic purposes (see Baker 1974, pp. 121ff.), but the 'atypical' is not necessarily degenerate, deformed or even a later development from the ancestral stock. 'Types' are invoked as well, to serve as the standard exemplars of such and such a species, family or class: but such types need not be typical, never mind perfect (see Baker 1974, p. 67). Quine's attempt to identify a biological kind with the set of all things 'to which [the paradigm] *a* is more similar than *a* is to [the foil] *b*' (Quine 1979, p. 9) is not in line with biological practice, unless a very strained sense is given to the term 'similar'. 'Those specimens that are types are merely those that happen to have had names based upon them; . . . the type of a name, falling within the range of variation of a taxon, may stand at one extreme of that taxon' (Jeffrey 1973, p. 18), and may therefore be more similar (phenomenally and genetically) to many things outside the taxon than to those inside.

Folk taxa are not foolish inventions: they are related to the uses we would make of things. For landscaping or woodworking purposes oak and pine alike are trees, and equally unlike daisies. Whether sea-birds are fish or fowl may matter a lot to priests and dieticians. If a particular cow is behaving in a manner quite unlike the others, or has an abnormal growth or a crumpled horn, we do well to check her health. Nor are folk taxa merely phenomenologically grouped classes of the sort that anyone might invent: they embody, in somewhat distorted form, a variety of ancient philosophical opinions. What we suppose to be common sense was once a radical invention (usually Plato's or Aristotle's). It is clear that folk taxa, however obvious they seem to us, and whatever philosophical insights they sometimes embody, need not be mirrored in a scientific taxonomy, and even when they are, the scientific taxon need not have the properties of the folk taxon. There are, in fact, at least six significant differences.

First, the folk taxon embodies an *a priori* concept of normality by comparison with which individuals or events are judged to be more- or less-abnormal or defective; thus 'our modern conceptions of health and disease and our notion of normality as something other than a statistical average enshrine Aristotle's model' (Sober 1980, p. 363). But in the scientific view nothing that happens is more- or less- 'natural': every creature of a given taxon is just as much a member of that taxon, however 'atypical' it is. Some taxa are remarkably homogeneous, their members homozygous at most genetic loci, and their populations polymorphic only for a few characters: *Rattus rattus* is an example. However, most individuals are heterozygotic, and most populations polymorphic for up to 80 per cent of their taxon's characters (White 1978, pp. 27f.). 'For example, individuals of the ground-finch *Geospiza fortis* are so variable in beak that they were for a long time considered to belong to at least two, and by some authorities to three or more separate species' (Lack 1947, p. 12).

Secondly, whereas in our folk taxonomy a thing is a tree if enough speakers of our language say so, membership of a scientific taxon depends on real genealogical connection, whatever we say about it. In folk taxonomy a tree is, crudely, a tree because it is judged by the standards appropriate in our linguistic community to be a large perennial plant having a single woody stem. Bonsai (Japanese miniaturized trees) and lightning-shattered oaks are trees because we choose to treat them so, because they have enough shared properties to make that classification useful. They are trees because they have (or in nature would have) single woody trunks: but they have such trunks because they share a particular ancestry, and it is because they do that that they are counted as members of particular genealogical taxa. 'Members of a taxon are similar because they share a common heritage; they do not belong to the taxon because they are similar' (Mayr 1969, pp. 65 ff.). Similarly, vegetables are (primarily) any plants 'whose root or fruit or leaf is [in the judgement of English speakers] (a) savoury, and (b) edible by human beings. The set of all vegetables has as its subsets some but not all species of the *Cruciferae* family, some but not all of the *Leguminosae* family etc. etc.' (Wiggins 1980, p. 172). They are not savoury or edible because they are vegetables, any more than a man is unmarried because he is a bachelor.

Thirdly, if all presently existing members of the folk taxon 'tree' perished without descendants, but cowslips at last evolved a woody trunk, there would (if English had survived) be trees again. However, the scientifically isolated taxa would have gone for good: neo-pterodactyls, to use Hull's (1978) example, would not be the same species, genus or family as the old pterosaurs, even if they were, for our purposes, indistinguishable. ' "*Homo sapiens*" . . . is a name, a proper name for a discrete, spatio-temporally bounded particular thing' (Rosenberg 1980, p. 120). Classes of the kind with which Quine and others have identified biological taxa do not begin and end with the birth or extinction of their members (Slote 1974, pp. 84f.).

A fourth difference between a biological kind and even a sophisticated version of our folk taxonomy has confused some recent commentators. Members of the folk taxon may not look alike, but may still be understood to share an underlying nature. Biological kinds are not even to be defined by their members' possession of a common genetic nature, something that would issue in perceptible similarity if all had gone well with the organisms' growth. Some commentators have admitted that the existence of sibling species such as *Drosophila pseudoobscura* and *Drosophila persimilis* demonstrates that the scientifically defined species of an individual is not a function of its outward appearance, but have gone on to claim that the 'real', natural kind of an individual is that set of creatures who share its nature (i.e. whose appearance and behaviour are caused by the same underlying principles): 'for the name to stand for a natural kind, everything depends on whether there is some nomological grounding for what it is to be of the kind' (Wiggins 1980, p. 80, after Putnam 1970). Unfortunately, whereas this doctrine serves well enough for the chemical elements, it does not meet with biological approval (see Dupre 1981). The physical stuffs we categorize as 'golden' constitute a natural kind, because there is a stuff (namely aggregates of atoms with a specific atomic number and structure) whose presence in greater or smaller proportion in the stuff we began with explains the phenomenal properties. Even atomic number is a vaguer and more probabilistic concept than optimistic systematizers once hoped (see Sober 1980), and biological kinds lack even that much 'underlying unity'. Even if we agree that there is a scientifically discoverable taxon (e.g. *Rattus rattus*), we do not thereby admit that there is any stuff (even an aggregate of DNA molecules) whose presence, however diluted, in all the members of that taxon explains the phenomenal features by which we (and for that matter, they) recognize a rat. Even if there were a stretch of DNA which is duplicated in every rat, that stretch would not be what guarantees their membership of the taxon (see Hull 1974b). Each rat does, indeed, have a genetic nature, and rats are (as it happens) very uniform, but there is no need to suppose that there is one element of that nature by virtue of which any rat is a member of the taxon. On the contrary, it is (in sexually reproducing species) precisely because all individuals do not have the same genetic nature that there is a species at all. The notional 'gene-pool' to which all members of a species contribute (and non-members hardly at all) is not (*pace* Trigg 1982, p. 96) what determines the natures of the individual organisms: some species have very heterogeneous pools and others have rather homogeneous ones, but both sorts are species.

Fifthly, in folk taxonomy a creature that is of one kind cannot also be of another, but the boundaries of scientifically defined taxa are not merely elastic (see Wiggins 1980, p. 32, after Sommerhof 1950), but vague. For the folk tax-onomist a deformed dog is still a dog, and will never be a seal: it survives at all only because there is an underlying structure which would, in nature and barring accidents, have produced a proper dog. If Growltiger is of one and the same kind as Rumpelteazer, and Rumpelteazer of the same kind as Macavity, then Growltiger and Macavity are also conspecifics, and share an underlying nature. But the existence of ring-species, or *Formenkreis* (Beckner 1959, pp. 61ff., see Baker 1974, pp. 82ff.) shows that this need not be so. 'Having the same nature as *x*' is a transitive relation; 'being of the same scientific taxon as *x*' is not. Were this not the case, evolution (in the Darwinian sense of descent with modification) could not have occurred.

Sixthly, the view which modern taxonomists frequently and with culpable inaccuracy (see Lloyd 1983, pp. 7–57) revile as Aristotelian is represented better as Platonic. Aristotle himself explained the character of a biological individual not by recourse to species-essences defined *per genus et differentiam*, but by the effect of the father's form upon the mother's material (see Balme 1980). However, according to the Platonic account there are real Forms of living crea-tures, having the power to influence the birth and development of physical organisms. No tangible lifeform is identical with the Form, or Ideal, to which it approximates, and the Form is not dependent for its existence on its having exemplars or copies. Whereas the taxon of *Tyrannosaurus rex* is irrecoverably extinct, the Form of that beast is an eternal verity which later lifeforms might 'resemble' to a greater or lesser degree. The Form of Vertebrate-at-Sea, for example, is regularly rediscovered (by osteichthyes, chrondichthyes, agnatha, ichthyosaurs, cetacea, . . .). On this account scientific investigation aims to find the Platonic essences, never perfectly embodied, which are the asymptotes of the hyperbolae traced by physical evolution. This Platonism, it seems to me, is still a serious option: certainly those taxonomists who sneer at it give no adequate reason for their scorn. Even the more sympathetic Oldroyd entirely mistakes the Platonic (and the Aristotelian) methods in describing them as 'talking round a problem until an acceptable "essential" definition of a thing or concept had been reached' (Oldroyd 1980, p. 261). But such Platonic Forms are not to be identified with actual genotypes, and their existence does not guarantee that what we now call, for example, the human species is really, and uniquely, guided by one such Ideal.

Those who believe that there are 'natural kinds' in the biological as well as in the chemical realm sometimes suggest that the alternative is to succumb to the Nietzschean view of 'truth' as 'a mobile army of metaphors' (Wiggins 1980, p. 81, see Oldroyd 1980, pp. 262ff.). All of our classes would then be indefinitely revisable, and founded only on how particular items happened to strike us, so that 'being a pygmy chimpanzee' would be as ineradicably tied to language and current fashion as 'being a vegetable, or a weed'. Humble realists who believe that there are truths to be found out, not just invented, then take comfort from the truism that there are real species of living creatures, and seek to interpret the thought typologically. But the implied contrast (Nietzsche versus Plato) is unfounded, and Trigg's conclusion (1982, p. 82) that those who disbelieve in species as natural kinds must be nominalists is false. There may be real universals, even real genetic factors shared by all or most or many members of a given species. There are, indeed, real species, 'groups of interbreeding natural populations that are reproductively isolated [though not necessarily absolutely so] from other such groups' (Mayr 1969, p. 25). Such genuinely interbreeding stocks are what Kant called *Realgattungen*, to distinguish them from morphological species, *Arten*, whether those latter were defined by surface similarity or subtler similarities of causal nature: 'Academic classification extends to classes, which it divides according to resemblances, while natural classification divides according to relationships, by taking reproduction into account' (I. Kant's *Gesammelte Schriften*, Vol. 2, pp. 427ff., cited by Baker 1974, pp. 81f.). We can guess that members of *Realgattungen* will resemble each other in a variety of ways, but their membership is not contingent on their resemblance at either the phenomenal or the causal level.

Realgattungen, as Kant suspected and as most of us believe, develop out of older stocks. Speciation, that is the development of barriers (social, geographical or physiological) to successful interbreeding, occurs both when a single interbreeding population is thereby divided (kladogenetic evolution) and when an ancestral population has so far changed its character as to lead us to suppose that ancestors and descendants could not now interbreed if they were in a position to do so (anagenetic or adastogenetic evolution). Some palaeontologists have concluded that they are operating with a distinctive concept of species, a 'palaeospecies', such that *Homo habilis*, *erectus* and *sapiens* are distinct species even though, so far as we know, there were no rival descendants of their immediate ancestors. Like Beckner (1959, p. 59), I doubt if any different concept is required: what we have is an inductive guess that these successive populations would not successfully interbreed, though particular members of the populations might. What the palaeospecies concept does do is bring to our attention the fact that even the most rigorously xenophobic of contemporary species are, once we bring their past to mind, merely *Rassen* (varieties) of a single *Formenkreis*, or ring-species. 'It is not possible', to adapt Otto Kleinschmidt, 'to distinguish sharply between good species and mere geographical races, because good species may often be geographical [or temporal] representatives of one another' (cited by Baker 1974, p. 82). Burma exaggerates the problem in claiming that a species is no more than 'an arbitrarily set-off segment of a continuous phyletic line' (Burma 1976, cited by Trigg 1982, p. 81), since the segments need not be arbitrarily set off. However, the divisions are not absolute.

Classes and biological taxa, accordingly, are not the same sort of thing, and the natural kinds that are perhaps to be found in chemistry should not necessarily be expected in biology. No-one can deny that there is an analogy between genetic code and atomic number: what the atomic structure is to the surface phenomena of samples of gold or water, the genetic structure is to the surface phenomena of Macavity or Growltiger. However, whereas samples of gold, to be true samples, must all have the same atomic structure, it is not true that even domestic cats (who are a lot more homogeneous than dogs) must all have the 'same' genetic structure to be true cats. There will be genetic resemblances, as there are phenomenal ones, but a genealogical, historical classification does not rely on those resemblances: where they exist, it explains them. We must distinguish *Arten* (morphospecies), *Realgattungen* (breeding stocks) and metaphysical, regulative Forms.

The unity of humankind

The body of social scientists and biologists who were called, in 1949, to lend their authority to UNESCO's moral and political ideals, declared firmly that 'mankind is one: all men [i.e. all humans] belong to the same species' (cited by Baker 1974, p. 65). The dictum, like an earlier declaration that 'all men are created equal', can be disputed, but my first concern is to understand it. Is it not also true (but who would bother to say so) that 'mammalkind (primatekind, hominoidea) is one: all mammals (primates, hominoids) belong to the same class (order, super-family)'? To be human at all is to be a member of a certain taxon, currently labelled '*Homo sapiens*': creatures who did not belong would not be human, though they might resemble many of us very closely. If mankind (i.e. humanity) exists as a distinguishable kind at all, it must be one (i.e. one species, genus or family), but it does not follow that 'humankind' could not name a higher taxon than the single species. Our guesses about *Homo neanderthalensis* shift with changing archaeological fashion: if that does name a separate species, then there were once other hominids that buried their dead and worshipped. If '*Homo habilis*' names the same species (the same breeding stock) as '*Homo sapiens*', then there were humans of our species who perhaps lacked some or most of our cultural capacities.

Clearly enough, we are faced by terminological confusion. The UNESCO savants, in the wake of a crass and horrible denial of our common nature, were concerned simply to say that all creatures born of woman must be expected to have much the same fundamental wants and talents. Thus, the statement 'all members of our species are human' implies that they all need food, drink, shelter, culture and companionship if they are to be happy, and that all can contribute to the on-going enterprise of human life. We are not to suppose that obvious physiological and cultural differences will render any member of our species alien, or undeserving. Creatures not of our species, by implicit contrast, lie beyond the pale: all human persons are to think that any conspecific is of more worth than any creature from another *Realgattung*, even if particular members of our species are not very different in outward show, or inner genetic nature, from the aliens.

In folk taxonomy humankind must embrace that set of creatures who have a common nature, namely humanity. That nature need not always be actualized: physical and chemical injuries alike may leave their victim dumb or deformed, but it is axiomatic that the victim would have joined the human game, were it not for the injury. What is 'natural' to a given kind is what members of that kind would do, under 'normal' or 'ideal' circumstances. Those circumstances, in turn, are to be defined as the ones in which members of the kind would realize their natures. If a creature's nature is its genetic code, then there will be some born into our species whose nature is irrevocably unhuman, such that it was never an open possibility that they should grow up to be language-using, cultural, God-fearing mammals. To believe that, but for fortune, they too would have been like us is only reasonable if we think that they are really immortal souls, housed (to their cost) in damaged instruments – and souls, moreover, of one simple sort, the transcendental ego which is, effectively, the Platonic Form of Humanity (see Merlan 1963). This belief may be useful practically: if we think that there is a 'real human' inside the apparent vegetable, we may expect (and so get) more of her, and treat her more as we would wish to be treated. It may also be a dangerous belief, encouraging the folk-taxonomic feeling that unusual creatures are defective. Seals are not merely deformed quadrupeds (though Aristotle was not wrong to see a relationship); our human-born monsters also have their own discoverable natures, their own contribution to the species-pool (see Hull 1978, p. 358).

Where the folk taxonomist supposes that all humans have a common causal nature, whether that is genetic or Platonic or both, the biologist speaks rather of 'one great breeding system through which genes flow and mix in each generation' (Wilson 1978, p. 50). Wilson himself goes on to interpret this gene-pool as constituting a shared human nature, illustrating the fourth confusion mentioned above. What is widely, though not universally, shared is simply the property of drawing from, and usually being able to contribute to the pool, and this property does not necessarily rest on any particular shared gene. It may be true, as I am inclined to think, that the nature of most present and probable members of our species is such that, as Wilson says, 'the qualities that we recognize as most distinctively mammalian – and human – make . . . a transition [to a permanent slave society] impossible. . . . Slaves under great stress insist on behaving like human beings instead of slave ants, gibbons, mandrills, or any other species' (Wilson 1978, p. 81, and see p. 199, see also Clark 1985a,b). However, Wilson knows well that these qualities are not necessarily possessed by all of our conspecifics, and might have noticed that some slave-societies have been very long-lived. The qualities which make such slave-societies unlikely to hold all humankind in thrall for ever are also possessed by many of our fellow-mammals. They do not constitute a human essence of the sort preferred by folk taxonomists. Insofar as our genes influence our lives, and are therefore – as Putnam (1970) claimed – rather like atomic structures, we are influenced by a nature we do not share with all humans, and do share with many non-humans. Humankind is not that sort of natural kind.

The unity of humankind (the biological taxon) does not rest in the possession of a common nature, but in being a breeding population such that my ancestors and my descendants alike may be yours as well. Not every imaginable human pair can expect viable offspring, but we are all embedded in a lineage such that any pair might reasonably expect to be able to share great-grandchildren or the like. This may result in the continued existence of widely shared qualities, but it does not always have to; nor can we be absolutely confident that past conspecifics were altogether like us. Wilson notes that 'human nature is just one hodgepodge out of many conceivable' (Wilson 1978, p. 23), although he also expresses an extraordinary confidence that 'if even a small fraction of the diagnostic human traits were stripped away, the result would probably be a disabling chaos'. Those traits, which are merely ones that 'have been recorded in every culture known to history and ethnography', might (for all that Wilson shows) be simply what they seem – cultural traits that, when described with sufficient vagueness, turn out for whatever reason to have been very common up to now. To suppose that such a list in any way limits our future is as futile as the cognate arguments that the forms of locomotion known by 1700 exhausted the possibilities, or that the presence of slaves in every human society till then – always excepting a few hunter–gatherer societies – shows that we cannot outlaw slavery. Without some evidence that 'age-grading, athletic sports, bodily adornment, calendar, cleanliness training, . . . trade, visiting, weaving and weather control' (Wilson 1978, p. 22, after G. P. Murdock) constitute an abiding syndrome, we must conclude that our genes have so far allowed these social forms, and may have predetermined them, but that we do not know which will drop from sight in some future culture, nor what other forms a changing gene-pool may allow or require. 'Maybe all triangles must have three angles, but not all reptiles must have a three-chambered heart, though in point of fact they might' (Hull 1974a, p. 79). Wilson correctly observes that 'maps of chimpanzee tool-making . . . might be placed without notice into a chapter on primitive culture in an anthropology textbook' (Wilson 1978, p. 31) – so eroding the barrier between human and non-human (see Foley 1984). The notional barrier between human and post-human (so to speak) is just as porous. We cannot fix the future progress of a *Realgattung*, any more than our forebears, when they were *Homo habilis*, could have precluded the possibility of their line's becoming *Homo sapiens*, and thereby having on average somewhat different blood groups, physiognomies and behavioural preferences. 'Since species evolve . . . they should be treated not as classes whose members satisfy some fixed set of con- ditions – not even a vague cluster of them – but as lineages, lines of descent, strings of imperfect copies of predecessors, among which there may not even be the manifestation of a set of central and distinctive, let alone necessary and suf- ficient, common properties' (Rosenberg 1980, pp. 122f.).

The Kantian or neo-Darwinian perspective has some ethical merit (see Hull 1978, *pace* Trigg 1982, p. 93). Once we realize that human variety is not an error, that there is no one sort of human being that is 'what a human being should be', and that we must expect our species always to be variegated, we can begin to think again about constructing social orders that will provide a place for all. It is because we have convinced ourselves that only avoidable accidents produce 'monsters' (Aristotle even thought that women were 'necessary deformities', not quite human) that we have designed our society around the free and healthy adult. We must instead begin to budget for a future where we shall always have 'monsters' – who are, of course, not monstrous at all, but merely variations within the range currently occupied by our *Realgattung*. We need a society that will have places – I do not mean asylums – for the aphasic, 'deformed', 'disturbed' and 'eccentric'. Variation is not a dysfunction of sexual reproduction, it is what sex is for (Sober 1980).

If individual members of our taxon may be without those properties that we have considered essential to humanity (a capacity to speak, to laugh, to make tools and to worship), might not whole populations? Rousseau and Monboddo thought it possible that there were human tribes which had not yet learned language, as there were others that had not learned to write or to use the wheel (Baker 1974, pp. 22f.). If speech and the other arts of life are not 'natural' to humankind, 'it is impossible we can refuse [orang-utans] the appellation of men'. Monboddo intended this dictum to have the humane effect that orang-utans and the like be treated respectfully, as being 'of our kind'. But once the ties between 'being of our species' and being 'human' (in the customary sense of 'language-using, time-binding, cultural, etc.') were loosened, what reason was there to treat even our conspecifics well? 'If the essence of humanity was defined as consisting in some specific quality, then it followed that any man who did not display that quality was sub-human, semi-animal' (Thomas 1983, p. 41). Kant himself, following a long and pernicious tradition, had decreed that only rational agents were of moral worth; their being of our *Realgattung* was not to the point. Some creatures of another species might turn out to be 'human' in the morally significant sense; many of our species might turn out to be 'sub-human'.

It is one of the minor ironies of history that 'enlightenment thinkers', who are popularly supposed to have released us from ethnocentric obscurantism, were very much readier than orthodox theologians to believe that chimpanzees were 'human', and negroes not. The belief that humankind was monophyletic – of one common descent – was preserved by orthodox believers. Contrast Voltaire on Hottentots (Baker 1974, p. 20), and Herder on the unity of humankind: 'Neither the *Pongo* nor the *Longimanus* is your brother; but truly the American and the Negro are' (Herder, in Baker 1974, p. 22). The conflict between those who are ready to see genetic differences within the human species, and those who emphasize the 'unity' of humankind still rages. If our conspecifics do not share a common nature, and if there is nothing to prevent the birth of atypical humans, then it may be that the nature of the Yanomamö or the Tibetan is not entirely ours. If we are bound to treat only those creatures well that 'share our nature', then we may find that some human tribes lie beyond the moral pale, as do particular individuals within our own tribe. The claim that Yanomamö or Tibetan are unlike 'us' is, of course, debatable. One of the oddest, and most disagreeable, features of Baker's learned and informative book is the way he appears to be retailing the horrors of the court of King Chaka (Baker 1974, pp. 389 ff.) or the Aztecs (pp. 524 f.) in order to show what 'Negrids' or 'Zentralids' are like – as though 'Europids' had never behaved as badly. Sadly, the evidence that Zulus and Aztecs are just like us is precisely that they behaved, on historical occasion, with appalling cruelty and greed. Baker's reliance on 19th-century explorers and missionaries for his 'first-hand' information on African tribes (no modern social anthropologist features in his extensive bibliography) produces a wildly distorted account of native character and achievement. A similar historical ignorance pervades more-recent, sociobiological work – as though none but Yanomamö males ever beat their wives, and none but Tibetans practised polyandry.

The recurrent fashion for discovering the 'unhuman' in other sections of humankind can be plausibly rebutted with evidence that all human groups so far discovered turn out to be very like the rest of us, and to contain much the same spread of characters and abilities. This may be less a discovery than a stipulation – groups that are not 'very like us' are simply not identified as human. We do not wait to see whether the populations could interbreed, or even ask whether they might not be able to understand each other well enough without the benefit of assertoric speech. 'Being human', in fact, remains a concept of folk taxonomy: to identify a creature as human is to stipulate that it be judged and treated according to the standards appropriate, within our linguistic community, to that sort of entity. Those standards include the requirement that we do not patronize a genuinely human being by supposing that he could do no other than he does. We treat people 'like animals' when we seek to control them merely by fear (or by desire), expect them to have no interests beyond the crudely physical, and do not ask them for an opinion.

The moral and political effects of allowing it to be thought that any biologically human population is less than 'human' have been so bad that it is understandable that liberals now insist upon Herder's thesis, and sneer at any purported evidence either that the biologically non-human could demonstrate any distinctively 'human' capacities, or that the biologically human could be without the characters and talents necessary for life in the liberal West. The price of this laudable insistence on moral humanism is a profound unease, even among those who are professionally committed to neo-Darwinian theory and scientific materialism (which are not, of course, the same thing), about any attempt to treat the characters and talents of human populations as explicable in something like the way that we might explain the behaviour of baboons or horses. It is asserted, in advance of any evidence worth mentioning, that our species has somehow escaped from the nexus of evolutionary selection, and become pure mind, governed only by the laws of reason and the purposes of conscious individuals. This was a rational and consistent position as long as we believed that the human soul, the Form of Humanity, was infused into our merely animal ancestry at some one point in time (as individual souls are, perhaps, infused in the developing embryo). It depended, in turn, on the judgement that those distinctively 'human' capacities were linked, and unanalysable. If, as seems both likely and in accordance with the profession of neo-Darwinism, such capacities are to be understood as piecemeal developments of earlier traits (see Clark 1982), we lack any definite reason to believe in a once-and-for-all infusion of Real Humanity. In fact, it may still be true that no human population has been isolated from all others for sufficiently long to be permanently cut off from the human gene-pool. Any character may turn up anywhere. However, the proportion of those characters in any given population may vary, and the nature of our descendants will not necessarily be ours (any more than birds are very much like dinosaurs). The genetic landscape, as it were, can no longer be conceived as an archipelago of isolated islets: it is a land of hills and valleys, where populations cluster around hill-tops and spill down the slopes (some steep, some gentle). Where one kind ends and another begins, in the valley between the adaptive peaks, is a matter of some indifference. The reality is the whole continent, Lifekind (Clark 1984).

'All men of good will', according to Eccles (1970, p. 1), 'would subscribe to the concept that we must strive to foster and develop the fullest possible life for mankind, not just here and now, but indefinitely into the future'. If 'mankind' here means the biological taxon of humankind, why should we make the 'well-being' (whatever it consists of) of that continuing taxon (which will perhaps one day be a family or even an order) our sole or major criterion of moral judgement? The words of another scientific savant are more to my own moral taste: 'The grand design of nature perceived broadly in four dimensions to include the forces that move the universe and created man, with special emphasis on evolution in our own biosphere, is something intrinsically good that it is right to preserve and enhance, and wrong to destroy or degrade' (Sperry 1983, p. 22). It is unfortunate that Sperry shows little sign of having thought through the moral implications of thus conceiving himself as the servant of being (Sprigge 1984, after Heidegger), but the moral thesis does have considerable resonance. Why bother only about our species, when we might instead concern ourselves with our order, or with the whole biosphere of which we are a part?

If, conversely, 'mankind' stands for all of those, of whatever descent and lineage, who display a devotion to the values that we serve – civility and rational debate, for example – we have to face the fact that not all biologically human beings can be expected to do so, and some biologically non-human ones might, at least in some degree. The problem, notoriously, is that the harder we make it to meet the qualifications of 'real humanity' (so as to exclude dolphins, chimpanzees, squids and honeybees), the more creatures of clearly human descent we also push beyond the pale. In the end either only the Wise are worth troubling about (and they, so far, are found only among the biologically human) or any individual with feelings and purposes of its own is a proper moral object. Either most human beings may rightly be treated 'like animals', when we deal with them at a practical level, and when we try to explain their behaviour; or a good many animals should not be treated like that either.

Humans in context, and transcendent selves

If humankind (the biological taxon) is at most only an accidental unity, and if humanity (the nominal essence which serves us well enough at the level of liberal

political theory) is only a collection of those traits which we expect to see in those
whom we choose to judge according to human standards, then the UNESCO
insistence on 'the unity of humankind' can only be a moral and political programme, not a report upon a relatively unknown species. Whether pygmy chimpanzees should be included in *Pan paniscus* or not matters hardly at all, and can be
settled easily enough, so far as the vagueness of the concept of 'conspecificity'
allows. Whether Neanderthals should be considered a distinct species or subspecies also matters little. To wonder whether Bushmen ('Sanids') and Caucasians ('Europids') might be of different species or subspecies, of which the former
is characterized by a greater degree of paidomorphosis even than the typical
'human' (see Baker 1974, pp. 307ff.), is politically dangerous. My suspicion is
that this rests on two factors. It depends first on the fact that we do have an
increased concern for creatures with whom we may imaginably or probably share
descendants as well as ancestors; secondly, that we mistakenly and even
unconsciously assume that to be of a different species is to be possessed of a different and probably inferior nature. It has been my main concern so far to dispose
of the idea that biological species are natural kinds in that sense. Our concern for
those creatures who might plausibly be co-parents or co-ancestors of our descendants should not be forgotten in any analysis of morality, or in any moral programme, but it can hardly be our sole concern. On the contrary, a wish to have
descendants rather like ourselves, and a corresponding care for those who might
helpfully contribute to our lineage, rests upon a desire that what we now value
should still be valued in the future. Sociobiological analysis of our system of
values has things quite the wrong way round: we do not value what we do in
order to have lots of descendants (as though that were our prime objective, no
matter what they were like), but desire heirs in order to preserve the life or lives
we value. A better understanding of how life is preserved should then lead to an
increased concern for all those beings who share the world with us: if the land
does not live, nothing that we value will (see Clark 1985b).

This second point – that we are dependent on the land and its creatures – has a
further, and directly anthropological, implication: that the correct context of
explanation is the whole ecosystem, not merely the notionally demarcated
species. To clarify this point we need to consider what explanation is. The
traditional humanist has sought explanations for cultural innovation and historical episode within the network of human discourse. To explain why Tibetans
practise polyandry, or why Cro-Magnons painted upon walls, it was necessary to
ask them, or to imagine what they (or we) might offer as an explanation. Such
humanistic explanations have been seen as inappropriate to the lives of chimpanzees or wolves: not only could we get no answer from them if we asked, but we
could not (it was said) suppose them capable even of offering themselves an
explanation. 'If a lion could speak', so it has been said, 'we could not understand
it' – a remark made, so far as can be seen, in total ignorance of what lions were
like, but tending to support the ancient prejudice that non-humans, because they
could not speak a human tongue, could not even be said to think or feel. Scientific materialists, having learnt to 'explain' animal behaviour with non-
intentional categories, without any need to wonder what sort of explanation the

animals would give, then began to doubt that the 'explanations' which human beings give were any more than folk-psychological hypotheses. Individual and social behaviour must be explained 'objectively', without recourse to mythical entities like hopes, desires, intentions or beliefs. If we retain the habit of intentional analysis it can only be in the spirit with which we retain Ptolemaic language about dawn and sunset. 'Real' explanations are to be found in sociobiological analyses of the statistical effects upon the gene-pool of particular forms of behaviour. That this view is wholly destructive of intellectual endeavour, including that of the enquiring biologist, seems to be impossible for some commentators to grasp.

Scientific materialism can be retained a little longer if we change the unit of explanation: the cause of the biologist's theorizing must, on pain of total incoherence, at least include the world concerning which she theorizes. She cannot be offering a particular theory simply because to do so gives her genes the best chance of appearing in subsequent generations. Part of the cause must be that it is likely to be true, and that she believes this because the world is what it is. Any satisfactory theory of knowledge or justified belief must include the proviso that one believes what one does because it is true, or because something else is true which would be improbable on any other hypothesis. In brief, a decent theory is one that is caused by features of the world we theorize about, one that we would be much more likely to have if it were true than if it were not.

From this it follows that good explanations of the events that we initially characterize as elements of human culture should not be internal to the species: they should link those events to the whole world-segment to which the events themselves are responses. If it is unfashionable to seek intentional explanation, and certainly very difficult when we deal with entities which cannot directly answer our probing questions, it is simply unsound to seek explanations of what 'people' do or did as if they were alone in the world. 'The explanation' of a cultural event, if it is not to be simply intentional, must deal with the whole 'ecological' community, which will include creatures of many species, and kinds. Past humanists could, not wholly unreasonably, explain the Lapps' treatment of reindeer simply by asking what the Lapps meant to do with them, and tacitly assuming that the reindeer had no relevant 'intentions'. Once the absence of any distinct 'natural kind' is recognized, we may acknowledge: first, that reindeer, too, may have simple purposes; secondly, that their behaviour and that of the Lapps alike may be explained objectively through sociobiological analysis; and, finally, that those creatures we demarcate as humans or as deer are only two subsets of all of the creatures there are in the relevant ecosystem. A properly materialist explanation of this or any other cultural form will reveal that 'human artefacts' are as much a product of the whole system as termite hills or the Everglades: no one being, perhaps, intended the result, and no one lineage necessarily profits from it.

If humankind is not a natural kind, but an assembly of interbreeding populations like any other species, existing within a series of ecosystems that are the proper units of explanation, then a number of traditional categories must be judged merely artificial. If oxygen is a natural kind, then so is oxygenation: if drink is not (being entirely relative to the needs and preferences of the speaker), then 'having a drink' is not. Correspondingly, if humankind is only a *Realgattung*, or even (taking its prehistoric past into account) a *Formenkreis*, and not a natural kind, then what becomes of slavery (as distinct from domestication), or cannibalism (as distinct from flesh-eating), or murder? European explorers, burdened or blessed with a folk taxonomy that laid emphasis on the moral and political unity of humankind, found it necessary to invent special explanations for such social categories as 'sacred cow' or family pig, and to think the natives simply mistaken in not 'seeing' the one human form in every normal adult of our species. Once we have acknowledged that a species is not a natural kind – not a set of individuals who share a common, underlying and causative nature – we can afford to allow that other linguistic communities have other views on who are 'people' (i.e. respected members of their community), just as they have other views about edible vegetables or trees. Either there is a natural kind of persons, which is not to be identified with the biological taxon *Homo sapiens*, or there is only a nominal, evaluative grouping. Either way we cannot merely dismiss other communities' taxonomies as 'biologically ignorant', as if they had just never noticed that deer were not human beings. The question is not why have so many human societies failed to see the difference between domesticating, killing and eating animals and enslaving, murdering and cannibalizing humans? It is rather, why do we make so much of any differences there are?

The answer – and the reason why so many contemporary liberals think it necessary to identify our species with a genuine natural kind – is that we in the West are the heirs to a metaphysical and religious tradition that was dogmatically certain that all those born of woman housed immortal souls that were equipped to share God's life. Every member of our species was also a member or potential member of the spiritual Israel. Everything in the world belonged to God, and to those whom God appointed as His friends. Such a transcendent soul could not be given in material generation, although it must, while still embodied, rely upon the body formed through ancestral ages. It is one further oddity that those moderns who regularly seek to dissociate themselves from these older doctrines of the soul (which they characterize as dualist or Cartesian, though there were dualists long before Descartes) still wish to maintain the moral divisons that only made sense upon the assumption of a distinctively human soul. If there is no such soul, and if each creature's character is fixed by its individual genetic inheritance and social experience, then there is no reason to distinguish sharply and generally between domestication and slavery, flesh-eating and cannibalism, the killing of an ox and the slaying of a man. Liberal humanists need to believe in the myth of a common human nature, but have abandoned belief in the human soul, and so equate that imagined natural kind with the human species. They should think again.

Essentialist accounts of humankind are still very popular, in scientific as well as political contexts. Efforts to define humans as tool-making animals, or language-users, or food-sharers, or time-binders and 'promising primates' (Wilson 1975, see Gowlett 1984) or the like all rest upon an unconscious assumption that there is some one feature which distinguishes 'human beings' from 'non-human beings'.

Aristotle knew better than that: generic kinds, such as Birds, Fishes, Quadrupeds and Humans, were characterized not by some one essential property, but by complexes of resemblances and homologous structures (the wings of eagle and penguin are homologous, those of eagle and bat only analogous). Such large-scale kinds play no explanatory part in Aristotle's biological theory, which rests instead upon the reproductive mechanisms of particular mating couples. As we advance upon the Aristotelian road, and come to treat morpho-species, generic kinds, *Arten*, as heuristic and expository conveniences, we have steadily less excuse for believing that the presence of our biological species can be detected simply by discovering instances of tool-making, food-sharing, exogamic structures or verbal activity. All of these may precede our species; any of them may, in theory, be absent from a given human population, although we may agree that if Monboddo had been right to identify orang-utans as humans, even as a distinctive subspecies, then there would be a large hybrid population by now.

There seem to me to be two ways which the decent explorer could pursue. The first is to accept the main tenor of this chapter: we live in a world of mutually dependent and competitive organisms, such that there are relatively enclosed gene-pools, and relatively stable species-forms within the *Realgattungen* that together make up the network of biological nature. We cannot assume that all 'human' communities should be explained one way, and all 'non-human' communities another, as if chimpanzees and whales were more like worms or amoebae than they were like humans, and all human groups more like each other than any of them are like baboons or chimpanzees. We cannot equate evidence of tool-making or even of ceremonial observance with evidence of some unique, shared nature such that we can then deduce what other properties the tool-makers and the like would have. We should not assume that slavery or cannibalism needs some special explanation, different from the sort of explanation we give for domestication or flesh-eating, nor yet that any of these institutions are somehow 'natural' ones (in anything but the banal sense that they frequently happen).

However, there is at least one other way of coping with our material: to take the ancient 'Platonic' viewpoint more seriously. Species are not themselves natural kinds that properly embody distinct Platonic Forms, but it may still be true that there are such Forms, and that they eternally influence what happens in this world of becoming. Our belief in the powers of speculative reason to see behind the phenomena and grasp real truths is hardly intelligible on any but the Platonic hypothesis. Our belief that we ourselves are genuine individuals, not merely momentary effects of particular biochemical conditions, seems to require that there are transcendent souls, bearing much the same relation to these bodies of ours, as particular instances of Living-Being-at-Sea bear to that eternal Form. That Stephen should have been of any other parents than he was, or even have been reared in any other culture than he was, is impossible: Stephen could not imaginably be James or Elizabeth, let alone Washoe or Moby Dick, and all moral or epistemological projects that rest upon my ability to think what it would be like to be someone or something else rest upon an absurdity – unless it is admitted that, although Stpehen could not have been James and the rest, *I* could have been.

My ability to imagine myself in other forms than this seems to require that I am not quite identical with this bodily organism (see Vendler 1984). Finally, our recognition of moral and epistemological obligation seems, as Kant insisted, to require the postulate of moral freedom, that our eternal Selves choose the whole world-system within which particular bodily events (our actions and assents) then seem to be necessary.

This metaphysical system has many merits, and is certainly not refuted by the scorn of those who have not troubled to understand it. If it is true, then real explanations lie at a higher level than we can easily reach. What does not seem to me to follow from it – and Plato himself did not suppose that it did – is the claim that all and only human beings (members of our species) embody such transcendent souls. Nor is this a biblical doctrine, nor one that non-literate societies usually accept: other creatures than the biologically human might be persons, might share a transcendent nature, even if 'being human' were 'being of a certain natural kind' (which it is not). For Plato, human beings were only the highest of a hierarchy of embodied souls: highest in that it was open to souls so embodied to remember who and what they were, immortal companions lost for a while in fantasy. Modern humanism is the tattered heir of Platonism: it is surely time that we chose whether to be honest Platonists or to accept the consequences of straightforwardly evolutionary thought.

References

Baker, J. R. 1974. *Race*. Oxford: Clarendon Press.

Balme, D. M. 1980. Aristotle's biology was not essentialist. *Archiv für Geschichte der Philosophie* **62**, 1–12.

Beckner, M. 1959. *The biological way of thought*. New York: Columbia University Press.

Burma, B. H. 1976. Reality, existence and classification. In *Concepts of species*, C. N. Slobodchikoff (ed.). Stroudsberg, Pennsylvania: Dowden, Hutchinson and Ross.

Clark, S. R. L. 1982. *The nature of the beast*. Oxford: Oxford University Press.

Clark, S. R. L. 1984. *From Athens to Jerusalem*. Oxford: Clarendon Press.

Clark, S. R. L. 1985a. Slaves and citizens. *Philosophy* **60**, 27–46.

Clark, S. R. L. 1985b. Hume, animals and the objectivity of morals. *Philosophical Quarterly* **35**, 117–33.

Dupre, J. 1981. Natural kinds and biological taxa. *Philosophical Review* **90**, 66–90.

Eccles, J. C. 1970. *Facing reality*. Berlin: Springer.

Foley, R. 1984. Putting people into perspective. In *Hominid evolution and community ecology*, R. Foley (ed.), 1–24. New York: Academic Press.

Gowlett, J. A. J. 1984. Mental abilities of early man. In *Hominid evolution and community ecology*, R. Foley (ed.), 167–92. New York: Academic Press.

Hull, D. 1974a. *Philosophy of biological science*. Englewood Cliffs, New Jersey: Prentice-Hall.

Hull, D. 1974b. Are species really individuals? *Systematic Zoology* **25**, 174–91.

Hull, D. 1978. A matter of individuality. *Philosophy of Science* **45**, 335–60.

Jeffrey, C. 1973. *Biological nomenclature*. London: Edward Arnold.

Lack, D. 1947. *Darwin's finches*. Cambridge: Cambridge University Press.

Lloyd, G. E. R. 1983. *Science, folklore and ideology*. Cambridge: Cambridge University Press.

Mayr, E. 1969. *Principles of systematic zoology*. New York: McGraw-Hill.

Merlan, P. 1963. *Monopsychism, mysticism and monoconsciousness*. The Hague: Nijhoff.

Oldroyd, D. R. 1980. *Darwinian impacts*. Milton Keynes: Open University Press.

Putnam, H. 1970. Is semantics possible? *Metaphilosophy* 1, 187–201.

Quine, W. V. 1969. Natural kinds. In *Essays in honour of C. G. Hempel*, N. Rescher (ed.), 5–23. Dordrecht: D. Reidel.

Rosenberg, A. 1980. *Sociobiology and the preemption of social science*. Baltimore: Johns Hopkins University Press.

Slote, M. A. 1974. *Metaphysics and essence*. Oxford: Basil Blackwell.

Sober, E. 1980. Evolution, population thinking and essentialism. *Philosophy of Science* **47**, 350–83.

Sommerhof, G. 1950. *Analytical biology*. Oxford: Clarendon Press.

Sperry, R. 1983. *Science and moral priority*. Oxford: Basil Blackwell.

Sprigge, T. L. 1984. *Theories of existence*. Harmondsworth: Penguin.

Thomas, K. 1983. *Man and the natural world*. London: Allen Lane.

Trigg, R. 1982. *The shaping of man*. Oxford: Basil Blackwell.

Vendler, Z. 1984. *The matter of minds*. Oxford: Clarendon Press.

White, M. J. D. 1978. *Modes of speciation*. San Francisco: Freeman, Cooper.

Wiggins, D. 1980. *Sameness and substance*. Oxford: Basil Blackwell.

Wilson, E. O. 1978. *On human nature*. Cambridge, Massachusetts: Harvard University Press.

Wilson, P. J. 1975. The promising primate. *Man* (New Series) **10**, 5–20.

3 *Beasts, brutes and monsters*

MARY MIDGLEY

The problem

What is an animal? Supposing that a child asks us this question, our answer will probably be wide, untroubled and hospitable. It can include you and me, and the dog and the birds outside, the worms in the garden and the whales and elephants, the polar bears and Blake's Tiger. However, at other times people use the concept very differently, drawing a hard, significant line across this continuum. 'You have behaved like animals!' says the judge to a set of defendants found guilty of highly complicated offences, such as driving a stolen car while under the influence of alcohol – offences which no non-human creature could even understand, never mind consider committing. What is the judge doing here? He is, it seems, banishing the offenders from the moral community. His meaning, as widely understood, will run roughly thus: 'You have offended against standards and ideals which are by no means just local rules of convenience. You have acted on motives which human beings are supposed either not to have at all or to prevent from ever giving rise to actions. You have crashed through all the barriers of culture, which alone preserve us all from a sea of abominable motivations. The horror of your act does not lie only in the harm you have done to your victims. It springs also from the degradation to which you have rashly laid yourselves open, and which may infect us all.'

If that is a fair interpretation of such common remarks, this notion of 'an animal' clearly carries us into areas of moral and emotional meaning which are both vast and, by their nature, threatening, so they are hard to explore. We are not dealing just with some casual ambiguity. We are trenching, by the very nature of the case, on matters about which it will frighten us to think. In the second use – the one which excludes humanity – the notion of an animal stands for the unhuman, the anti-human. It is a symbol for the forces which we fear in our own nature, and do not regard as a true part of it. It displays those forces as continuous with ones which we fear in the world around us – with floods, earthquakes and volcanoes – and thereby dramatizes their power. By speaking of those forces as 'animal', we imply that they are in some way alien to us, therefore incomprehensible. But the peculiar alarm which they produce suggests also that they are *not* altogether alien – that we too carry the seeds of them in our nature, and are liable to feel their stirrings if offenders are allowed to set us their inhuman example. 'Our animal nature' exists already as a Trojan horse within the human gates. Only constant vigilance can stop it playing an active part in human life.

Clearly any concept riven by an ambivalence as deep as this is not going to yield us a clear, simple, central meaning. It is more likely to serve us as a forest of instructive examples in our attempt to understand a rampant and important confusion. The word 'animal', though it exists as a term of science, does most of its work in areas which are far from being detached and scientific. It serves continually as a reference point in the forming of our communal self-image. Both of its uses contribute to this. In its first, inclusive, use it names a class to which we all belong. In its second it names one to which we do not belong, and whose characteristic properties can be used to supply a foil, a dramatic contrast lighting up the human image.

Origins

The history of the word shows plainly the problems underlying this double use. In Latin *animal* was used to translate the Greek word *zöon*, a living creature. Although both these words are sometimes used in the exclusive, contemptuous sense I have noted a modern judge as using – to describe objectionable human beings – they seem more often to occur in the mild, inclusive, purely descriptive sense, simply to denote any living creature. It is interesting that the Greek word *zographos*, a painter, means one who depicts any living creature, the difference between people and other animals being for this purpose overlooked. This, of course, is how Aristotle and his successors used *zöon* and *animal* in the scientific enquiries which were the source of our modern zoology. Thus, during the Middle Ages the word *animal* crept gradually into scholarly use as a term of art, and thence into everyday English. The *Oxford English Dictionary* cites it first from 1398 – 'All that is comprehended of flesh and of sprite of life . . . is called *animall*, a beest' – but comments that the word hardly appears as a substantive before the end of the 16th century, and is not found in the King James Bible of 1611. The words in normal use were still *beast* and *brute*, both with the exclusive sense only. The inclusive one had still to be built up, and clearly there were great difficulties in doing this. Thus, one of the first substantive uses which the dictionary does give is where Shakespeare's Hamlet declares 'What a piece of work is a man! . . . the paragon of animals!',[1] and this is followed by a remark from Milton: 'Man hath his daily work, while other animals unactive range'.[2] Subsequent examples also balance the painful thought of human inclusion by consoling notions of contrast and pre-eminence within the class. At the same time the exclusive use had already spread itself fully to *animal* from *brute* and *beast*, carrying all of its old connotations of alienation and disgust. Thus, Shakespeare's *As You Like It* opens with Orlando's indignant speech of protest against his brother Oliver's neglect of his education – a task with which their dying father had charged him – 'Call you that keeping for a gentleman of my birth, that differs not from the stalling of an ox? His horses are bred better; . . . I, his brother, gain nothing under him but growth, for the which his animals on his dunghills are as much bound to him as I'.[3] Also, in his *Love's Labour's Lost* – 'His intellect is not replenished; he is only an animal, only sensible in the duller parts'.[4] In its adjectival use, too, the word is ambivalent. As the dictionary unhappily remarks, 'the mediaeval use of "animalis" varied from "bestial" to "spiritual", and English "animal" (adjective) had an equally wide range'. As meaning what had life or soul, the word pointed upwards. As meaning the only non-human things with life or soul which people actually knew, it pointed downwards and could not easily be used with entire equanimity.

Outer darkness

These excursions into the word's history are not a distraction. The range of fears and conflicts which they show us is of the first importance for our theme. The notion of the species-barrier, as it emerges, is inevitably linked with that of the border of value. What is admirable for humans is naturally viewed as typically human, and because social life poses us great difficulties, and culture is hardly won, the notion of the great dark outside non-human area is bound to be frightening. This area includes, in uncertain relation, the unacceptable parts of our own nature and the entire natures of the other animate beings around us. Thus, an obvious and familiar horror attends situations such as the one which Orlando describes, where human beings are 'treated like animals', or (alternatively) do things which only properly belong to animals. This kind of situation is monstrous. Oliver's offence is 'unnatural', not just in the sense of treating his brother no better than a stranger, but in the worse sense of treating him no better than a being of another species. Similarly, drunken drivers or others who are said to have 'behaved like animals' or 'made beasts of themselves' are felt to have degraded their very nature and admitted sinister outside forces to the supposedly safe citadels of civilization.

It will be obvious that this is not the only way in which human beings can consider other species, and I shall return later to the other, more hospitable and constructive ways in which, within our own culture, we do consider them. However, I want to stress first the hostile, exclusive attitude, because I think it is much more influential than we realize. Having deep roots in our everyday emotions, it plays an unacknowledged and distorting part in discussions which are supposed to be purely theoretical. The symbolism I have mentioned constantly brings irrelevant emotional factors into our attempts to conceptualize the species-barrier. The chief emotion involved is, I think, our fear of our own vast and ill-understood nature. We have, of course, certain working notions on this difficult topic, notions which enable us to carry on life reasonably quite a lot of the time. However, in difficult cases these notions constantly fail us, precipitating us into theoretical and (still more obviously) practical disaster. The bold confidence with which Enlightenment thinkers approached such topics has not proved justified. In spite of the enormous achievements of the past two centuries, if we think seriously today we must surely find ourselves in essential agreement with Pope's view of Man:

> – A being darkly wise and rudely great, . . .
> He hangs between, in doubt to act or rest,
> In doubt to deem himself a god or beast. . .
> Sole judge of truth, in endless error hurled,
> The glory, jest and riddle of the world.[5]

In the Enlightenment a prodigious effort was made to simplify this distracting picture by treating the darker aspects of human life as historical accidents – mere effects of unnecessary moral and political failures – passing 'products of the system'. Had this project entirely succeeded, perhaps we might today have been able to look at other animals dispassionately, as something quite separate from ourselves, but in spite of many important local gains, it could not so succeed. Instead, the advance of science connected us more closely than ever before with those animals, through the theory of evolution. To Darwin it seemed obvious that this move indicated strong and significant continuity between their nature and that of humans; that a scientific spirit called for the abandonment of prejudice against serious comparisons between the two, and that far the best prospect for understanding human nature lay in assimilating the conceptual schemes used for these studies, and developing both through systematic comparison.

Soon after his death, however, the tide turned against all such thinking and, until the development of ethology in the present century, almost all of those scholars whose studies brought them to the species-barrier united in insisting that the gap should be viewed as unbridgeably wide. Many factors combined to produce this volte-face,[6] the most forceful of the intellectual ones being probably the increasing specialization which went with the establishment of professional science, and its accompanying discrediting of more comprehensive, Darwinian thinkers as mere 'naturalists'. It is my present suggestion that we cannot hope to understand what the species-barrier means to us unless we consider emotional factors as well as intellectual ones. The notion of 'an animal' is a deeply and incurably emotive one. Darwin was exceptional, not just in his scientific capacity, but in his awareness of such emotional traps, and in the broad and generous spirit which often enabled him to escape them. Since his approach was written off as amateurish, scientists who suppose themselves to be thoroughly detached and impartial have, I suspect, often fallen into these traps. Chronic, endemic exaggeration of the difference between our own species and others seems to me to be such a case. I want to examine now one particular aspect of it, namely the discrepancy which now exists between what is treated as a *parsimonious* explanation for a piece of human behaviour, and what counts as such when the behaviour is that of some other animal.

Widening the gap

In the human case the normal, indeed practically the only licensed, form of explanation is in terms either of culture or of free will, or both. Anyone who suggests that an innate tendency might be even a contributing cause finds the burden of proof placed entirely on this suggestion and made exceptionally heavy. To put it another way, any explanation which invokes culture, however vague, abstract, far-fetched, infertile and implausible it may be, is readily accepted; while explanation in terms of innate tendencies, however careful, rigorous, well-documented and specific, is ignored.[7] However, for animal psychology exactly the opposite position obtains. Here, what is tabu is the range of concepts which describe the conscious, cognitive side of experience. The preferred, safe kind of explanation is that from innate programming. Again, this preferred kind of explanation may be left as loose as the user pleases, while if anything cognitive is mentioned, standards of rigour at once soar into a stratosphere where few arguments could hope to follow them.[8]

This situation will be so familiar to many readers that they will wonder how these rulings can possibly be questioned. Fortunately, however, in both areas the tide is turning, and complacent acceptance will not last anybody for much longer. In the field of animal psychology Donald Griffin has called attention to the immense oddity of supposing that it is *more* parsimonious to account for highly complex and flexible behaviour by supposing a program elaborate enough to predict and provide for every eventuality than by making the much more natural assumption that the creature has enough brain to have some idea what it is doing. As he points out, the attempt to make pre-programming account for everything has only been made to look plausible by constant misdescription – by abstract, highly simplified accounts of what creatures do, which are repeatedly shown up as inadequate when anybody takes the trouble to observe them longer and more carefully. For instance, he points out that the work of leaf-cutter ants is far more subtle and complex than it is usually described as being. Such highly complicated performances by relatively simple animals can indeed be accounted for to some extent by positing that they possess inborn 'neural templates' which they use as patterns. However, considering the skill and flexibility with which they adapt these patterns to suit varying conditions and materials, it is scarcely plausible to suggest that the template reigns alone and can, so to speak, work itself.

Can we reasonably infer from the varied, effective and highly integrated behaviour of leaf-cutter ants that they might think consciously about burrow-construction, leaf-gathering, fungus-gardening or other specialized activities? As in other instances, prevailing biological opinion is vehemently negative. Yet the *principles of adaptive economy . . .* may appropriately be called on in this instance. The workers of leaf-cutter ants are tiny creatures, and their entire central nervous system is less than a millimetre in diameter. Even such a miniature brain contains many thousands of neurones, but ants must do many other things besides gathering leaves and tending fungus gardens. *Can the genetic instructions stored in such a diminutive central nervous system prescribe all of the detailed motor actions carried out by one of these ants?* Or is it more plausible to suppose that their DNA programs the development of simple generalizations such as 'Search for juicy green leaves', or 'Nibble away bits of fungus that do not smell right', rather than specifying every flexion and extension of all six appendages? . . . Explaining instinctive behaviour in terms of conscious efforts to match neural templates may be *more parsimonious* than postulating a complete set of specifications for motor actions that will produce the characteristic structure under all probable conditions. Conscious efforts to match a template may be more economical and efficient. . . . *It is always dangerous for biologists to assume that only one of two or more types of explanation must apply universally.* (Griffin 1984, pp. 105, 116, emphasis added.)

Or again, there is the well-known case of birds which lead predators away from their broods by distraction behaviour, acting as if they were unable to fly properly till they have diverted the threat well away from the danger area. Notoriously, they do this well, apparently adapting their behaviour with great skill to the predator's responses. They often succeed in losing the hunter, and show an apparent knowledge of this by dropping their masquerade suddenly and completely, flying back directly to the nest as soon as the job is done. However, scientists have gone to great lengths to account for this quite widespread practice without invoking conscious intention. Instead, they posit an explanation in terms of conflict behaviour. This involves supposing that clashes between the bird's inborn drives to attack the predator and to escape it just happen to result in this strangely convenient effect of distracting it instead. Griffin comments:

> Why has conflict between motivations been so commonly accepted as an adequate explanation and, at least by implication, one that does away with any need to suppose that the bird has the slightest idea what it is doing? Perhaps the preference tells us more about the scientists than about the birds. If we pull ourselves out of this negative dogmatism, we can begin to ask what birds engaged in predator-distraction behaviour might be feeling and thinking. . . . [He discusses this, and continues] The thoughts I am ascribing to the birds under these conditions are quite simple ones, but *it is often taken for granted that purely mechanical, reflex-like behaviour would be a more parsimonious explanation* than even crude subjective feelings or conscious thoughts. But to account for predator-distraction by plovers, we must dream up *complex and tortuous chains of mechanical reflexes.* Simple thoughts could guide a great deal of appropriate behaviour without nearly such complex mental gymnastics on the part of the ethologist or the animal. (Griffin 1984, p. 94, emphasis added.)[9]

Which costs more?

The question which Griffin raises here is extremely important. Is it in fact necessarily more economical to account for the behaviour of animals without invoking their consciousness? If so, what makes it so? What kind of economy do we actually need here? What (more generally) does scientific parsimony always require of us? This parsimony evidently cannot be a purely negative ideal. It is not a mere general preference for omitting elements from any explanation. If it were, the best explanation would always be the shortest, and we would best account for the working of a car by invoking automotive force, or perhaps by simply saying 'it goes'. Where our ignorance is complete there are advantages in this way of proceeding, but it cannot properly be called explanation. Nor, again, does parsimony merely consist of refusing to use more than one pattern of explanation – in economizing on one's basic methods of thought. Griffin rightly calls attention to the dangers of this, to the misleading effect of that sense of familiarity which can make a particular way of thinking seem proper and inevitable merely because it is familiar, when the subject-matter demands something quite different. The merely negative effect of removing subjective elements from the explanation has, therefore, no special value in itself. What is needed is to remove *irrelevant* elements, leaving the relevant ones, and we still have to show why subjective elements are the irrelevant ones.

A reason which seems to influence many people here is a rather simple confusion about the status of subjectivity – an impression that to study subjectivity, or to mention it seriously, is the same thing as 'being subjective' – that is, being uncritically influenced by one's own feelings and moods. This is the same mistake as supposing that the study of folly must be a foolish study, or the study of evil conduct an evil one, or in general (as Dr Johnson put it) that 'who drives fat oxen should himself be fat'.[10] Behind this simple error there lies the slightly more substantial objection of a difficulty in seeing how we can know anything about the subjective states of others. That our knowledge of them is limited and must not be exaggerated by pretentious claims is true and important. However, if we really had no such knowledge, our world would be totally different from what it is, and we should not possess any concepts for understanding our own subjective states either. To pretend to suspend judgement on these questions is in fact mere humbug. If a torturer excused her activities by claiming ignorance of pain on the grounds that nobody knows anything about the subjective sensations of others, she would not convince any human audience. An audience of scientists need not aim at providing an exception to this rule.

Solipsists and sceptics

Solipsism, the belief that one is oneself the only existing conscious subject, may not be internally inconsistent, but it is incompatible with so many basic conditions of human life that nobody can intelligibly adopt it. The same thing (we should notice) is true of total scepticism about the subjective life of others, even if it were combined with a theoretical admission that they may have one. It makes no more sense for us to claim that we doubt whether people manifesting strong, typical cases of anger or fear are in subjective states falling somewhere within the family of those which we recognize from our own experience and the expressions of others as characteristic of these passions, than it does to profess similar scepticism about the presence of the chairs and tables around us. In neither case can we dream up a convincing alternative which will connect with the rest of what we know. To accept something we have to be able to do this. It is idle to claim that these people may very well be feeling just as we (or rather I) would feel when waking gradually from sleep in a comfortable bed, or when eating an ice-cream, because those states have a totally different context in the elaborate, shared system of emotional logic by which we all live, and without which subjective states cannot be described at all. Of course, we can sometimes be deceived, whether by pretence or by misperceiving; we are not infallible, but this possibility of deception must be viewed against the background of generally regular, reasonably reliable and usable, organized information which we call our knowledge.

Whether it concerns furniture or feelings, our claim to knowledge is moderate and unpretentious because it is explicitly limited. We admit – indeed we know – that our ignorance about the table is enormous, as is also our ignorance about the fear and anger even of our friends. In both cases we think that some of the mysteries will remain always impenetrable to us, but to say this is to contrast these mysteries both with the crude general knowledge which serves us for the mere identification of manifest phenomena and with much other, more detailed knowledge which careful investigation will provide.

Descartes' sceptical, solipsistic, negative approach to problems about knowledge has done a great deal of useful work in its time. But when it is uncritically relied upon, its weaknesses are crippling; and wherever it is still used, so to say, *raw* – uncorrected by a full apprehension of the deeply social nature of our thinking – it makes mayhem. Its dramatic appeal, its penchant for stark black-and-white antitheses which strike the imagination, makes it especially dangerous. Because of this, patches of it still linger in far too many sheltered spots in the social sciences, which ought of all others to be the most keenly aware of its faults. The dramatization of the species-barrier, which is our present topic, depends on several of these traditional arbitrary rulings. Its core is, of course, Descartes' own wildly perverse view that all non-human animals are merely unconscious machines[11] – a view just excusable in the context of the creationist biology of his day and the manic euphoria produced by the emergence of good clockwork, but not, one might have supposed, destined to survive Darwin. What most protects such thinking today is, it seems, another legacy from Descartes, though a degenerate one – an uncritical respect for scepticism as such. Scepticism means here not what Descartes himself meant by it, namely critical doubt and questioning, but simply dogmatic denial. To many scholars denying something seems in itself to be more respectable than asserting it. The conception of parsimony which we have been examining often seems to centre on this idea, recommending simply an austere refusal to assert.

Fixing the burden of proof

This does not make sense. All propositions can be put either in positive or in negative form, so that the most resolute denier never stops asserting things, and often extremely startling things. What makes this notion of parsimony look usable is that it is always applied selectively, to cover propositions which offend against what we have initially decided to be probable. This initial decision is an absolutely necessary precondition for critical thinking. In itself, there is nothing disreputable or irrational about it. What is disreputable is to fail to be aware of it. We are accountable for our background presuppositions, and it is our business to work our hardest to make them explicit, so that they come within the range of criticism. As the history of thought shows us, we shall never succeed entirely; other generations will easily see what we ought not to have taken for granted. It also shows us that efforts of this kind are vital to constructive thinking, that many errors really can be spotted in this way, and that failure to attempt this difficult criticism results in wasted labour and scientific disaster. It is an unfortunate feature of the current ideal of science, as essentially consisting in precise and detailed work, that it diverts attention from this background thinking, without which detailed science loses its way completely.

Because the history of thought shows us so many of these errors, there should not be anything entirely surprising, nor anything offensive to psychologists, about my present suggestions, and certainly not about Griffin's question. What, he asks, makes it specially parsimonious to exclude the idea of conscious understanding from the scientific conception of an animal? He goes on to point out a number of ways in which this exclusion proves, on examination, to be not more but less parsimonious than its more natural alternatives.

What remains? Unquestionably there does remain a non-scientific but power-ful tendency to resent and fear all close comparison between our own species and any other. Unquestionably, we often tend to feel – at times extremely strongly – that the gap between our own species and all others is enormous and unbridge-able. This feeling is one of many which provide raw material for our thought, an impression of a kind which may turn out when unpacked to contain excellent sense, but which may equally vanish into thin air on closer inspection. Com-monly, the fate of such general impressions falls somewhere between the two extremes; they contain some sense and some nonsense. What we must *not* do, however, is to leave them unexamined if there is reason to suspect that they may be influencing our judgements. In cases like the present, that is surely extremely probable. It is remarkable how, in scientific discussions of this topic, the charge of bias and emotional influence is always confidently levelled at the people who do consider animals as capable of thought, and never contemplated as one which might be affecting their opponents.

Ignoring elephants

An extraordinary effect of this habit is the cheerful contempt with which it is usual to treat the evidence of people who spend their lives dealing successfully with extremely demanding animals. As far as I know, it is quite unknown for people with this kind of experience to endorse the psychologists' view of their animals as mindless, unthinking machines. Ought not this fact to give the psy-chologists pause? Is it not the business of a science to produce views which are supported, not contradicted, by the most testing forms of experience which involve their subject-matter, never mind if such testing takes place outside laboratories? To give an example, the kind of view which these practical people express is fairly represented by this passage from the memoirs of one of them:

> An elephant does not work mechanically, like many animals. He never stops learning, because he is always thinking. Not even a really good sheep-dog can compare with an elephant in intelligence. . . . His little actions are

always revealing an intelligence which finds impromptu solutions for difficulties. (Williams 1950, p. 58.)

This author constantly discusses the characters of his elephants in the same sort of terms as those of the people with whom he works, and makes many interesting comparisons between them. Is he, then, some dreamy armchair anecdotalist? He is not. He has spent all of his working life in the service of the Bombay Burma Corporation, mostly in remote jungle stations in charge of teams hauling teak logs through difficult country. During World War II, however, he varied this experience by commanding elephant teams building bridges which were vital to the survival of the army, becoming the military's most valued expert on elephant use – a task for which he is publicly thanked by Field-Marshal Sir William Slim in the introduction to his book. Contrary to what some psychologists appear to think, people like this do not have disorganized minds, infested by sentimentality and superstition, nor are they uncritical. They ask 'how do elephants think?' not out of ignorance, but because they both understand the question and know that the answer matters to them. The question is not – as Cartesian sceptics suggest – a remote one, private to each individual elephant. It concerns an essential aspect of the behaviour of any conscious subject, and no-one who deals with such a conscious subject can afford to ignore it. In the case of our fellow humans we know this very well, and the Behaviourist attempt to ignore it is perhaps now recognized as humbug. We do not pretend to be solipsists, and the sceptical pretence of ignorance about the content of other people's conscious thinking is maintained only for certain very narrow theoretical purposes. In the case of other species, however, as Griffin remarks, a kind of 'species solipsism' is felt to be more plausible, simply (I suspect) because it has not yet been subjected to much critical scrutiny (Griffin 1984, p. 28, Humphrey 1976, 1978).

In conclusion: I have devoted most of this chapter to discussing that 'species solipsism', and the general sense of alienation from other species which underlies it, because I think this is a very important factor, though a negative one, affecting all of the positive conceptions which we form of them. Insofar as it constitutes an obstacle to our free thinking on these subjects, it is something of which we badly need to be aware. How far it actually does constitute such an obstacle is, of course, very much a matter of opinion, and the influence certainly varies greatly in different areas. As I see it, a somewhat uncontrolled and unconscious ambivalence exists. Quite often we are moved by a strong Darwinian or Franciscan sense of kinship with other living things, which can be as influential as the distancing and revulsion which at other times replaces it. However, what is really worrying at present is the impression many people have that the revulsion accords better with science. These people seem to believe, first, that science ought not to be guided by emotion and, secondly, that whereas love and admiration are emotions, disgust and contempt are not. Accordingly, all enquirers who have loved their subject-matter, from the Greek astronomers gazing at the stars to field-naturalists who love their birds and beetles, would be anti-scientific, and should be replaced by others who are indifferent to them. However, since indifference would drive people away from the study altogether, it may seem that the best a scientist can hope for is actively to dislike his subject-matter, and help to remove the good opinion which others have ignorantly formed of it.

Obviously, this is a foolish attitude, and to express it explicitly is perhaps to guard against it sufficiently. Nevertheless, unexpressed attitudes of this kind do haunt us, and it is an important part of what I have to say here that we do need to guard against them, whatever may be thought about the particular example I have been discussing. However, one of the reasons why I have chosen to dwell on that example is that I think it does unrecognized harm in the current discussions about the moral responsibilities of humans towards animals. When reformers who are disturbed about particular aspects of our current treatment of animals protest about them, they have to use our existing moral language which is, of course, largely adapted to describing moral relations among human beings. This can at once have the effect that I mentioned in discussing the protest of Orlando – it can sound monstrous. People hearing such protests for the first time often take refuge from their scandalized reaction in laughter – 'are you really making this fuss about *frogs*?'. Now frogs, in fact, have quite an advanced nervous system, and when they are roughly cut in half – as was happening all over India until the roaring trade in frogs' legs for the epicure market of the West was recently made illegal – the discarded half takes much longer to die than would be the case for a mammal. Does this matter? The trade was, of course, made illegal because of the appalling effect on agriculture of this wholesale massacre of the prime insectivores which protected the crops. The idea that an objection could be brought on behalf of the frogs themselves would to many seem obscure, and indeed bizarre. However, in the West, we cannot actually take refuge in the innocent sense of total mystification about this which for people in some other cultures may really be appropriate. This is the kind of thing about which we are actually ambivalent. At some times we see the frogs' objection quite plainly, and if (for instance) one of our children were to start cutting them up for fun, we should state that objection firmly. Similarly, if intelligent alien beings were to start cutting us up, we should probably think that we had a genuine grievance against them. In Indian culture a similar ambivalence appears, as the sophisticated doctrines of Buddhism make obvious.

This is not a simple subject. I would like to end by urging that, in all such debates, we make very serious efforts not to be guided merely by our sense of what is familiar. This is a topic to which human beings have never properly attended, and on which it takes great efforts to fix our minds fairly. It is natural that on such matters traditional thinking is superficial and unsatisfactory. It is our business not to rest content with it, but to amend it. The moral community to which we take ourselves to belong is not a single, clear, fixed one, but one of very varying and shadowy boundaries. The difference between our species and the various others around us is not simple or obvious either, but extremely complex and obscure. Elephants, too, are different from most other animals, and so are albatrosses. All serious study of any species ought to send us back to the drawing-board.

Notes

1   *Hamlet*, II.ii.306–12.
2   *Paradise Lost*, Book IV.1.621. It is worth noting the implausibility of this remark in relation to (say) beavers or birds with young.
3   *As You Like It*, I.i.12–16.
4   *Love's Labour's Lost*, IV.ii.27.
5   *Essay on Man*, Epistle ii.1.1.
6   A process admirably traced in Boakes (1984).
7   I shall say no more about this arm of the divergence here, having treated it fully elsewhere (Midgley 1979, 1981, 1984). However, I have not previously stressed so explicitly the relationship between the two arms, which I think to be a very important one.
8   The oddities of this approach, and especially the misuse made in it of the concept of anthropomorphism, are further discussed in Midgley (1983) chapters 8–12. See especially p. 115.
9   Excerpts from D. R. Griffin (1984) *Animal Thinking* are reprinted by kind permission of the author and the publisher, Harvard University Press.
10 Boswell's *Life of Johnson*, vol. iv, p. 313.
11 Descartes, *Discourse on Method*, closing pages to Part V (1911–12, I: 115–18). See also two letters by him, to the Marquess of Newcastle (23 November 1646) and to Henry More (5 February 1649) in Descartes (1970). These selections are conveniently reprinted in Regan & Singer (1976). For Descartes' general sceptical and ego-centred method, see his *Meditations on First Philosophy*, Meditation 1, and the *Discourse on Method*, Chapter 4.

References

Boakes, R. 1984. *From Darwin to behaviourism: psychology and the minds of animals.* Cambridge: Cambridge University Press.
Descartes, R. 1911–12. *Philosophical works of Descartes* (transl. E. S. Haldane and G. R. T. Ross). London: Cambridge University Press.
Descartes, R. 1970. *Descartes: philosophical letters* (transl. and ed. A. Kenny). Oxford: Oxford University Press.
Griffin, D. R. 1984. *Animal thinking.* Cambridge, Massachusetts: Harvard University Press.
Humphrey, N. K. 1976. The social function of intellect. In *Growing points in ethology*, P. P. G. Bateson and R. A. Hinde (eds), 303–17. Cambridge: Cambridge University Press.
Humphrey, N. K. 1978. Nature's psychologists. *New Scientist* **78**, 900–3.
Midgley, M. 1979. *Beast and man: the roots of human nature.* Brighton: Harvester Press.
Midgley, M. 1981. *Heart and mind: the varieties of moral experience.* Brighton: Harvester Press.
Midgley, M. 1983. *Animals and why they matter: a journey around the species barrier.* Harmondsworth: Penguin.
Midgley, M. 1984. *Wickedness: a philosophical essay.* London: Routledge and Kegan Paul.
Regan, T. & P. Singer (eds) 1976. *Animal rights and human obligations.* Englewood Cliffs, New Jersey: Prentice–Hall.
Williams, J. H. 1950. *Elephant Bill.* London: Rupert Hart-Davis.

4 *Animality, humanity, morality, society*

RICHARD TAPPER

Humans as animals

> Animals have always been central to the process by which men form an image of themselves . . . the animals supply examples for the mind as well as food for the body; they carry not only loads but also principles. . . . The first metaphor was animal . . . the essential relation between man and animal was metaphoric. Within that relation what the two terms – man and animal – shared in common revealed what differentiated them. . . . What distinguished men from animals was born of their relationship with them. (Berger 1971, pp. 1042, 1043; 1977, pp. 504, 505.)

> The crux of the explanation of the apparent universality of animals as images of the profoundest symbolic significance would seem, I argue, to lie in the fact that 'the animal' is both within us, as part of our enduring biological heritage as human beings, and also by definition, outside and beyond human society. (Willis 1974, p. 9.)

> We are not just rather like animals; we are animals. Our differences from other species may be striking, but comparisons with them have always been, and must be, crucial to our view of ourselves. (Midgley 1979, p. xiii.)

> The brute creation provided the most readily-available point of reference for the continuous process of human self-definition. Neither the same as humans, nor wholly dissimilar, the animals offered an almost inexhaustible fund of symbolic meaning. (Thomas 1983, p. 40.)

These statements – by an art historian and critic, a social anthropologist, a philosopher and a social historian, respectively – indicate an apparently unanimous interest in the notion of 'animals as metaphor'. They are somewhat randomly drawn from an outpouring of writings over the last 20 years or so, in a wide variety of disciplines, on the perennial Great Question: what is human nature? Most of this literature has been concerned, not with the 'metaphor' issue, but with the basic, empirical and positivist question most simply posed as, how animal is man? In this chapter I make no attempt to answer the question, but rather pursue the anthropologically more fundamental issue of the different ways in which people in different societies ask and answer it. In other words, I am interested in the cultural variation in definitions of 'humanity' and 'animality', and in constructions of 'animals' and animal society as metaphors of human morality and society.

The history of constructions of 'nature' in the West, and of changing attitudes towards animals, has been traced recently by Thomas (1983) and Serpell (1986).

Medieval and Renaissance theology and philosophy – rooted in the Bible and Aristotle, and confirmed by Descartes, Spinoza and Kant – were wholly anthropocentric: nature was created for the interests of humanity, 'every animal was intended to serve some human purpose, if not practical, then moral or aesthetic' (Thomas 1983, p. 19). Man, made in the image of God and endowed with reason, was fundamentally different in kind from other forms of life, which he was entitled to treat as he chose.

In the early modern period the growing scientific interest in natural history led to a recognition of the physical similarities between humans and other animals. Moreover, 'the growth of towns and the emergence of a new industrial order in which animals became increasingly marginal to the processes of production' (Thomas 1983, p. 181) engendered an awareness of moral duties owed to animals. Anthropomorphism began to replace anthropocentrism. When Darwin caused a confrontation between the two perspectives, the intellectual battle was already won.

The recently renewed debate on these issues has closely followed advances in research, notably in those disciplines concerned with animal behaviour and consciousness: ethology, primatology, sociobiology and psychology. There has been new movement on that frontier of the human sciences touching on the difference, if any, between humans and other animals.

The debate has been particularly fierce recently around sociobiology, whose practitioners have seemed to argue an extreme position, that there is little or nothing important in human culture that does not have biological, hence animal roots.[1] Not surprisingly, there has been a strong reaction to this from some social and cultural anthropologists, who seem to have a vested interest in a particular predefinition of the frontier. They take it for granted that humans are a special kind of animal, uniquely possessed of 'culture' in the sense of a system of meanings and symbols: all that is cultural, hence specifically human, is the domain of anthropology; all that is animal, unless it forms part of human culture, is not. Such anthropologists cannot accept that animals have 'culture' in this sense, nor that culture and its variations and complexities can be understood as products of evolutionary adaptation under natural selection. For them, human nature *is* cultural diversity.

In recent and widely read discussions of the moral relations between humans and animals, philosophers such as Midgley (1979, 1983) and Clark (1984) have reviewed the debate, but they have tended to present it in terms of an opposition between polar extremes: the 'blank-paper', all-is-culture libertarianism of the anthropologists and sociologists, versus the biological determinism of ethologists and sociobiologists. Rightly castigating both positions as shallow and simplistic, they have chosen to steer something of a middle course between them, urging those studying both animal and human behaviour to adopt a 'more carefully philosophical' approach (Clark 1984, p. v).

Of course, the extreme views attributed to each side in the debate are caricatures. Rebuttals of the naive and extravagant claims of the early sociobiologists have forced many to modify their ambition of annexing the social sciences, while redefining their discipline as 'behavioural ecology' or 'socio-ecology' (see Foley

1986). As for social and cultural anthropologists, among whom I include myself, it is not so much that we do not hold a 'blank-paper' view of humanity, but that as anthropologists our perspective on, and interest in, the problem are rather different. Apart from a few who have taken an extreme 'cultural' stance, and a few who have jumped wholeheartedly on the sociobiology bandwagon, most of us have stood aside from the debate. Our detachment is perhaps due to a sensation of *déjà vu*: when we hear the arguments, we are reminded of experiences in the field, of debates we have witnessed or in which we have participated, in some New Guinea men's house, or (in my case) huddled around a smoky fire in a felt tent on top of a mountain in Iran; debates about whether dogs understand what people say to them, whether bears can talk, whether camels bear grudges, how wolves learn to attack from both sides of the flock at once. . . . What interests anthropologists about such debates is less the 'scientific accuracy' of the answers than the context of the discussion and the relevance of the terms of the debate to human social relations.

In other words, when anthropologists hear philosophers (or others) speculating on the animal nature of humanity or moralizing about 'animal rights', we cannot but locate their views in the cross-cultural context to which some philosophers have remained remarkably blind. As anthropologists we do not ask how far humans are animals – that is, how far they share with animals basic drives such as aggression, fear and sexuality – though we grant this to be a major philosophical and ethical problem; nor do we ask how far animals are conscious, social, moral, cultural or articulate. Rather, we are concerned with how these questions are constructed in different societies; that is, with where different societies locate their humanity. We stand back to ask: is the Great Question – What is human nature? – a *universal* question? What sorts of answers are given, and is the question asked and answered in ways that are related to other apsects of culture and society? For us, the views of modern Western philosophers are just further examples of cultural variation, which need to be explained in both social and historical terms.

Too often the question has been posed (by anthropologists among others) in the form: how does humanity perceive nature? This carries the 'common-sense' presumptions that nature is an objective given, and further, that humanity is one, a species with a common nature despite cultural diversity. However, it has long been established that notions of both nature and humanity are highly variable and changing cultural constructions, and that in many societies they are not constructed at all.

Totemic thought

How do other peoples phrase the problem of humanity? With the less philosophically inclined, we have to search in categories, metaphors, and modes of socialization. One widely accepted premise (see, for example, Leach 1982, ch. 2 and pp. 116f.) is that in every society children have to learn how to distinguish Self from Other; and 'people like me' (kin and friends) from 'people not like me' (strangers, enemies and witches); and 'people' from 'not people' (usually animals). Freud noted (of European society) that 'children show no trace of arrogance which urges adult civilized men to draw a hard-and-fast line between their own nature and that of all other animals. Children have no scruples over allowing animals to rank as their full equals' (quoted by Hines & Bustad 1986, p. 5). It appears, moreover, to be established that

> during the first years of life [children] do not appear to be able to make a clear distinction between humans and non-humans, and even as early as two years of age will begin responding socially towards animals such as family pets and treating them, to all intents and purposes, as if they were persons. (Serpell 1986, p. 139, see also ch. 11).

However, various rather more complex formulations of the relation between people and animals are possible, and are indeed found. For example, the straightforward Cartesian dualism familiar to the West, yielding the series of homologous oppositions culture : nature :: people : animals (:: male : female :: reason : passion . . .)[2] is perhaps historically rare – and indeed the denial of it is currently popular: people *are* animals, animals have rights like people. In other cultures a continuum may be constructed, or a more complex series of distinctions. For example, 'people' are divided into some that are 'like us' and others that are 'like animals'; or 'animals' are divided into 'tame animals' that are 'like people' and 'wild animals' that are not; or 'tame animals' are divided into 'pets' that are 'like people' and 'livestock' that are not. The various distinctions may be treated as analogies: each Other may be likened to each other: 'strangers' are 'wild animals' and 'witches'. . . . As Douglas (1975, p. 289) suggests,

> in each constructed world of nature, the contrast between man and not-man provides an analogy for the contrast between the member of the human community and the outsider. In the last most inclusive set of categories, nature represents the outsider.

However, these analogies remain metaphoric, they are not identifications. Strangers, even witches, are in some ways 'people', and 'wild animals' have something in common with 'tame animals'. What interest us are the markers that are introduced to distinguish these metaphorical analogues from each other, and from 'people like us'.

In considering cultural constructions of relations between people and animals, and the use of animals as metaphors for human society, we are of course in the anthropological realm of 'totemic thought'. Lévi-Strauss (1964, 1966) has argued that animals figure so commonly in totemic discourse, not as Malinowski, Radcliffe-Brown and Fortes proposed, because they are good to eat, but because they are good to think with. He also maintained that systems of classification of animals are not, as Durkheim and Mauss (1963) suggested, derived from social categories, but rather that categories drawn from a system of classification of nature are employed to express the nature of relations between human groups and individuals.

If this argument (that animals are good for thinking) is valid, and I think it is, then we need to enquire further, thinking to what purpose? Clearly, that purpose is not just classification and the creation of order, but also teaching and learning morality – or, as Tambiah puts it, 'to forge a system of moral conduct and to resolve the problem of man in nature' (1969, p. 457, cf. Fernandez 1971).

Animals, or rather cultural constructions of them, are used as metaphors for this moralizing and socializing purpose in two rather different, even contradictory, ways. Sometimes certain animals are idealized and used as models of order and morality, in animal stories and myths (cf. Sperber 1975). The animals are treated as agents and social beings, with motives, values and morals; and differences between them and people are implicitly denied. By contrast animals are sometimes represented as the Other, the Beast, the Brute, the model of disorder or the way things should not be done. Animals are ideal for both of these purposes, because they can be seen to perform the same basic functions as people (eating, excreting, moving, copulating, being born, giving birth, dying, . . .) in ways that people conceivably could, yet which are forbidden to them by the rules that are fundamental to any cultural and moral system. It is 'culture' in this sense that separates people from other animals.

Animals are good to teach and learn with, particularly in those central areas of life clouded by taboos and inhibitions. It is not so long ago that the realities of sex and procreation were so unmentionable in the English family that children were gently initiated into the harsh truth through stories of birds and bees and the stork. As Serpell (1986, p. 139, referring to Sharefkin & Ruchlis 1974 and Blanchard 1982) points out, children

> can readily relate to real or imagined feelings in animals, when they often have great difficulty in relating to or comprehending the feelings of other people. This fact is clearly recognized by the authors and publishers of children's literature who frequently use anthropomorphic animal characters, rather than more realistic images, as a medium for conveying social values and rules.

In effect such animal stories serve a threefold purpose: through *non-human metaphor* they allow teachers and learners to avoid articulating difficult or embarrassing truths about humanity; at another level they *create a distinction* between humans and other animals; and they *reinforce human morality* by giving it a 'natural' basis.

Sapir (1977) has suggested a caveat to what he calls Lévi-Strauss' 'shibboleth' that animals are good to think with: fine, he says, but only when there are animals about. I would question this: there are always animals about, even if they exist only as *images in the mind*. My caveat, or rather elaboration of the 'shibboleth', would be that animals are good to think with, and good to teach with, but the way in which they are used (and thought *of*) varies both with people's familiarity with them and also with the availability of other possible human models, other ethnic groups, classes and social categories, either for emulation as ideals or for derogation as Others.

Human–animal relations of production

Familiarity with animals is a function, I suggest, of aspects of the economic system, or at least of the nature of *human–animal relations of production*. A Marxian classification of social and economic systems by *mode of production* is not apposite, since its central component, comprising *human* social relations of production, does not take account of relations of production between humans and animals, the feature I want to examine here. More useful, I suggest, is to cast a Marxian frame around the classic typology of production systems, which *are* characterized by specific human–animal relations of production. These systems are hunting and gathering, pastoralism, agriculture and urban–industrial production.

Here I follow a suggestion made by Ingold, who points out that higher animals can *act*, and that 'in this capability resides the potential for animals to be *tamed* by man: that is, to enter into social relations of domination defined by man's subjugation of the animal's will to suit his own purposes' (Marx 1964, p. 102). Marx, he reminds us, 'denied the possibility of this form of relationship between man and animals on the grounds that animals lack will', and therefore classified domestic animals alongside primitive tools, as instruments of labour (Marx 1930, p. 172). This, Ingold rightly objects,

> is to relegate animals to the status of mindless machines. In truth, the domestic animal is no more the physical conductor of its master's activity than is the slave: both constitute labour itself rather than its instruments, and are therefore bound by social relations of production. (Ingold 1980, p. 88, also 1979, 1983.)

The specific relations he considers are those involved in the three aspects of domestication he distinguishes as taming, herding and breeding. Except when he describes (only half-seriously) the relations between Chukchi pastoralists and their herds as involving 'class exploitation' (Ingold 1980, p. 234), he does not pursue Marxian categories in the context of human–animal relations. I suggest we should do just that.

At the extremes, of simple hunter–gatherer bands on the one hand and urban–industrial society on the other, Marxian categories of human social relations of production also apply to those between humans and animals; in the intermediate types (peasant agriculture, pastoral nomadism and ranching) we shall find that things are rather different.

Hunter–gatherers live in complementary relations with the other animal species in their environment, not particularly close to any of them, but with an extensive knowledge of the habits of all species. Objectively they are predators, but hunters' relations with their prey are often culturally constructed as ones of reciprocal exchange and co-operation in the mutual production of each others' existence. In this respect at least, such relations resemble those entailed in Marx's notion of the Germanic or communal system.

Some hunters tame certain animals (such as dogs or reindeer) to help with the hunt. Individual animals are taken out of their natural species community and subjugated to provide labour for the human production process. These, unlike other tamed animals that hunting peoples also frequently keep as pets, are treated as slaves, their feeding and reproduction under the control of their human masters. This 'slave-based' or 'ancient' system of production relations between people and animals also characterizes those cultivators who use draught animals.[3]

More-extensive livestock-rearing by pastoralists involves animals that are not tamed but are herded in communities and following their natural inclinations to move, congregate, graze and breed. Again, these are subservient to and controlled by human masters, but the relation is like a contract or transaction in which the masters 'protect' the herds in return for a 'rent'. This resembles the Marxian conception of feudal relations between lord and serfs.

Ingold makes a clear distinction between 'tamed' and 'herded' animals. The former enter 'social' relations with their owners, whether as helpers in the hunt or as farm labour; the latter have only ecological relations with their masters – but here he is writing of the carnivorous pastoralists of the north (Ingold 1980, pp. 88f.). Most pastoralists keep livestock for both milk and meat, hence they have both social and ecological relations with them. However, farmers and pastoralists, like hunters with their 'tamed' animal labour, often conduct a variety of relations with animals. For example, farmers keep herds for meat and milk, pastoralists rear 'tame' animals for household and transport purposes, and both farmers and pastoralists may hunt 'wild animals', both game and predators.

In ranching, the modern form of pastoralism, human–animal relations are again different. Animals are herded in large numbers, extensively, and with no close personal relations with the owners of the ranch. They are considerably more autonomous than in pastoralism: in earlier, more-open ranching the animals were in effect undomesticated, and ranged, grazed and bred with no control other than the annual round-up for branding, castrating and the 'extraction of surplus'. In later, closed systems there is more control, exercised not under the contractual system inherent in pastoralism, but by use of superior force (even violence) and technology (Ingold 1980, pp. 235f., Strickon 1965). These seem to me typical – paradoxically for a modern offshoot of capitalism – of Asiatic–Oriental relations of production. Indeed, the cattle 'barons' of the Texas ranges should perhaps be termed 'sultans' – or 'moguls', like their oil-rich successors.

Urban–industrial society, finally, is dependent for animal products on battery- or factory-farming. The animals that feed us are reduced to machines, kept in artificial conditions in which the concern of the owners is profit through cost-effective organization of the animals' productive labour and reproduction. These are clearly exploitative relations on classic capitalist lines (cf. Serpel 1986, ch. 11).

In all this the relations discussed have been those of the (usually) male owners and the animal labour. Among the various simplifications and omissions necessitated in a chapter of this length, I have left out of account the intermediary human workers, the hired herdsmen, cowboys, butchers and other members of the owner's family. Nor have I considered the possibility of zoomorphic animal views of their human masters (Ingold 1980, p. 36). My concern is rather with how, in these various systems of human–animal relations of production, animality and humanity are socially constructed, and with the ways in which animals are used metaphorically, as Others or models.

Animals as metaphor in different production systems

Nomadic hunter–gatherer societies are usually homogeneous, with low population density and few human Others in the environment. Human groups are expected to follow the same basic moral rules, though they may be involved in relations of ritual exchange or raiding. However, animal species – and, indeed, other features of the environment – provide a treasury of contrasts for the modelling of difference. Interspecific differences are an apt metaphor for differences between human groups or individuals, with the neat intellectual contrast that while animal species cannot interbreed, human groups 'must'. This is Lévi-Strauss' classic understanding of totemism in the context of exogamous lineages, typically among hunter–gatherer societies. At the same time various animal Others may be used for teaching morality: the !Kung, for example, deprecate eating alone as the behaviour of a lion. Discussion of animal metaphor in such societies leads into further classic anthropological questions concerning taboo, sacrifice, and ideas of common ancestry, but I will not pursue these further here.

Settled farmers, typically, see themselves at the centre of a series of circles of decreasing familiarity: from home, farm and village to the wild periphery where danger threatens. Leach (1964), Tambiah (1969) and others, developing a theory of taboo, have given detailed accounts of farming societies in which such social–spatial classifications are assimilated to a homologous series of animal classes. For example, the degree of edibility of the animals (taboo : edible within limits : normally edible : inedible) corresponds with the degree of sexual availability of humans at the same social distance (prohibited by incest taboo : restricted sexual access : marriage preference : the unknown). In such systems not only are draught animals (ox, buffalo or horse) metaphorically 'slaves' in our scheme of relations of production, but they also correspond to the animal category 'edible within limits' and the social category 'restricted sexual access'; while livestock (pigs, cattle or sheep), kept 'under contract' for their edible products, and hence approximating 'serfs' in our scheme, correspond to the social category 'preferred for the marriage contract'.

The distinctive feature of pastoralism is that two communities, one human and one animal, coexist in what is usually described as a relation of symbiosis, but which I have characterized as feudal relations of production between lords and serfs: the owners protect and control their herds, extracting 'rent' in the form of produce, wealth values and (on ritual occasions of sacrifice) meat. For the most part pastoralists live in a homogeneous social environment that is almost as empty of human Others as that of hunters. Settled, agricultural or urban society is glimpsed from afar, if at all. Animals, by contrast, are more immediately available as models than in any other type of society. Pastoralists are thus a particularly interesting case. The implications of their relations with their animals for their conceptions of humanity have been remarkably neglected by their ethnographers, who have focused on the economic and ceremonial, but rarely on the cognitive and metaphoric, uses of animals.

Intellectually, the pastoralist symbiosis with livestock has two edges. Whether they are thought of as part of human society or humans as part of theirs, they provide an ideal model for humanity. However, as is shown for instance in Evans-Pritchard's classic description of the 'bovine idiom' of Nuer discourse on social relations, it seems that although on one level the distinction of humans from animals is being denied and their identity explicitly affirmed, on another level a distinction is made. This again comes out clearly in Evans-Pritchard's (1940, p. 37, 1956, pp. 258–60) account: the herds are replicas of human society, yet they are matrilineal and uxorilocal (the cows are the stable core of the herd), whereas their human counterparts organize themselves in patrilineal, virilocal terms (the men are the stable core of the community). Humans and animals are identified at one level but differentiated at another. For Willis (1974, pp. 9, 120, cf. Beidelman 1966),

The image of the symbolic animal is therefore necessarily a dualistic image, structurally homologous with the duality in human society and the human self between the real and the ultimate ideal, the actual and the longed for, even if subconsciously. . . . The distinctive peculiarity of animals is that, being at once close to man and strange to him, both akin to him and unalterably not-man, they are able to alternate, as objects of human thought, between the contiguity of the metonymic mode and the distanced, analogical mode of the metaphor. This means that, as symbols, animals have the convenient faculty of representing both existential and normative aspects of human experience, as well as their interrelation; what is beyond society, the ultimate ends of action, and the incorporation of such values in the structure of social perception and relations.

I would argue a different point: it is because pastoralists live in the closest intimacy with their herds, and because the herds 'naturally' are organized in ways that their owners cannot but construct as matrilineal and uxorilocal, that the pastoralists must organize themselves patrilineally and virilocally, in terms that thus define the 'animality' of the herds.

Engels argued long ago, following Morgan, that the domestication of animals and the emergence of pastoralism, with the development of wealth in animals, led to the replacement of matriliny and matriarchy by patriliny and patriarchy, which he called 'the world historical defeat of the female sex' (1972, p. 129, cf. Morgan 1877, p. 345). It seems to me equally plausible to argue an intellectualist explanation for the prevalence among pastoralists of patriliny and patriarchy: human pastoralist society necessarily constructs itself in this way to provide an otherwise absent distinction of humanity from animality.[4]

In this respect, again, ranching contrasts markedly with pastoralism. Ranching, it will be recalled, is characterized by 'Asiatic' relations of production between the owners and the semi-wild herd community. One of the most powerful modern myths is that of the cowboy, the aggressive, macho, gun-toting individualist, engaged in competitive struggle not only with the human and animal predators (rustlers and Indians, and the wolves and bears of the wild), but with the very steers and broncos of the ranch. This struggle, no doubt influenced by the circuses, tournaments, bear-fights and bullfights of European tradition, has been glorified in the modern rodeo, where man and beast are matched as opponents in a ritualized – and gratuitously cruel – 'taming' of the wild.[5]

Urban–industrial society, complex, differentiated and dense, offers a wide variety of human Others: different classes and ethnic groups are all stereotyped for emulative or pejorative use by teachers or parents. In a society which offers little experience of what animals are 'really' like, they become stylized or idealized humans: hence the role of pets, zoos, and animal toys, the prevalence of animals in children's stories, and the universal success of both animal cartoons and wildlife documentaries. At the same time animal metaphors of 'bestiality' proliferate, focusing particularly on 'vermin', but also on factory-farmed livestock, with special emphasis on the pig (cf. Serpell 1986, ch. 1, Leach 1964). The animals of the mind remain with us, while real animals have become marginalized. As Berger (1977, p. 123) points out,

> the marginalisation of animals is today being followed by the marginalisation and disposal of the only class who, throughout history, has remained familiar with animals and maintained the wisdom which accompanies that familiarity.

He means peasant farmers, but I would add pastoralists.

The marginalization of animals is not complete, of course. Pets are at the centre of modern urban society, but there they are treated as fellow-humans, just as humans very close to each other sometimes treat each other as 'pets'. Pets are found in all kinds of societies, as Serpell has recently shown, but it is surely significant that there has been a recent shift in Britain and the USA towards giving pets human names, the final reversal of the Nuer mode of naming people after favourite livestock.[6] At the same time their sexual and dietary habits have been radically transformed: they are almost all speyed or neutered, and are taught to develop a 'taste' for human-defined flavours in artificial (canned) food. Any manifestation of 'animal' behaviour is embarrassing and checked.

The role of pets is complemented by animal toys, wildlife films and zoos. Berger notes that earlier animal toys were few and mainly stylized and symbolic: now they are highly realistic. 'The manufacture of realistic animal toys coincides, more or less, with the establishment of public zoos' (Berger 1977, p. 122). Enormously popular documentary films bring into the urban home vivid visual and aural images of wild animals – the wilder and more 'natural' the better.

However, in zoos the 'real thing' involves another marginalization, an artificial representation. Zoo animals have no need to hunt for food or to fight for mates, all is supplied. There is no competition with other animals or with humans, hence the indifference displayed by most zoo animals to their human visitors – quite the opposite of their attitude in the wild. The animals are objectified and individualized. Even when there are groups – a troop of monkeys or a pride of lions – these groups are artificially isolated from danger and competition.

Whether pets or zoo animals, the 'live' creatures we observe in urban society are treated as individuals, as specimens; and urban society also individualizes and marginalizes people. Children are taken to zoos and are shown wild-animal films, ostensibly to teach them about the 'natural' life of animals. However, in effect zoo animals provide the metaphors for learning about the social life of humans. In zoos and documentaries what children (and adults) are most interested in is the display by animals (especially primates and higher mammals) of recognizably *human* behaviour and personality characteristics: feeding, copulating, mothering, playing and fighting.

It is the same with animal stories. From Beatrix Potter's *Peter Rabbit* to George Orwell's *Animal Farm*, the stories are not about animals as such, but about the cultural rules, relationships and problems of human society. In the world of Donald Duck, as Berger (1977, p. 665) says, 'the pettiness of current social practices is *universalized* by being projected onto the animal kingdom . . . their physical features apart, these animals have been absorbed into the so-called silent majority'. The attraction of Shultz's Snoopy is his humanity. Even Richard Adams' *Watership Down* and *The plague dogs*, and to a lesser extent *Shardik*, which come closest of all to depicting 'what it is really like' to be a rabbit, a dog or a bear, are at base, and explicitly, about *human* problems and power relations. As Orwell (1970, p. 459) himself declared, however, 'the true struggle is between animals and humans'.[7]

Anthropomorphism and ethnocentrism

The obverse of the role of animal stories in our society is played by moral philosophers in their discussions of human nature and animal rights. Part of the concern of writers like Midgley is the misconception, in popular Western discourse, of animals as evil. She argues (Midgley 1979, 1983) that humans are capable of worse and more-motivated evil than animals, hence that the use of animal models of 'beastliness' and 'brutality' is inappropriate and unfair; and that the degree to which humans are animals can be assessed in terms of 'natural' characteristics such as aggression.

I have argued that any position, any set of ideas about human nature and the relation of humanity to animals, is a function of economic imperatives, on the one hand, and the social and political environment on the other. This argument is by no means novel: it is supported, for example, by Thomas (1983, p. 189) in his *Man and the natural world*, where he traces changing constructions of 'nature' in England from 1500 to 1800, showing among other things not only that accepted attitudes reflected current practices and class differences, but also that early pressures for reform – for example, opposition to battery-farming – were motivated by self-interest. The modern case for 'animal liberation' is put in similar terms (Rowan & Tannenbaum 1986, p. 32, discussing Singer 1976, cf. Serpell 1986).

Thomas locates his discussion very carefully within particular cultural contexts, and at the same time is aware of how far other cultures and other times ask other questions and give other answers. Some philosophers seem to lack this perspective and betray a remarkable ethnocentricity. Midgley (1979), for example, in her stimulating but at times infuriating *Beast and man*, asks about 'the roots of human nature', but for her, 'humanity' – 'we' – are 'civilized Western man', and particularly the 20th-century, urban middle class. She uses 'man' – 'humanity' – very freely in this sense. Sometimes she is more explicit: referring, for example, to the idea of man the hunter as morally equal to wolf the hunter, she commits the following solecism: 'There are tribes [*sic*] that do think this way, but it is Western thought that I am exploring' (Midgley 1979, p. 31). This is later compounded by a standard philosopher's (Freudian?) myth of 'primitive man' with 'weak inhibitions' and consequent sense of guilt: 'the preoccupation of our early literature with bloodshed, guilt and vengeance suggests to me that these problems occupied man from a very early time' (Midgley 1979, pp. 40f.). Elsewhere in the book, 'modern man' and 'our own society' are reiterated without regard to cultural variation. In the concluding chapter there is a defence of 'anthropomorphism' – the imputation of human (but implicitly 20th-century, urban, middle-class) emotions and perceptions to other animals – with a consideration of various other possible 'morphisms'; it is significant that 'ethnomorphism' is not among them (Midgley 1979, pp. 344f., cf. 1983, ch. 11, Serpell 1986, pp. 138f.).

Moral philosophers look to ethology to tell them what animals are 'really' like, in order to discover what is natural about human behaviour. Referring to researchers such as Lorenz, Berger (1971, p. 1043) insists: 'Today animals are studied in laboratories and the findings are used to excuse, in so far as they are philosophical and popular, our present social nature'. Behaviourists, he says, 'imprison the very concept of man within the limits of what they conclude from their artificial tests with animals' (Berger 1977, p. 664). As Leach (1982, p. 99) puts it,

> ethologists tend to describe their observations in language which takes the anthropomorphic analogy for granted. They regularly assert that the significance of an observed action is *symbolic* (rather than functional) and they start with a basic assumption that emotions and attitudes are just as much observable characteristics as colours or structures.

Ethologists and sociobiologists, whether working with ants or with chimpanzees, do not appear to be able to tackle the fundamental anthropological problem of translation. Wittgenstein's remark that 'if lions could speak, we could not understand them' has been quoted in relation to the problem of human cognitive relativity (Bloch 1977, p. 283, see also ch. 2, this book), but it is more directly relevant here. If, in describing behaviour in an alien *human* culture in terms derived from our own, we run the constant risk of misrepresenting or completely mistaking thoughts, emotions, meanings and motivations, how much more is this likely to be the case when describing *non-human* behaviour, when an articulated language of 'native categories' is not even accessible for translation, and the only terms available are those of human language, and indeed those of a particular human culture. Modern philosophers and ethologists rightly decry the medieval anthropocentrism that stressed the uniqueness of humans and permitted the exploitation of animals, but they should not be allowed to resurrect the equally egregious – and unscientific – error of anthropomorphism, which not only treats animals as humans but also, by ignoring human cultural differences, privileges as supremely 'human' the cultural categories of the investigator.

Moral philosophers should surely be asked to be 'more carefully anthropological' in their approach to the question of the animality of humans, and to consider the possibility that the question is not a universal one and that the answers that are offered have a social and cultural context.

In effect, the ideas of many moral philosophers and sociobiologists are part of the same tradition as are animal stories for children, with their ancestry in the bestiaries and fables against which the philosophers inveigh. They both represent, as Sahlins (1976a, p. 106) has written of sociobiology, kinds of modern Western 'Scientific Totemism'. They are not interested in cultural variations, which are embarrassing to their simplistic and ethnocentric arguments. They differ from children's stories in that the latter do not pretend to a universality, and are not trying to teach what animals are 'really' like, whereas the philosophers, and the sociobiologists in particular, know or say nothing of cross-cultural variation in the cultural construction of humanity and animality, which has been my central concern in this chapter.

Notes

An early draft of this chapter was part of a lecture delivered at the Center for Middle East Studies and the College of Liberal Arts at the University of Texas at Austin; it was also presented at a seminar in the School of Oriental and African Studies, University of London. I am grateful for helpful comments received on both occasions, and also to Tim Ingold for his extensive comments and criticisms. The faults in the present version remain my own.

1   See, for example, Wilson (1975, 1978), Dawkins (1979), Sahlins (1976a), Bock (1980), Leach (1982, ch. 3) and Geertz (1984, pp. 268f.).

2   See various chapters in MacCormack & Strathern (1980), and Ortner & Whitehead (1981); cf. Midgley (1983, ch. 7).

3   Andrew Turton reminds me that the Romans classified slaves as *instrumentum genus vocale*, and cattle as *instrumentum genus semi-vocale*; other 'tools', e.g. *plaustra*, wagons, were *instrumentum mutum* (see Varro, *De re rustica*).

4   This argument was suggested in Tapper (1979, p. 293) and is elaborated in a forthcoming paper.

5   See Lawrence (1982) on the rodeo, and Lawrence (1986) on bears; cf. Azoy (1982) on *buzkashi* in Afghanistan; Douglass (1984) on bullfighting in Spain.

6   Serpell (1986); see Lévi-Strauss (1966, pp. 204f.), Thomas (1983, ch. 3) and Sahlins
      (1976b, p. 170) on the naming of pets. Levinson (1972) and his followers take a much
      more positive perspective on the role of pets in modern urban society; see Hines &
      Bustad (1986) and Katcher (1986).
7   Animals in fiction are discussed briefly by Burt & Harding (1986).

References

Azoy, G. W. 1982. *Buzkashi: game and power in Afghanistan*. Philadelphia, Pennsylvania:
    University of Pennsylvania Press.
Beidelman, T. O. 1966. The ox and Nuer sacrifice. *Man (New Series)* **1**, 453–67.
Berger, J. 1971. Animal world. *New Society* (25 November), 1042–3.
Berger, J. 1977. Animals as metaphor. Vanishing animals. Why zoos disappoint. *New
    Society* (10 March), 504–5; (31 March), 664–5; (21 April), 122–3.
Blanchard, J. S. 1982. Anthropomorphism in beginning readers. *The Reading Teacher*
    35, 5.
Bloch, M. 1977. The past and the present in the present. *Man (New Series)* **12**,
    278–92.
Bock, K. 1980. *Human nature and history: a response to sociobiology*. New York: Columbia
    University Press.
Burt, M. K. & C. Harding 1986. Images of attachment: the human–animal bond in the
    arts. *National Forum (Phi Kappa Phi Journal)* **66** (1), 11–13.
Clark, S. R. L. 1984. *The nature of the beast: are animals moral?* Oxford: Oxford
    University Press.
Dawkins, R. 1979. *The selfish gene*. Oxford: Oxford University Press.
Douglas, M. 1975. *Implicit meanings: essays in anthropology*. London: Routledge &
    Kegan Paul.
Douglass, C. B. 1984. Toro muerto, vaca es: an interpretation of the Spanish bullfight.
    American Ethnologist **11** (2), 242–58.
Durkheim, E. & M. Mauss 1963. *Primitive classification*. Chicago, Illinois: University of
    Chicago Press.
Engels, F. 1972. *The origin of the family, private property and the state*, E. Leacock (ed.).
    London: Lawrence and Wishart.
Evans-Pritchard, E. E. 1940. *The Nuer*. Oxford: Oxford University Press.
Evans-Pritchard, E. E. 1956. *Nuer religion*. Oxford: Oxford University Press.
Fernandez, J. 1971. Persuasions and performances: of the beast in every body . . . and the
    metaphors of every man. In *Myth, symbol and culture*, C. Geertz (ed.), 39–60. New
    York: Norton.
Foley, R. 1986. Anthropology and behavioural ecology. *Anthropology Today* **2** (6),
    13–5.
Geertz, C. 1984. Anti anti-relativism. *American Anthropologist* **86**, 263–78.
Hines, L. M. & L. K. Bustad 1986. Historical perspectives on human-animal interactions.
    National Forum **66** (1), 4–6.
Ingold, T. 1979. The social and ecological relations of culture-bearing organisms: an
    essay in evolutionary dynamics. In *Social and ecological systems*, P. C. Burnham & R. F.
    Ellen (eds), 271–91. London: Academic Press.
Ingold, T. 1980. *Hunters, pastoralists and ranchers*. Cambridge: Cambridge University
    Press.

Ingold, T. 1983. The architect and the bee: reflections on the work of animals and men. *Man (New Series)* **18**, 1–20.

Katcher, A. H. 1986. People and companion animal dialogue: style and physiological response. *National Forum* **66** (1), 7–10.

Lawrence, E. A. 1982. *Rodeo: an anthropologist looks at the wild and the tame*. Chicago, Illinois: University of Chicago Press.

Lawrence, E. A. 1986. Relationships with animals: the impact of human culture. *National Forum* **66** (1), 14–18.

Leach, E. R. 1964. Anthropological aspects of language: animal categories and verbal abuse. In *New directions in the study of language*, E. R. Lenneberg (ed.), 23–63. Cambridge, Massachusetts: MIT Press.

Leach, E. R. 1982. *Social anthropology*. London: Fontana.

Levinson, B. 1972. *Pets and human development*. Springfield, Illinois: Charles C. Thomas.

Lévi-Strauss, C. 1964. *Totemism*. London: Merlin.

Lévi-Strauss, C. 1966. *The savage mind*. London: Weidenfeld and Nicolson.

MacCormack, C. & M. Strathern (eds) 1980. *Nature, culture and gender*. Cambridge: Cambridge University Press.

Marx, K. 1930. *Capital*. London: Dent.

Marx, K. 1964. *Pre-capitalist economic formations*, E. Hobsbawm (ed.). London: Lawrence & Wishart.

Midgley, M. 1979. *Beast and man: the roots of human nature*. Brighton: Harvester Press.

Midgley, M. 1983. *Animals and why they matter: a journey around the species barrier*. Harmondsworth: Penguin.

Morgan, L. H. 1877. *Ancient society*. New York: Holt.

Ortner, S. B. & H. Whitehead (eds) 1981. *Sexual meanings: the cultural construction of gender and sexuality*. Cambridge: Cambridge University Press.

Orwell, G. 1970. *Collected essays, etc.* Vol. 1. Harmondsworth: Penguin.

Rowan, A. & J. Tannenbaum 1986. Animal rights. *National Forum* **66** (1), 30–3.

Sahlins, M. 1976a. *The use and abuse of biology*. London: Tavistock.

Sahlins, M. 1976b. *Culture and practical reason*. Chicago, Illinois: Chicago University Press.

Sapir, J. D. 1977. Fecal animals: an example of complementary totemism. *Man (New Series)* **12**, 1–21.

Serpell, J. 1986. *In the company of animals*. Oxford: Basil Blackwell.

Sharefkin, B. D. & K. Ruchlis 1974. Anthropomorphism in the lower grades. *Science and children* (March).

Singer, P. 1976. *Animal liberation*. London: Cape.

Sperber, D. 1975. Pourquoi les animaux parfaits, les hybrides et les monstres sont-ils bons à penser symboliquement? *L'Homme* **15** (2), 5–34.

Strickon, A. 1965. The Euro-American ranching complex. In *Man, culture and animals*, A. Leeds & A. P. Vayda (eds), 229–58. Washington, DC: American Association for the Advancement of Science.

Tambiah, S. J. 1969. Animals are good to think and good to prohibit. *Ethnology* **8**, 424–59.

Tapper, R. 1979. *Pasture and politics: economics, conflict and ritual among Shahsevan nomads of northwestern Iran*. London: Academic Press.

Thomas, K. 1983. *Man and the natural world: changing attitudes in England 1500–1800*. London: Allen Lane.

Willis, R. G. 1974. *Man and beast*. London: Hart-Davis, MacGibbon.
Wilson, E. O. 1975. *Sociobiology: the new synthesis*. Cambridge, Massachusetts: Harvard University Press.
Wilson, E. O. 1978. *On human nature*. Cambridge, Massachusetts: Harvard University Press.

5 'Animal' in biological and semiotic perspective

THOMAS A. SEBEOK

Whatever else an animal may be, it is clear that each is a living system, or sub-system, a complex array of atoms organized and maintained according to certain principles, the most important among these being negative entropy. The classic statement emphasizing this fact is to be found in Schrödinger's famous book, *What is life?* (1946, p. 77), where he addresses an 'organism's astonishing gift of concentrating a "stream of order" on itself and thus escaping the decay into atomic chaos – of "drinking orderliness" from a suitable environment'.

The importance of Schrödinger's formulation, with its stress on the generation of order, seems to me to derive from two crucial implications. First, in invoking the notion of entropy, which in statistical mechanics is fundamental to the Second Law of Thermodynamics, it authenticates that life conforms to the basic laws of physics (Ling 1934). Secondly, since negative entropy is closely coupled with the notion (or, more accurately, *a* notion) of information – that which 'embodies, expresses, and often specifies order' (Medawar & Medawar 1983, p. 205) – it demonstrates the salience of semiotics to an understanding of life. Schrödinger himself (1946, p. 79) hinted at the latter when he remarked on the power of a group of atoms – he called them a 'tiny central office' – to produce 'orderly events' in the isolated cell, and then went on to ask: 'do they not resemble stations of a local government dispersed through the body, communicating with each other with great ease, thanks to the code that is common to all of them?'.

If the subject matter of semiotics 'is the exchange of any messages whatever and of the systems of signs which underlie them' (Sebeok 1985, p. 1), the amount of information is 'a measure of the degree of order which is peculiarly associated with those patterns which are distributed as messages in time' (Wiener 1950, p. 21). In short, life couples two transmutative processes, one energetic or physical, the other informational or semiosic. The former has to do with the conversion of low-entropy articles, integrating energy flowing from external sources, into high-entropy waste products disgorged into other open systems; the latter points to the transformation of signs into (as a rule) more-developed signs (an identification of organisms with signs that goes back at least to Peirce 1868).

There are two additional striking properties of life. One of these is hierarchical organization (cf. Bonner 1969, Salthe 1985). This is a universal characteristic which life shares with the rest of the cosmos and which defines, in the overall architecture of the universe, its position on a continuum of scale between the vanishingly small (leptons, photons and quarks) and the indefinitely large (galactic superclusters).

The second conspicuous property lies in the contrast between, and fundamental invariance in, life's subjacent biochemistry (a virtually uniform pool of 20 amino acids) and the prodigal variety in the individual expressions thereof, the latter depending on shifts in the environmental context within the global biosphere.

Given that all animals are composed of matter in a 'living state', it is equally clear that by no means all lifeforms are animals. Competing definitions of life abound (e.g. Miller 1978), as well as miscellaneous paradigms to account for its origin (e.g. Schopf 1983), but these need not be discussed here. Indeed, such an exercise may not even serve any useful purpose, as Pirie (1937) has argued, especially considering the existence of borderline phenomena, comparable with the transition from, say, green to yellow or acid to alkaline. The supposedly iron-clad distinction between life and non-life becomes fuzzy not only if you look back far enough in time, but also in the light of recent developments in commingling and breeding lifeforms (including man) with manufactured objects, as is breathtakingly envisioned by Margulis & Sagan (1986b).

The place of animals among other living systems and their distinctive features do, however, require consideration. Macrotaxonomy, the craft of classifying, is a vast (if not always fashionable) field of endeavour, masterfully explored in the realm of biology by Mayr (1982). However, the sole biologically valid classification of animals, since Darwin, is of subordinate classes whose members are united by common heritage or descent at one level of ancestry into superordinate classes whose members are united at the next ascending level. In Darwin's own words, 'all true classification is genealogical' (1859, p. 420, see also Ch. 2).

There are many competing representations of evolutionary relations on all levels, and all of these are doubtless provisional. For example, the Linnaean plant versus animal dichotomy has been argued on quite different grounds by naturalists since the 18th century. Mayr (1965, pp. 418–20) lists 11 clusters of distinctive features among the more important differences which have been variously adduced. This notwithstanding, he concludes by noting that 'it is important to emphasize that the species of animals and plants are nevertheless essentially similar. Plants and animals are virtually identical in their genetic and cytological mechanisms'.

Thus, the choice of a classification scheme is ultimately (although, of course, within limits) a personal matter. I favour the one which seems to me to provide the maximum heuristic guidance. That is the codification proposed by Whittaker (1959), refined by him a decade later (1969).

Whittaker reviews the broad, conventional two-way classification of all organisms – into plants and animals – and enumerates its drawbacks, as well as those of an alternative quadripartite scheme proposed by Copeland (e.g. 1956). He then puts forward a pentad of his own, which, although having certain recognized deficiencies as well, seems to me the most comprehensive and cogent system worked out thus far. Whittaker's classification is based on a combination of two sets of distinctions, concerning respectively *levels* of organization and *types* of organization. The first is derived from the principle of hierarchy already mentioned. The second relates to three principal modes of nutrition, that is, to three different ways in which information (negentropy) is maintained by extracting order out of the environment.

This second set of distinctions sorts macroscopic entities into three complementary categories, called Superkingdoms, within the pervasive latticed configuration of the terrestrial biosphere. These are:

I. *Plants*, or producers, which derive their food from inorganic sources, by photosynthesis.

II. *Animals*, or ingestors, which derive their food – preformed organic compounds – from other organisms. They may be subdivided into three classes:

(A)   If they eat plants, we call them herbivores.
(B)   If they eat animals that eat plants, we call them carnivores (or predators).
(C)   If they eat both, we call them omnivores.

Animals are designated 'ingestors' because they incorporate food into their bodies, where the intake is then digested.

III. *Fungi*, or decomposers, in opposition to animals, do not incorporate food into their bodies, but they 'secrete digestive enzymes into the environment to break down their food externally and they absorb the resulting small molecules from solution' (Margulis 1981, p. 32).

On this macroscopic scale animals can be catalogued as intermediate transforming agents midway between two polar opposite lifeforms: the composers, or organisms that 'build up', and the decomposers, or organisms that 'break down'. Bernard (1878, pp. 1, 37) once coined a pair of slogans, paradoxically entailing both production, *La vie, c'est la création*, and decay, *La vie, c'est la mort*. Of animals, it may well be added, *La vie, c'est l'entremise!*[1]

Most remaining lifeforms can be negatively defined as non-plants, non-animals and non-fungi. By application of the first principle of hierarchy, these fall into one of two groups.

IV. *Protoctists*, comprising the remaining eukaryotes, all of them being microorganisms lacking embryogenesis but displaying alimentary heterogeneity, including the familiar triad of photosynthetic, ingesting as well as absorbing species (here belong algae, protozoa, slime moulds and nets, etc.).

V. *Prokaryotes*, the Monera, where bacteria belong, are generally single-celled creatures which, although nutritionally diverse, are incapable of ingestion (see also Margulis & Sagan 1986a).[2]

Let me now consider further the classification of animals. In addition to Whittaker's double characterization: first, by level of entitation – a term coined by the physiologist Gerard (1969, pp. 218–19) to mean 'the identification of entity', and which he considered vastly more important than the concept of quantitation – and secondly, by nutritional mode, two further principles may be introduced; one embryological, the other biosemiosic. The former is stated by Margulis (1981, p. 32) thus: 'in all animals, the zygote formed by the fertilization

of the female by the male gamete develops into a ball of cells called a blastula',
which unambiguously separates animals from all other forms by virtue of
their development.

All animates are bombarded by signs emanating from their environment,
which includes a *milieu intérieur*, as well as, of course, other animates sharing their
environment, some conspecific, some not (for further pertinent particulars, see
Sebeok 1986a, ch. 3). Such inputs are eventually transmuted into outputs consisting of strings of further signs. This sign-process is called semiosis. The pioneer
explorer of the decisive role of semiosis in the origin and operation of life processes was Jakob von Uexküll (1864–1944), who was also a pre-eminent founder
of modern ethology. He advanced a highly original and integrated theory of
semiosis in the framework of what came to be known as *Umweltforschung*, the
study of phenomenal worlds, self-worlds or the subjective universe.[3]

Although *Umwelt* research has focused almost wholly on animals including
humans (e.g. Sebeok 1977), plants are also discussed, contrastively if briefly, and
there have been allusions even to plasmodial slime moulds – now in a phylum of
the Protoctista, although classified by Uexküll and others among the Fungi
(Uexküll 1982, pp. 35f.). As Uexküll has maintained (1982, pp. 33f.), and Krampen (1981) later greatly elaborated, plants differ from animals in that they lack a
'functional cycle' (Uexküll 1980, ch. 3) which would link receptor organs via a
mesh of nerve fibres to effector organs. They are rather immersed directly in
their habitat. The relationships of a plant with its habitat, or casing, 'are
altogether different from those of the animals with their Umwelts'. However,
Krampen (1981, p. 203), concludes that the 'vegetative world is nevertheless
structured according to a base semiotics which cuts across all living beings, plants,
animals, and humans alike'. He argues that while plants exhibit predominantly
indexical signs, in animals both indexical and iconic signs appear, whereas human
sign-processes encompass the entire gamut from indexicality via iconicity to sym-
bolicity.[4] However this may be – and in my opinion the entire subject cries out
for more empirical investigation – it is already obvious that, at least as a working
assumption, one must suppose that there are bound to be substantive differences
among the several branches of biosemiotics (or biocommunication, as in
Tembrock 1971): endosemiotics (Uexküll 1980, p. 291, 1986, p. 204),
zoosemiotics (Sebeok 1963), phytosemiotics (Krampen 1981) and, *in posse*,
mycosemiotics.[5]

These and related subfields are very unevenly developed. The literature of
zoosemiotics alone – even discounting human communication – is so prodigious
that no summary can be attempted here, although one point pertinent to the topic
of this chapter perhaps does need to be emphasized.

It seems to me beyond reasonable doubt that the symbiotic theory of the origin
and evolution of cells is correct. This means that eukaryotic forms composed of
nucleated cells – including such advanced forms as animals – evolved in consequence of certain symbioses between ancestral prokaryotes in the Proterozoic
Aeon, by about 800 million years ago, and thereafter continued to diversify (see
Margulis & Sagan 1986a, especially chs. 8 and 9).

'Symbiosis', including commensalism, mutualism and so forth, is plainly a form of semiosis: 'mutual cooperation is often facilitated by simple forms of *communication* between the participants', as *The Oxford companion* puts it, with undue caution (McFarland 1982, p. 540). Biologists appear reluctant to describe it as such, yet the most obvious fact about symbionts is that they are types of communicants. They are organisms of different species living together, in ceaseless informative commerce, for most of the life-cycles of each, and to their mutual benefit. 'Semiochemical effects occur between organisms of all types' (Albone 1984, p. 2; for the sharing of semiochemicals in human bonding-related behaviour, see Nicholson 1984). Their exchanges are accomplished by chemical messengers of precision and subtlety; the topics of their 'conversations' have to do largely with territory or reproduction. The exosemiotic chemical signals yoking microorganisms together – hormonal and chemical neurotransmitters – evolved in lifeforms such as animals into specialized and localized endosemiotic cells within the body tissue (Krieger 1983, p. 977). Such cells facilitate exceedingly complex mutual communicative interactions between the immune and nervous systems, known as 'neuroimmunomodulation'. Research in this area has far-reaching clinical as well as philosophical implications, some of which I have reviewed elsewhere (Sebeok 1981).

Mayr (1982, p. 146) defines *taxonomy* as 'the theory and practice of delimiting kinds of organisms and of classifying them'. However, this kind of enterprise, fathered in its evolutionary perspective by Darwin, is but a segment of the far more venerable as well as unbounded science of *systematics* which, as Simpson (1961, cf. Mayr 1982, p. 145) taught it, has diversity as its subject matter. Systems of classification may depend on a whole variety of alternative, presumably complementary, approaches. For example, given that multiple biochemical pathways emerged for the biosynthesis of chlorophyll, plants can be reclassified according to how they fabricate their photosynthetic pigments. As Lowenstein (1984, p. 541) for one has cogently claimed, comparisons based on DNA or on proteins can be vastly fecund, especially when it comes to 'the inclusion of extinct species in phylogenies, the identification of species in fossil studies and museum collections, and broad systematic analysis of living animals and plants'.

In short, all organisms – especially plants, animals and fungi – pertain at once to a plurality of codes, each of which is capable of being transmuted into every other. To paraphrase a striking passage from one of Lévi-Strauss' latest books (1985, p. 228), 'like a text less intelligible in one language than in several, from many different versions, rendered simultaneously, there might flow a sense richer and more profound than each of the partial and distorted meanings that any single version, taken in isolation, might yield to us'.[6] Although his observation was meant to apply to myths, viewed as formulaic networks, the same surely holds for groupings of animals into at once biologically relevant assemblages and into anthropologically as well as semiotically relevant folk arrangements, such as were discussed, for instance, for English animal categories by Leach (1964), or to adumbrate the 'meaning of life' in assorted African societies, by Willis (1974). Lévi-Strauss (1962, pp. 57, 59, 1966, pp. 42–3) has remarked on the 'evidence of thought which is experienced in all the exercises of speculation and resembles that of the naturalists and alchemists of antiquity and the middle ages. . . . Native classifications are not only methodical and based on carefully built up theoretical knowledge. They are also at times comparable, from a formal point of view, to those still in use in zoology and botany'. Thus, it is hardly surprising that Aristotle classified whales as fish, and that, despite their replacement in 1693 by John Ray (refined by Linné in 1758) into that class of vertebrates biologists call the Mammalia, infraclass Eutheria, order Cetacea, most laymen still believe that whales are, indeed, fish. Whales are, of course, both, and other entities – as Moby Dick – to boot.

The transience from code to code can become critical. In certain societies a plant can substitute for an animal, as a cucumber for an ox in the well-known case of the Nuer (Evans-Pritchard 1956) and, as elsewhere in Africa, a token of a plentiful animal species can take the place of a religiously prescribed but rare one. *A fortiori* a beast can stand in, symbolically, for a human in a sacrificial rite. Nor should one overlook liminoid creatures belonging to overlapping codes – Turner (1974, p. 253) singles out the centaur Cheiron as a classical prototype epitomizing such liminality – which render the would-be cataloguer's chore so wearisome. Just how much they do so is beautifully explored in Vercors' penetrating novel centring on an imaginary creature named *Paranthropus erectus* (Bruller 1953).

Brown (1984) is concerned with folk zoological lifeforms. Appendix B to his book contains a rich source of lexical data on zoological lifeform coding from more than 220 globally scattered languages, postulating six stages of terminological growth, ranging, for example, from no zoological forms to a mammal – 'wug' (i.e. worm + bug) dichotomy, on to a bird–fish–snake trichotomy, and so forth.

To appreciate what counts as an animal for man and in what ways, finally requires a concentrated semiotic enquiry, which can only be hinted at in the following paragraphs. An animal is upgraded to a cultural object, an object of value, as a by-product of structuring, ordering and classifying: the animal, in short, becomes a *marker* in MacCannell's (1976, p. 110) sense, a chunk of concentrated information, a signifier segregated from a signified by virtue of 'the superimposition of a system of social values' (*ibid*, p. 119).

From this point of view it seems promising to consider the many and varied circumstances under which man may encounter animals. In what follows I shall identify and briefly comment on some of the most common situations. The following list is presented in no particular order, and is certainly not all-embracing. Moreover, the different situations are not necessarily exclusive, and may partially coincide.

(a) *Man as predator*. Man preys upon or even annihilates an animal species, for different reasons. Some, like antelopes, may be hunted down as game; certain carnivores, such as the East African crocodile, are condemned as 'vermin' (a distancing label, discussed by Serpell (1986, pp. 159–62) under the heading of justificatory 'misrepresentation'); primates are overused in medical research; marsupials are killed for their hides; and cetaceans are exploited for their oil. In effect, every time a population of animals is exterminated, the draining of the gene-pool is concurrently and irreversibly accompanied by the elimination of a unique communicative code.

(b) *Man as prey*. Man becomes the casualty of an animal's depredations: e.g. human malaria is caused by any of four sporozoites (parasitic protozoans). Each is transmitted from human to human by a female *Anopheles* mosquito, which injects saliva containing plasmodian sporozoites as it bites (even today, more people die every year of mosquito-borne disease than from any other single cause; cf. Stanier *et al.* 1985, p. 646). Another forceful illustration is provided by Geist's speculations on the prehistoric bears of native North America, and their possible role in delaying human colonization of that continent (Geist 1986).

(c) *Man as 'partner'*. Man coexists with an animal in some sort of partnership (see Katcher & Beck 1983), as for example in a purely guest–host relationship (as aquarium fishes with their master) or in a nexus of mutual dependence (such as in bee keeping; a Seeing Eye dog working in the service of a blind person; dogs used for hauling, such as Arctic sled-dogs; dogs or cheetahs used for tracking; birds as fishing partners, such as a cormorant catching fish for a Japanese fisherman in exchange for a food reward matching the size of the catch; or as hunting partners, such as the raptors described by Frederick II (1194–1250) in his classic and innovative account, *De arte venandi cum avibus*; pets as therapists (Beck & Katcher 1983, ch. 8, Serpell 1986, ch. 6); and the like).

A special set of subproblems in this category can be identified when animals are used as sexual partners by either men or women, a phenomenon known as 'cross-species attachment' (Money 1986, pp. 75f.). Bestiality, or the carnal exploitation of animals, has been known at least since Apuleius (cf. an 'ancient pre-Columbian custom among Indians of the Caribbean coast of Columbia', cited by Money (*ibid.*), 'that associates the attainment of manhood with the exercise of copulating with donkeys'). Zoophilic acts, involving cattle, horses or donkeys, dogs, monkeys, or barnyard fowl, are a common theme of pornographic literature; there is also a variant called 'formicophilia', 'in which arousal and orgasm are dependent on the sensations produced by small creatures like snails, frogs, ants or other insects creeping, crawling, or nibbling the genitalia and perianal area, and the nipples' (*ibid.*). In some urban environments animals are used as social facilitators, or catalysts; thus, dogs are used by European female as well as male street-walkers to assist in striking up conversations with potential clients. The curious Western phenomenon of pet cemeteries could further be mentioned here.

(d) *Sport and entertainment*. Animals have been long and variously used for human amusement: in Roman circuses (gladiators wrestling with big cats), bullfighting rings, wrestling with alligators, promotion of cock fights and frog-jumping contests. Here, too, belong horse- and dog-races and, perhaps marginally, birdwatching, (urban) pigeon feeding and, more generally, safaris with photographic intent.

(e) *Parasitism*. This may work in either direction:

(i) The activities of man in relation to the reindeer, for instance, can be described as those of a social parasite; interspecific associations, in relation to parasitism and other concepts, are discussed by Ingold (1980, pp. 30f.). He writes: 'It is a matter of personal experience, since when I was first in the field in Lapland, an old reindeer named Enoch made a habit of coming round, at 11 o'clock every morning, to visit the place where I regularly urinated outside my cabin' (personal communication).

(ii) Each of us has about as many organisms on the surface of our skin as there are people on earth. The mite *Demodex*, crab lice, fleas and bedbugs are a few samples of the teeming miniature parasitic population sharing the ecological niche constituted by human bodies (Andrews 1976).[7]

(f) *Conspecificity.* An animal may accept a human as a conspecific; this is also known as 'zoomorphism'. As early as 1910, Heinroth described the attachment of incubator-hatched greylag goslings to human beings. These goslings reject any goose or gander as parent objects, opting instead to look upon humans as their exclusive parents. Many other hand-reared birds were later found to have transferred their adult sexual behaviour toward their human caretakers. Morris & Morris (1966, pp. 182ff.) have recounted attempts by a 'fully humanized' female panda, Chi-Chi, to mate with her keepers; and the sexual advances of a male dolphin, Peter, towards his female trainer, Margaret Howe, were recorded in her published protocol (Lilly 1967, p. 282). The latter episode was represented as an accomplished, although fictional, aquatic congress in Ted Mooney's 1981 novel, *Easy travel to other planets* (cf. also (c), above).

(g) *Insentience.* An animal may define a human as a part of its inanimate *Umwelt*, as when young birds will perch on the keeper's head or even on his outstretched arm, as though it were a branch. Fascinating behaviours of this sort were extensively analysed by Hediger (1969, pp. 81–3), who explains one of the tricks performed by snake-charmers on the basis of this principle of misapprehending a human limb for an insensate substrate. According to Hediger, mammals such as the koala may also regard humans as a place for climbing, and make use of them accordingly. Especially intriguing is Hediger's discussion (*ibid.*, pp. 91–5) of the 'centaur-like fusion' of man and motor vehicles, especially in the context of big-game reserves, and of how wild animals view such relatively novel combinations.

(h) *Taming,* defined as the reduction or possibly total elimination of an animal's flight reaction from man, may be deliberately induced. This is an indispensable precondition for both training and domestication. In the latter not only the care and feeding, but most particularly the breeding of an animal – or the communication of genetic information from one generation to the next – have to some degree come under human control. When the biologically altered domesticated animal breeds out of control, it is referred to as 'feral', as opposed to 'wild'.

(i) *Training.* Man's training of animals may take one of two counterpolar forms

(i) A rat forced to swim under water to escape drowning is taught to take the alley in a submerged Y-maze when the correct decision is indicated by the brighter of two alleys; a porpoise is brought under behavioural control to locate and retrieve underwater objects. Such efforts are called *appren-*

tissage, loosely rendered as 'scientific' or 'laboratory training' (cf. Silverman 1978) or, in German, *wissenschaftliche Dressur*.

(ii) A horse is taught to perform a comedy act for the purposes of exhibition (cf. Bouissac 1985, ch. IV); a porpoise is taught to play basketball. Such efforts are called *dressage*, or circus (viz. oceanarium) training, or *höhere Dressur* (as with the Lippizaners, of the Spanish Riding School).

Note that *apprentissage* and *dressage* are fundamentally distinct ways of shaping behaviour, although from a semiotic point of view they constitute complementary measures, in particular as regards their pragmatic import. This distinction was intuitively appreciated by Heini Hediger as early as 1935, in his dissertation, and was later materially advanced in several of his published writings (for example, Hediger 1979, p. 286). For instance, Hediger insightfully emphasized that *apprentissage* entails a reduction of the animal–man nexus to as close to zero as feasible. *Dressage*, conversely, requires a maximum intensification of the ligature, with the richest possible emotional involvement. This is one dimension of semiotic variation.

Apropos *dressage*, Breland and Breland (1966, p. 108) relate an arresting informal observation concerning the emotional component of a parrot's vocalization. In the exhibition in question the bird picks up a toy telephone, holds it up to his ear, and says 'Hello!'. Afterwards he receives a peanut. It was noted that every time the bird said 'Hello!', 'the pupils of his eyes contracted and dilated remarkably'. The sign is emitted solely in an emotionally charged situation, for the pupil-size cue may not occur if the bird is 'talking' merely for peanuts (kindred observations have been made of domestic cats).

A second dimension of semiotic variation lies, in Hediger's words, between 'Dressur ohne Affektaufwand' (or without affective display) and 'Dressur mit bedeutendem Affektaufwand' (or with significant affective display).

There are many other juxtapositions of human and animal which could fruitfully be examined; concerning some of these there of course already exist more- or less-substantial studies (see ch. 4, this book). These areas include the representation of animals in mythology, oral and written literature, cartoons, on the stage and in the performing arts generally (especially the cinema and television), or in the shape of dolls, puppets, toys and robots. Animals are often featured, by design, in magazine and TV advertising.

Moreover, there exist countless studies dealing with interactions between humans and particular sets of demarcated animals, individual anthropomorphic animals and classes of exploited captives, such as primates (Erwin *et al.* 1979), or species in the aggregate (Clutton-Brock 1981, Craig 1981, Houpt & Wolski 1982, ch. 2), birds in general (Murton 1971), or horses in particular (Lawrence 1985). A synthesis of this vast literature, especially in its fascinating semiotic ramifications, is long overdue.

Saint Augustine was once asked: what is time? He answered: 'If no-one asks me, I know; if I wish to explain it to one that asks, I know not'.

To recapitulate, the central purpose of this chapter was to enquire what, broadly speaking, an animal is. That question ought to be preceded by another: what is life? Although there may not be an absolutely rigorous distinction between inanimate matter and matter in a living state, it is clear enough that animates undergo semiosis, i.e. they exchange, among other items, messages, which are strings of signs.

Paying heed, first, to biologically valid (meaning strictly genealogical) classificatory schemes, five major lifeforms were distinguished, among which, on the macro-level, the mediating position of animals between plants and fungi was accentuated. The critical relevance of *Umweltforschung* to an understanding of animals was mentioned, but was not further developed. The recalcitrant term *Umwelt* had best be rendered in English by the word 'model' (as recently expounded in Sebeok 1986c). The biologist's notion of symbiosis, it was also suggested, is equivalent to the philosopher's notion of semiosis.

Turning back to systematics, of which taxonomy is but one component, animals were reassessed from the standpoint of folk classification. In this perspective it was argued that an animal always belongs at once to a multiple array of codes, some natural, or 'scientific', others disparately cultural. Far from being irreconcilable, such codes complement one another. Therefore, it is perfectly in order, as one illustration, to regard a whale as being simultaneously a mammal and a fish, as well as, moreover, an enigmatic creature of man's imagination.

The anthropological, or semiotic, definitions of 'animal' acquire concreteness and saliency within different types of man–animal confrontation, but their enumeration cannot be carried out exhaustively in the compass of a brief essay such as this. Nevertheless, even the very incomplete and preliminary listing attempted here may serve to elicit further investigation.

Notes

1   In semiosis, signs tend to function in a trinity of mutually exclusive classes as the intermediate transforming agents between 'objects' and 'interpretants'. This is highly pertinent to Peirce's man–sign (more broadly, animal–sign) analogy. For a recent discussion by an anthropologist, see Singer (1984, especially pp. 1–2, 55–6, 61).

2   It is at present unclear whether the recently discovered thermophillic ('black smoker') bacteria of the East Pacific Rise, employing symbiotic chemosynthesis, thus surviving in utter independence of the sun (i.e. of photosynthesis) and seemingly constituting the only closed geothermal (terrestrial) ecosystem not integrated with the rest of life, can or cannot be grouped with 'ordinary' bacteria (see Baross & Deming 1983, Jannasch & Mottl 1985). The giant worms subsisting, by absorption, upon these microbial symbionts thus also derive their energy from underwater volcanoes, not sunlight.

3   Among his many writings, Uexküll (1982), creatively amplified by his elder son, Thure, is both one of the most important and readily accessible in English; see also Uexküll (1980, pp. 291–388), 'Die Umweltlehre als Theorie der Zeichenprozesse'; Lorenz (1971, pp. 273–7); and Sebeok (1979, ch. 10).

4   Peirce's trichotomous classification of signs into iconic, indexical, and symbolic is

fundamental in semiotics. It has been discussed by many commentators, notably Burks (1949), Ayer (1968, pp. 149–58), Sebeok (1975) and, most recently, Hookway (1985, ch. IV); see also the entries under each of these three lemmata, and Joseph Ransdell's article on Peirce, in Sebeok (1986b).

5   See Bonner (1963) for semiosis in the *Acrasieae* – however classified, they must be reckoned aggregation organisms *par excellence*. See also Stanier *et al.* (1985, pp. 543f.).

6   'Comme un texte peu intelligible en une seule langue, s'il est rendu simultanément dans plusieurs, laissera peut-être émaner de ces versions différentes un sens plus riche et plus profond qu'aucun de ceux, partiels et mutilés, auqel chaque version prise à part eût permis d'accéder.'

7   In the framework of Uexküll, the ecological niche could best be described as '*Umwelt*-from-outside', from the standpoint of the observer of the subject concerned. (Compare Gibson's concept of the niche as a set of affordances, discussed in ch. 9 of this book – *Ed.*)

References

Albone, E. S. 1984. *Mammalian semiochemistry: the investigation of chemical signals between mammals*. Chichester: Wiley.

Andrews, M. 1976. *The life that lives on man*. New York: Taplinger.

Ayer, F. J. 1968. *The origins of pragmatism: studies in the philosophy of Charles Sanders Peirce and William James*. London: Macmillan.

Baross, J. A. & J. W. Demming 1983. Growth of 'black smoker' bacteria at temperatures of at least 250°C. *Nature* **303**, 423–6.

Beck, A. & A. Katcher 1983. *Between pets and people: the importance of animal companionship*. New York: G. P. Putnam's Sons.

Bernard, C. 1878. *Leçons sur les phénomènes de la vie communs aux animaux et aux végétaux*. Paris: Baillière.

Bonner, J. T. 1963. How slime molds communicate. *Scientific American* **209**, 284–93.

Bonner, J. T. 1969. *The scale of nature*. New York: Harper & Row.

Bouissac, P. 1985. *Circus and culture: a semiotic approach*. Lanham: University Press of America.

Breland, K. & M. Breland 1966. *Animal behaviour*. London: Collier-Macmillan.

Brown, C. H. 1984. *Language and living things: uniformities in folk classification and naming*. New Brunswick: Rutgers University Press.

Bruller, J. [Vercors] 1953. *You shall know them*. Boston, Massachusetts: Little, Brown & Co.

Burks, A. W. 1949. Icon, index, and symbol. *Philosophy and Phenomenological Research* **9**, 673–89.

Clutton-Brock, J. 1981. *Domesticated animals from early times*. London: British Museum (Natural History).

Copeland, H. F. 1956. *The classification of lower organisms*. Palo Alto, California: Pacific Books.

Craig, J. V. 1981. *Domestic animal behavior: causes and implications for animal care and management*. Englewood Cliffs, New Jersey: Prentice-Hall.

Darwin, C. 1859. *On the origin of species by means of natural selection or the preservation of favoured races in the struggle for life*. London: John Murray.

Erwin, J., T. L. Maple & G. Mitchell 1979. *Captivity and behavior: primates in breeding colonies, laboratories, and zoos*. New York: Van Nostrand Reinhold.

Evans-Pritchard, E. E. 1956. *Nuer Religion*. Oxford: Oxford University Press.

Geist, V. 1986. Did large predators keep humans out of North America? Precirculated paper. In *Cultural attitudes to animals including birds, fish and invertebrates*. World Archaeological Congress, vol. 1 (mimeo).

Gerard, W. R. 1969. Hierarchy, entitation, and levels. In *Hierarchical structures*, L. L. Whyte, A. G. Wilson & D. Wilson (eds), 215–28. New York: American Elsevier.

Hediger, H. 1969. *Man and animal in the zoo: zoo biology*. New York: Delacorte Press.

Hediger, H. 1979. *Beobachtungen zur Tierpsychologie im Zoo und im Zirkus*. Berlin: Henschelverlag.

Heinroth, O. 1910. Beiträge zur Biologie, namentlich Ethologie und Psychologie der Anatiden. *Verhandlungen des V. Internationalen Ornithologen-Kongress*, 589–702. Berlin.

Hookway, C. 1985. *Peirce*. London: Routledge & Kegan Paul.

Houpt, K. A. & T. R. Wolski 1982. *Domestic animal behavior for veterinarians and animal scientists*. Ames, Iowa: Iowa State University Press.

Ingold, T. 1980. *Hunters, pastoralists and ranchers: reindeer economies and their transformations*. Cambridge: Cambridge University Press.

Jannasch, H. W. & M. J. Mottl 1985. Geomicrobiology of deep-sea hydrothermal vents. *Science* **229**, 717–725.

Katcher, A. H. & A. M. Beck (eds) 1983. *New perspectives on our lives with companion animals*. Philadelphia, Pennsylvania: University of Pennsylvania Press.

Krampen, M. 1981. Phytosemiotics. *Semiotica* **36**, 187–209.

Krieger, D. T. 1983. Brain peptides: what, where, and why? *Science* **222**, 975–85.

Lawrence, E. A. 1985. *Hoofbeats and society: studies in human–horse interactions*. Bloomington, Indiana: Indiana University Press.

Leach, E. 1964. Anthropological aspects of language: animal categories and verbal abuse. In *New directions in the study of language*, E. H. Lenneberg (ed.), 23–63. Cambridge, Massachusetts: MIT Press.

Lévi-Strauss, C. 1962. *La pensée sauvage*. Paris: Plon. (English version [1966] *The savage mind*. Chicago, Illinois: University of Chicago Press.)

Lévi-Strauss, C. 1985. *La potière jalouse*. Paris: Plon.

Lilly, J. 1967. *The mind of the dolphin: a nonhuman intelligence*. Garden City: Doubleday.

Ling, G. N. 1984. *In search of the physical basis of life*. New York and London: Plenum Press.

Lorenz, K. 1971. *Studies in animal and human behaviour*, Vol. II. Cambridge, Massachusetts: Harvard University Press.

Lowenstein, J. M. 1984. Molecular approaches to the identification of species. *American Scientist* **73**, 541–7.

MacCannell, D. 1976. *The tourist: a new theory of the leisure class*. New York: Schocken Books.

McFarland, D. (ed.) 1982. *The Oxford companion to animal behaviour*. Oxford: Oxford University Press.

Margulis, L. 1981. *Symbiosis in cell evolution: life and its environment on the early Earth*. San Francisco, California: Freeman.

Margulis, L. & D. Sagan 1986a. *Microcosmos: four billion years of evolution from our microbial ancestors*. New York: Summit Books.

Margulis, L. & D. Sagan 1986b. Strange fruit on the tree of life. *The Sciences* **26** (3), 38–45.

Mayr, E. 1965. *Animal species and evolution*. Cambridge, Massachusetts: Harvard University Press.

Mayr, E. 1982. *The growth of biological thought: diversity, evolution, and inheritance*. Cambridge, Massachusetts: Harvard University Press.

Medawar, P. B. & J. S. Medawar 1983. *Aristotle to zoos: a philosophical dictionary of biology*. Cambridge, Massachusetts: Harvard University Press.

Miller, J. G. 1978. *Living systems*. New York: McGraw-Hill.

Money, J. 1986. *Lovemaps: clinical concepts of sexual/erotic health and pathology, paraphilia, and gender transposition in childhood, adolescence, and maturity*. New York: Irvington.

Mooney, T. 1981. *Easy travel to other planets*. New York: Farrar, Straus, Giroux.

Morris, R. & D. Morris 1966. *Men and pandas*. New York: New American Library.

Murton, R. K. 1971. *Man and birds*. London: Collins.

Nicholson, B. 1984. Does kissing aid human bonding by semiochemical addiction? *British Journal of Dermatology* **111**, 623–7.

Peirce, C. S. 1868. Some consequences of four incapacities. *Journal of Speculative Philosophy* **2**, 140–51.

Pirie, N. W. 1937. The meaninglessness of the terms life and living. In *Perspectives in biochemistry*, J. Needham & D. E. Green (eds), 11–22. Cambridge: Cambridge University Press.

Salthe, S. N. 1985. *Evolving hierarchical systems: their structure and representation*. New York: Columbia University Press.

Schopf, J. W. (ed.) 1983. *Earth's earliest biosphere: its origin and evolution*. Princeton, New Jersey: Princeton University Press.

Schrödinger, E. 1946. *What is Life?* Cambridge: Cambridge University Press.

Sebeok, T. A. 1963. Communication among social bees; porpoises and sonar; man and dolphin. *Language* **39**, 448–66.

Sebeok, T. A. 1975. Six species of signs: some propositions and strictures. *Semiotica* **13**, 233–60.

Sebeok, T. A. 1977. Zoosemiotic components of human communication. In *How animals communicate*, T. A. Sebeok (ed.), Chapter 38. Bloomington, Indiana: Indiana University Press.

Sebeok, T. A. 1979. *The sign and its masters*. Austin, Texas: University of Texas Press.

Sebeok, T. A. 1981. The ultimate enigma of 'Clever Hans': the union of nature and culture. In *The Clever Hans phenomenon: communication with horses, whales, apes, and people*, T. A. Sebeok & R. Rosenthal (eds), *Annals of the New York Academy of Sciences* **364**, 199–205. New York: New York Academy of Sciences.

Sebeok, T. A. 1985. *Contributions to the doctrine of signs*. Lanham: University Press of America.

Sebeok, T. A. 1986a. *I think I am a verb: more contributions to the doctrine of signs*. New York and London: Plenum Press.

Sebeok, T. A. (ed.) 1986b. *Encyclopedic dictionary of semiotics*, Vols 1–3. Berlin: Mouton de Gruyter.

Sebeok, T. A. 1986c. The problem of the origin of language in an evolutionary frame. *Language Sciences* **8**, 169–76.

Serpell, J. 1986. *In the company of animals: a study of human–animal relationships*. Oxford: Blackwell.

Silverman, P. 1978. *Animal behaviour in the laboratory*. New York: Pica Press.

Simpson, G. G. 1961. *Principles of animal taxonomy*. New York: Columbia University Press.

Singer, M. 1984. *Man's glassy essence: explorations in semiotic anthropology*. Bloomington,

Indiana: Indiana University Press.

Stanier, R. Y., J. L. Ingraham, M. L. Wheelis & P. R. Painter 1985. *The microbial world*. Englewood Cliffs, New Jersey: Prentice-Hall.

Tembrock, G. 1971. *Biokommunikation: Informationsvertragung im biologischen Bereich*. Berlin: Akademie-Verlag.

Turner, V. 1974. *Dramas, fields, and metaphors: symbolic action in human society*. Ithaca, New York: Cornell University Press.

Uexküll, J. von 1982 [1940]. The theory of meaning [transl. by B. Stone & H. Weiner from *Bedeutungslehre*, T. von Uexküll (ed.)]. *Semiotica* **42**, 1–87.

Uexküll, T. von 1980. *Kompositionslehre der Natur*. Frankfurt: Verlag Ullstein (Propylaen).

Uexküll, T. von 1986. Medicine and semiotics. *Semiotica* **61**, 201–17.

Whittaker, R. H. 1959. On the broad classification of organisms. *Quarterly Review of Biology* **34**, 210–66.

Whittaker, R. H. 1969. New concepts of kingdoms of organisms. *Science* **163**, 150–60.

Wiener, N. 1950. *The human use of human beings*. Boston, Massachusetts: Houghton Mifflin.

Willis, R. G. 1974. *Man and beast*. London: Hart-Davis, MacGibbon.

6 *Animals' attitudes to people*

JENNIE COY

Introduction

The central theme of this chapter is the close interaction of people and animals, which enables them to predict each other's actions. The first section defines what I mean by an animal. I then go on to discuss the close interaction of two individual animals, whether of the same species or different species, which might involve one individual attempting to attribute thoughts to the other in order to predict its actions. The close interactions of people with prey, or of people with dom- esticated animals – corresponding to Sebeok's first and third dyads, respectively (in Ch. 5) – are those which I, as a biologist studying the history of hunted and domesticated animals, find the most interesting.

Accordingly, in the second section I concentrate on the role that humans play in these interactions, and discuss our capacity to be aware of, and indeed to empathize with, the thoughts or feelings of fellow animals. In the third section I discuss to what extent this is reciprocated by other species, especially vertebrates, for we cannot accept the specist assumption that the traffic is in only one direc- tion. The way in which specism has coloured the debate on this issue, both now and in the past, is considered briefly in the final section.

What I mean by an animal

Like most of my contemporaries trained in the mainstream biology of the 1950s, I regard the term 'animal' as including people. In everyday thoughts and conver- sation I tend to think of people as having animals inside them, and certainly do not subscribe to the view common in popular literature that other species have little people inside them, nor can I see the need to postulate the existence of a soul for any of us animals. I presume that the differences between people and other animals involve different degrees of complexity and differences in organization. Above all, people are different from other animals, first because of the scope of their conscious thinking, which allows enormous flexibility in their behaviour, and, secondly, in having evolved a complex language in which they speculate a great deal. This capacity to devise and implement new patterns of behaviour has meant that change itself can become a goal of human behaviour; something which may have disastrous consequences for the survival not only of the species, but also of the world.

In his discussion of animal awareness Griffin (1981, p. 32) remarks that there is no evidence to show that other species are not self-aware. Yet, as he points out, there has been much resistance, even from among those studying animal behaviour, to allowing mentality to other animals (*ibid.*, pp. 88f.). Discussing the

evolutionary continuity of mental experience and the possibility of our recognis-
ing such attributes as hope and long-term anticipation in animals, Griffin suggests
that the hypothesis that animals have thoughts would enable us to understand a
great deal more about how animals manage to achieve a consistently adaptive response to highly variable environmental conditions (Griffin 1981, pp. 102f.,
1984, p. 94), and that a comparative approach to the study of mental experience
may prove to be more rewarding than behavioural research, which decides in
advance that consciousness in animals is something about which we can never
know (Griffin 1984, p. 12). As Midgley points out in Chapter 3 of this book,
Griffin has shifted the burden of proof to those who would deny that
animals think.

I am inclined initially to regard Griffin's ideas with some scepticism, since
many of his assertions strike me as just as dogmatic as those of the behaviourists
which he rejects. Dogma is no substitute for scientific observation or experiment.
However, Griffin admits that he remains open-minded and agnostic (Griffin
1981, p. 171), and stresses that his views of animal consciousness are mere
hypotheses. On this basis, presumably any 'soul' hypothesis would need to be
animal-wide. With these reservations I can accept most of what Griffin says in
Animal thinking. Much of his discussion is an attempt to redress the balance.

If a change of hypothesis is all that Griffin is suggesting, then I can go along
with him and shall use this kind of hypothesis (that other species engage in conscious thinking to some extent) as the background to my subsequent discussions.
In the past I would have decided that it would do me no good to use the words
'conscious' or 'self-aware', as these were naughty words for a biologist to use
unless they could be demonstrated beyond doubt. I am no longer convinced
of this.

People interacting with other species

I shall begin by talking about our own species, and then consider whether the
behaviour I have discussed is likely to occur in other species and, if such can be
proved, whether this would be likely to alter our views of processes of interaction
between people and other species.

As scientists and participants in academic debate, we do not dissent from the
theory that human beings can think and are aware of their thought processes to
the extent that they wish to communicate them to their fellow humans. We
become aware of ourselves as separate entities from our parents during infancy.
The high level of conscious awareness, manifested at least in humans and the
great apes, is linked with a strong sense of 'self'.

Following Wood-Gush, we can define self-awareness as 'the ability to abstract
and form a conceptual framework of the environment so that an animal can see
itself and its actions in relation to its environment' (Wood-Gush *et al.* 1981, p.
46). An individual equipped with this ability can distinguish the present 'here and
now' and possible futures, projected as the outcomes of alternative strategies, and

is thus able to make choices between them and produce more-relevant behaviour. This conscious juggling and plotting can go on in the human mind at the same time as quite complicated activities which do not appear to require full-time conscious direction.

It is not remarkable that most of us can walk *and* chew gum; a lot of other species can do the equivalent. What is extraordinary is our ability to watch TV, knit, read a book and be aware of the progress of three separate conversations taking place in the same room. Yet this is just spreading our 'consciousness' thinly and operating in much the same way as a computer operating a large number of workstations. Because of their ability for conscious thinking, people are good at co-operating in tasks (such as collective hunting) in which they have to keep aware of the actions of a number of other individuals at once. This requires each participant not only to consider the possible consequences of what he or she might do, but also to predict the actions of all of the others.

Such prediction depends on the inferences that we make about the attitudes or feelings of other persons through the evidence of their speech, non-verbal behaviour, or both. Experience gradually leads us to suspect that their attitudes as revealed to us through their behaviour do not always represent what they really feel, but rather what they would have us think they feel. This duplicity may not be unique to humans, if such animal activities as predator distraction by birds could be shown to be consciously motivated (Griffin 1984, pp. 90–4).

The very subtlety of our own appreciation of what may be going on in another mind suggests a long and important history for this behaviour. We may suppose that, since increasing ability to predict the action of other individuals would have been critical for survival, the development of self-awareness would have been favoured by natural selection, and that this may have been a major factor in the evolution of cerebral complexity. Moreover, there is a selective advantage in being able to anticipate the behaviour not only of other humans, but also of other species – especially if they are potential prey, competitors or predators. For example, when hunting or scavenging, in competition with other scavengers, it is very useful to be able to predict what prey or competitors will do. Most predators evolve alternative behaviours to cover a variety of possibilities of prey response. So do animals in other relationships discussed by Sebeok in Chapter 5 of this book. The interest shown in the prey's behaviour is a logical extension of the awareness of conspecifics. We might hypothesize, on these grounds, that animals capable of greater intraspecific empathy will be more likely to develop a similar empathetic understanding of individuals of other species.

Awareness across the species boundary would similarly have been an asset for humans when domestication began to take place. However, whether the close interspecific association with which we are concerned is that of predation or domestication, it is clear that the adaptation involved could never be one-way. Rather, we might expect a co-evolutionary adaptation of both humans and other species. The co-evolution that has taken place, and must still be taking place, has been little studied: there is still scope for research into the communication and interaction involved in current hunting, herding and farming.

Other species interacting with people

Individuals of many species show some ability to distinguish 'self' from 'non-self', through sounds, smells or sonar, in that they can use complex methods of communication and receive feedback on the identity of other individuals, or even on their 'states of mind' with respect to certain aspects of behaviour.

In interactions with people, a certain level of awareness would be necessary for us to describe the other species as having any sort of 'attitude' to people (either individually or as a group). There would have to be a threshold of awareness above which the other species could really be said to be a participant rather than a recipient. If domestication entails participatory behaviour, then we would be justified in concluding that the potential domesticate, and not just the people, must be 'ready' for domestication if it is to occur.

To be able to co-operate as described above for humans, an animal has to be sufficiently aware of itself: first, to place itself in relation to the environment; secondly, to perceive itself as having an effect on that environment; and, thirdly, to be aware of the other individual as separate from itself. An animal which had evolved this facility might be expected to attempt to relate its behaviour to that of other individuals; in fact, this exercise itself would probably have played an important part in the evolution of self-awareness.

There is some evidence, from work on apes and dolphins, for the existence of this sense of 'self' in other species. It is therefore possible that individuals of other species have sufficient ability of conscious projection to impute likely actions to their conspecifics. It is another step forward in consciousness to carry this out successfully in an interspecific encounter. We know that members of many other species, certainly other vertebrates, can correctly interpret specific human actions. The birds in our gardens and fields are quick to interpret some of our activities as possible soil-turning, and our household pets will respond to the noise of a cupboard or refrigerator opening from a long way off. What is important in these cases is the extent to which the animals are plotting alternative strategies in a conscious way. The flexibility of such interactions needs rigorous testing. In the predation and domestication relationships discussed earlier, co-evolution would proceed very rapidly if both species were self-aware.

It would also be interesting to know whether the depth to which intraspecific empathy occurs governs to any extent the relationship of that species with other species, including humans. It is possible that species with a higher level of intraspecific awareness may be more adaptable in both interacting with predators and prey, and interacting with people.

When it comes to interpreting the behaviour of another species, this is something we are increasingly likely to attempt the closer the behaviour patterns of that species are to our own. This is particularly true of human attempts to interpret the non-verbal communication (or just facial expressions) of other species. Sometimes our interpretations are probably correct, because the behaviour concerned closely resembles our own. Yet, even with behaviourally close species we can misinterpret, as Clutton-Brock (1981, p. 41) points out with regard to dominance behaviour in dogs.

However, most early domesticates in Europe were previously prey or very like them, so that their behaviour would already have been known to people to some extent. Ungulates are not behaviourally close to us, and they are probably somewhat different in the organization of their nervous systems. Yet these are the species with which we became most closely involved.

It could be the level of the animal's ability to predict human behaviour (or its level of awareness) which distinguishes the successfully domesticated species from those not domesticated. If they were more aware, in the sense of having a higher capacity to predict the behaviour of their own species and even that of hunters, then they could also have been more difficult prey. However, the same ability, which enables animals to evade hunters, could be turned to the opposite use if the advantage of close association with people outweighed the danger. Contact with humans could have been a strategy for individual survival during periods of radical environmental change. The ability of a species, or a particular population of a species, to predict the behaviour of people could thus be closely linked with ease of domestication.

Changing views of animals' attitudes

I originally approached this subject when I was searching through European texts on hunting and domestication for clues on people's ideas about animals' attitudes, and for evidence of overt specism. Pre-Darwinian views of other animals often credited them with certain qualities of mind, and some early hunters and domesticators are not exempt from this. However, such views often got out of hand, and those interpretations most worthy of consideration should surely be those from people with the closest experience of working with animals – the painters in the caves and the earliest practical writers on hunting and animal-keeping.

Successful hunters, herders and farmers were the earliest natural scientists, and their views of the species they interacted with are usually well balanced. Hunting texts often include a wide coverage of natural history – as in the Norman manuscripts of Gaston Phebus, where the animal itself is described first, followed by a description of how it is hunted (Tilander 1977). Arthur Stringer, an Irish keeper writing at the beginning of the 18th century, takes great care to throw doubt on theories of animal behaviour current at that time – which imputed very detailed conscious thinking to the animals concerned – when he did not consider the evidence sufficient to support them. Discussing various contemporary stories of how hunted stags go to extraordinary lengths to avoid leaving scent, he decides that such a contrived explanation does not fit his perception of the brain processes of a stag, and declares: 'In the main I am satisfied it is unreasonable for any man that understands deer to believe it' and, moreover, 'nor did I ever see any thing in a stag that looked so like policy' (Fairley 1977, p. 136).

The literature on domestication tends to reflect the ethos of the time in which it was written. As Clutton-Brock (1981, p. 124) points out, 19th-century views of the camel were heavily biased by man's certainty of the superiority of man. This contradicts the attribution by these views of the worst aspects of human nature to -

beasts that they regarded as highly inferior. This contradiction is paralleled in British writings on animal welfare in both the 19th and 20th centuries, where a protective attitude towards 'dumb beasts' is coupled with suggestions that mammals, at least, have the full suite of human emotions, including their attitudes to chronic pain.

Recent European literature on domestication makes only feeble attempts to attribute malice to species other than our own. It also presents more of a picture of co-evolution to mutualism, which assures us that specism has at least been recognized as a pitfall, if not actively attacked. Most of the writers of these texts sit comfortably within the current traditions of mainstream Western biological thought.

As a sideline, but directly related to our own overpowering desire for empathy with other species, it is relevant to note the enormous popular literature in many European languages which puts thoughts or words into animals' minds. At its worst, such literature often implies that members of the other species are so self-aware that a particular individual or even a species as a whole may be 'vicious'. If this means 'involving malice', then it is probably inaccurate; nevertheless, literature of this type, which insists on throwing our own bad points on the shoulders of others, is still remarkably popular. The continuing popularity of characters like 'Lassie' (the canine equivalent of 'Superman') shows us the other side of this interesting coin. The degree to which we 'put words into animals' mouths' in past and present European literature makes a fascinating study, and is a guide to *our* changing attitudes to *them* (in Ch. 4).

In conclusion, I wish to stress how important it is for us to understand those other species with which we have the closest links. They are the most likely species to reveal the nature of animals' attitudes to people. However, it is not easy, for example, to interpret from their facial expressions whether sheep are content, and we have to use other behavioural evidence – although much contemporary experimental work merely uses weight gain as an indicator. This does not stop people, especially good stock-keepers, from trying to guess at other animals' attitudes, but we are now coming to realize that very little is known about the behaviour of the common domestic species. Most experimental work has been related to production, and therefore is not concerned with the attitudes of the animals themselves, except in an indirect way. Neither has it been designed to relate changes in behaviour to a single variable (Kiley-Worthington 1977, p. 107).

To some extent the evolution to ranching that has occurred for many of these species means that we are no longer so close that we need to be aware of their existence or have any sort of attitude towards them, or they to us. It is sad to see such an influential popularizer as Donald Griffin saying that the study of wild animals under natural conditions is the only worthy study (Griffin 1984, p. 13). I am sure it is research on laboratory rats that he is attacking, since there is now ample evidence that for some farm animals a great deal of the behavioural repertoire of their ancestors is intact (e.g. Wood-Gush & Stolba 1981). Experimental behavioural work on domestic animals is essential, both to illuminate what went on in the past, when we were both involved in a closer relationship, and to improve what is currently, for many of them, an unenviable lot.

Surely a further development in awareness is necessary now. *We* need to be so self-aware that we can appreciate the differences between ourselves and them. We need to pay more attention to the design of behavioural experiments, to unravel the complexities of the behaviour both of humans and of the common domesticates.

In attempting to unravel our own mental functions, behavioural investigations of species which have different ways of functioning may play a useful part. However, we are probably misleading ourselves if we think that their behaviour is just simpler. Although I stressed that the differences between ourselves and other species are ones of complexity and organization, it is important to point out that, while we are generally more complex in our thinking abilities, there are many complex things which some species can do better. Pigeons can reorientate and recognize patterns (including those involved in intelligence tests) more quickly than we can, because they do it in a different way, although, as far as we know, they are not doing it for the same reasons (Hollard & Delius 1982). Other species are *different*, and we tend to underestimate the complexity of their behaviour. We are doing animals a wrong in thinking that we can automatically know, therefore, what gives them pleasure and satisfaction.

The analytic and empathetic behaviour that, as I have attempted to show, is well developed in humans leads us to relate to other species in subtle ways. In these relationships we tend to 'put words into their mouths'. It is important to be aware of the evolutionary origins and importance of this interesting aspect of human behaviour. However, we should also be prepared to concede that other species may do it too, be prepared to investigate the extent to which they do it, and discover whether those with the closest relationship to ourselves are unique in some way.

Bibliography

Clutton-Brock, J. 1981. *Domesticated animals from early times*. London: Heinemann/British Museum (Natural History).

Fairley, J. (ed.) 1977. *The experienced huntsman*, by Arthur Stringer (first published 1714). Belfast: Blackstaff Press.

Griffin, D. R. 1981. *The question of animal awareness*. New York: Rockefeller University Press.

Griffin, D. R. 1984. *Animal thinking*. Cambridge, Massachusetts: Harvard University Press.

Hollard, V. D. & J. D. Delius 1982. Rotational invariance in visual pattern recognition by pigeons and humans. *Science* **218**, 804–6.

Kiley-Worthington, M. 1977. *Behavioural problems of farm animals*. Stocksfield, Northumberland: Oriel Press.

Tilander, G. 1971. Livre de chasse. Gaston Phebus. *Cynegetica* XVIII. Karlshan.

Wood-Gush, D. G. M. & A. Stolba 1981. The assessment of behavioural needs of pigs under free-range and confined conditions. *Applied Animal Ethology* **7**, 380–9.

Wood-Gush, D. G. M., M. Dawkins & R. Ewbank 1981. *Self-awareness in domesticated animals*. South Mimms, Hertfordshire: Universities Federation for Animal Welfare.

7 *The animal in the study of humanity*

TIM INGOLD

Learning, symbolism and the limits of humanity

The study of culture, we commonly suppose, is a branch of anthropology, that is of the study of humanity. Most people seem to agree that the source of human pre-eminence (if human beings *are* pre-eminent) lies in the phenomena of culture, and that the task of anthropology is to study them; yet nobody can agree on what culture actually is. Definitions of culture are legion: one compilation, attempted more than 30 years ago, amassed no fewer than 161 different definitions (Kroeber & Kluckhohn 1952). By now there must be at least twice as many. Part of the problem is that many of the simpler definitions, such as that 'culture is learned (or acquired) behaviour', conspicuously fail to isolate anything that is specifically human, or merely sidestep the issue by substituting one problematic term (learning) for another (culture).

That much of the behaviour of non-human primates is acquired by a learning process is plainly evident to anyone who has worked with them. Moreover, there is no obvious break in learning abilities between primates and other mammalian species (Harlow 1958). Among birds the non-genetic transmission of components of song is well-established (Thorpe 1961, pp. 71–92). Going further down the scale, it may be recalled that in his latter years, Charles Darwin performed an ingenious series of experiments that conclusively demonstrated the existence of quite advanced learning capacities in earthworms (Reed 1982). A century later we find Bonner, in a beautiful book on *The evolution of culture in animals*, admitting rather reluctantly that although the colony of bacteria in his Petri dish do not exactly learn, 'they do have the basic response system' (Bonner 1980, p. 56)!

If earthworms learn, and if culture is learned behaviour, it follows that earthworms have culture. What, then, becomes of our cherished idea that the study of culture is an aspect of the study of humanity? To solve the problem, as some writers do, by distinguishing between the 'proto-culture' of non-human animals (Hallowell 1962) and the 'euculture' of human beings (Lumsden & Wilson 1981, p. 3) hardly helps, unless we can adduce independent criteria by which these kinds of culture are to be set apart. One possible solution, much favoured by contemporary anthropology, is to refocus the definition of culture upon the notion of the *symbol*. Its primary reference is then no longer to non-genetic (or 'social') modes of behavioural transmission, but to the conceptual organization of experience, or 'the imposition of an arbitrary framework of symbolic meaning upon reality' (Geertz 1964, p. 39, see also Holloway 1969, p. 395). What most anthropologists have failed to realize, however, is that the opposite of symbolically encoded behaviour is *not* genetically transmitted, or crudely 'instinctive' behaviour. For although all learning depends on the association of individuals, only when it involves teaching does it depend on the articulation of a symbolic blueprint or model for conduct. No such model is required for observational learning, of the kind that is common to both humans and non-human animals. Hence the boundaries between instinct and learning, as modes of intergenerational transmission of behavioural instructions, and between practices that are and are not grounded in a symbolically constructed matrix, *do not coincide*.

The latter boundary, I would argue, is what is generally implied in the distinction between the innate and the artificial; an artefact being defined as any object that results from the imposition of prior conceptual form upon material substance (Ingold 1986a, pp. 344–7). Thus, confusion arises because of the non-congruence of the two oppositions: instinctive versus learned, and innate versus artificial. The gross assumption of so many anthropological texts, that whatever cannot be claimed for the symbolic must be relegated to the instinctive, simply will not do, since it leaves altogether out of account the vast field of behaviour that is transmitted by learning (and which consequently will not be manifested by individuals deprived of contact with conspecifics at crucial moments of ontogenetic development), but which is *not* underwritten by a prior symbolic plan.

Moreover, this field of behaviour, which we could call *traditional*, overlaps the boundary between human and non-human conduct. On the one hand, we find local or regional traditions – or 'behaviour dialects' as they are sometimes known in ethological literature – not only among such 'almost human' animals as chimpanzees, but in social species (for example, of birds) far removed from man in the scale of nature (Beck 1982). On the other hand, a great deal of human behaviour, considered to be 'cultural' merely because it is learned, is effectively innate rather than symbolically grounded. It follows that neither of the oppositions I have mentioned, instinctive versus learned and innate versus artificial, serves to isolate the domain of the specifically human. The former is far too broad, whereas the latter is too narrow, isolating not the totality but only a small subset of the totality of human works.

I endorse the view that the production of artefacts depends on a capacity for symbolic thought unique to *Homo sapiens*, a capacity that is based in the faculty of language; and I believe this has enormous implications for human evolution and human history. Amongst other things, it allows for innovation by deliberate invention rather than accidents of blind variation, for the transmission of design by teaching rather than imitative learning, hence for the active acquisition of culture rather than the passive absorption of tradition, which in turn is responsible for the cumulative or progressive growth of knowledge which is surely an undeniable and unique feature of the history of humankind. However – and this is no minor qualification – we should not be misled by these far-reaching consequences of the symbolic faculty into thinking that it underlies everything that we do. My contention, to the contrary, is that it underlies only a small though highly significant fraction of what we do, whereas for the most part human conduct does not differ all that substantially from the conduct of non-human animals.

Lewis Henry Morgan and the engineering of the beaver

It was the grandfather of modern cultural anthropology, E. B. Tylor, who in 1871 enunciated the now classic definition of culture as those 'capabilities and habits acquired by man as a member of society' (Tylor 1871, I, p. 1). Tylor's definition has since been construed and misconstrued in countless ways; be it noted, however, that he always referred to culture in the singular rather than the plural, as a property not of particular local populations, but of mankind as a whole, and that in this sense it was used as a synonym for 'civilization' (Stocking 1968, pp. 73f.). For Tylor, therefore, culture referred to the progressive development of human knowledge in its various fields – of science, art, law, morality, and so on. Like most thinkers of his day, schooled in the philosophy of the enlightenment, Tylor believed that human beings, alone in the animal kingdom, were endowed with the quality of mind and that the greater or lesser 'cultivation' of this quality accounted for the differences between peoples on a universal scale of degrees of civilization. The evolution of culture was therefore equated with the advance of mind, along uniform channels, within a constant bodily form. Only subsequently, following the publication of Darwin's *The descent of man*, did Tylor's views begin to shift towards the position that mental progress was a function of advance in inherited bodily form, and particularly in the form and complexity of the organ of thinking: the brain. This view, applied to the differences between human populations rather than between human beings and other animals, underlay the virulent racism of the late 19th century.

On the other side of the Atlantic rather similar ideas were being propounded by Lewis Henry Morgan, who ranks equally with Tylor as one of the founders of the discipline of anthropology as we know it today. Morgan's *Ancient society* (1963 [1877]) is very well known, though this owes a good deal to the historical accident that Marx and Engels, when they eventually came to read it, claimed to find in it the key to their materialist theory of history. In fact, Morgan's account of the evolution of society was anything but materialist, since it rested on the idea of the progressive cultivation of so-called 'germs of thought'. To find the source of that idea, we have to turn to an earlier and much less well-known work by Morgan, published in 1868 under the title *The American beaver and his works*. This splendid monograph on the behaviour and constructive abilities of the beaver is still re-garded as an authoritative work on the subject. Morgan's interest in the beaver actually came about as a result of his involvement, as a director and stockholder, in a railroad company that was building a line to the iron-mining districts on the shores of Lake Superior. The line passed through virgin forest full of beavers, so that in connection with his duties for the company Morgan had ample opportunities to observe them at work. Like all other observers of this remark-able animal, he was enormously impressed by the industry and ingenuity they displayed in constructing their dams and lodges, which he described with painstaking precision (Fig. 7.1).

However, Morgan's beaver book is not only descriptive, for it ends with a remarkable chapter in which he reflects on the intelligence and cognitive capacities of non-human animals, as they compare with those of humans. In this

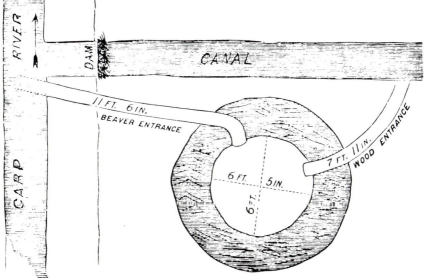

Ground Plan of Lodge

Measurements.

Diameter of chamber parallel with canal............ 6 feet 5 inches.
Transverse diameter.. 6 "
Height of chamber at centre............................. 1 foot 9 inches.
Level of floor below ground............................. 6 "
Height of floor above water in entrances...... ...... 4 "

Figure 7.1 Ground plan and dimensions of one of the beaver lodges observed by Morgan. Reproduced from Morgan (1868, p. 153).

he took a line which, for its time, was quite unusual. The conventional view, yet to be shaken by Darwin's revelations in *The origin of species*, was that every species had been separately brought into being by God at the time of Creation, and had retained ever since its essential bodily form. Now Morgan was as convinced of this as anybody; and like so many of his contemporaries, he also believed that the human body was the place of abode for an incorporeal essence, known as 'mind' or 'spirit' – or in Morgan's own words 'the thinking principle' – whose cultivation amounted to the process of civilization. Unlike Tylor, however, Morgan felt that the thinking principle was *not* unique to humanity. To the contrary, he believed that the Creator had endowed *all* animal species, and not mankind alone, with a mind as well as a body. If anything convinced him of this, it was his observations of the technical accomplishments of the beaver.

If civilized people differ from animals, Morgan surmised, the difference lies in the *degree* to which mind has developed, not in the presence of mind in humans as against its absence in non-human animals. For some reason the animals' mental progress has taken place at snail's pace compared with that of mankind, but this should not be taken to imply that animals have failed to make any progress at all since the days of the Creation. As for primitive humans, Morgan considered their degree of mental advance to be equivalent to, if not actually lower than, that of many animals. Indeed, in this respect he thought the beaver compared quite favourably with most so-called 'savages' (Fig. 7.2).

I cannot refrain from citing a delightful passage from Morgan's book, in which he depicts the mental processes of the beaver at work:

A beaver seeing a birch-tree full of spreading branches, which to his longing eyes seem quite desirable, may be supposed to say within himself: 'if I cut this tree through with my teeth it will fall, and then I can secure its limbs for my winter subsistence.' But it is necessary that he should carry his thinking

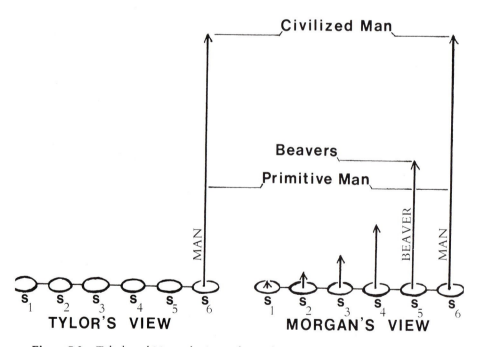

Figure 7.2 Tylor's and Morgan's views of mental progress. S_1–S_6 are species linked in an ascending chain of being (S_6 is the human species). Vertical arrows represent the advance of mind, within a constant bodily frame. In Morgan's view both beavers and other non-human animals have minds of their own, which are also advancing, albeit slowly compared with the mind of man. However, beavers have already overtaken the most primitive men, as is shown by the ingenuity of their technical accomplishments.

beyond this stage, and ascertain whether it is sufficiently near to his pond, or to some canal connected therewith, to enable him to transport the limbs, when cut into lengths, to the vicinity of his lodge. (Morgan 1868, p. 262.)

According to Morgan, then, the beaver is a perfectly self-conscious, intentional agent; indeed, a consummate engineer, fully capable of planning out in his mind a complex sequence of instrumental operations *before* even beginning to put them into effect. 'When a beaver stands for a moment and looks upon his work', Morgan (1868, p. 256) went on, 'he shows himself capable of holding his thoughts before his beaver mind; in other words, he is conscious of his own mental processes'.

However, if the beaver thinks or, more to the point, if he *knows* what he thinks, why can he not tell us about it? Why is he incapable of communicating his thoughts to an observer? For Morgan the answer was perfectly plain: because he lacks the requisite speech-apparatus. In man this apparatus involves structures of the larynx, mouth and ears, which are built into the bodily equipment that all normal humans possess. By contrast, the beaver has the mind to think, but lacks the bodily equipment to broadcast his thoughts. The same also goes for all other animals which, even if not so intelligent as the beaver, still possess a thinking principle. For this reason, and not wishing to be disrespectful towards the animals, Morgan preferred to call them *mutes*.

As it happened, the weight of opinion soon swung against Morgan. A psychology strongly influenced by the ideas of Darwin sought to demonstrate precisely the opposite of what he had argued: namely that if humans differ from non-human animals in degree rather than kind, it is not because they all share a spiritual essence or thinking principle, but because the human mind itself should be seen as nothing more than the functioning of a bodily organ, the brain. In a sense, where Morgan had sought to upgrade animals, the Darwinians sought to downgrade man. It was against this strongly Darwinian current that the anthropology of the early 20th century had to fight once more for the recognition of a distinctively human essence, lying in what came to be called – in place of the ancient notion of spirit – the 'capacity for culture'.

One of the strongest champions of this position was A. L. Kroeber, and in a classic paper of 1917 on 'The Superorganic' we find him returning once more to the engineering of beavers:

The beaver is a better architect than many a savage tribe. He fells larger trees, he drags them farther, he builds a closer house. . . . But the essential point is not that after all a man can do more than a beaver, or a beaver as much as a man; it is that what a beaver accomplishes he does by one means, and a man by another. . . . Who would be so rash as to affirm that ten thousand generations of example would convert the beaver from what he is into a carpenter or a bricklayer – or, allowing for his physical deficiency in the lack of hands, into a planning engineer! (Kroeber 1952, p. 31.)

Kroeber's point about the planning engineer is this: the beaver *does not* and *cannot* construct an imaginary blueprint of his future accommodation, whereas this is something of which even the most 'primitive' human is capable. The human engineer constructs a plan in advance of the execution; the beaver lives merely to execute plans designed – in the absence of a designer – through the play of variation under natural selection.

Kroeber's remarks on the uniqueness of human works were by no means novel. They were, in fact, anticipated by Marx in a celebrated passage from the first volume of *Capital*, where he seeks to establish a form of labour peculiar to the human species:

> A spider carries on operations resembling those of the weaver, and many a human architect is put to shame by the skill with which a bee constructs her cell. But what from the very first distinguishes the most incompetent architect from the best of bees, is that the architect has built a cell in his head before he constructs it in wax. (Marx 1930, pp. 169f.)

That is to say, the human architect, who here denotes cultural man, carries a blueprint of the task to be performed, prior to its performance, whereas the non-human animal does not (Ingold 1986b, pp. 16–39). Thus, the Gothic vault, to borrow an example from Bock (1980, pp. 182f.), is literally man-made, in the sense that its presence may be explained 'by reference to the doings of persons'. Neither the web nor the hive could be said, in the same sense, to be 'spider-made' or 'bee-made'. However, human beings do not always act like architects or engineers, so that Marx's distinction could just as well be carried over into the domain of human conduct, to separate the novel products of intentional design from the habitual replication of traditional forms. This would be equivalent to Alexander's (1964, p. 36) contrast between 'selfconscious' and 'unselfconscious' processes, and corresponds to ours between the artificial and the innate.

Donald Griffin and the language of bees

There was a long period in the present century during which mainstream biology appeared content to share with cultural anthropology a view of non-human animals as virtually mindless automata. Insofar as anthropologists sought to emphasize the specifically human attribution of the symbolic imagination and its products, by drawing a contrast with the apparent disabilities of non-human animals, the rather negative characterization of the latter was only reinforced. Those who denied the absoluteness of the Rubicon were inclined, like Darwin, to doubt that there was anything more to human cognition than the functioning of the machinery of the brain, rather than to follow Morgan in suggesting that non-human animals might have autonomous faculties of reason and intellect such as we recognize in ourselves. However, in recent years there has been much renewed interest in animal thinking (Walker 1983), and many scholars are coming round to the idea that non-human animals do, indeed, have minds of their own, even if they do not express the idea in quite the same way as did Morgan. The result is a direct challenge both to the predominantly behaviourist stance of ethology and animal psychology, and to the prevailing anthropological conception of human uniqueness.

One of the most interesting and outspoken contributors to this area of debate has been Griffin (1976, 1984). He puts the question of animal consciousness in the following way: 'Do animals have any sort of mental awareness of probable future events, and do they make conscious choices with the intent to produce certain results?' (Griffin 1977, p. 31). Posing the question thus, he is really asking whether animals engage in rational deliberation, and whether they have a reflective self-awareness. In suspecting that they do, Griffin's position does not differ very much from what Morgan (1868, p. 271) asserted a century previously, that the animal 'sets the body in motion to execute a resolution previously reached by a process of reasoning'. The problem is: how are we to know whether the animal is thinking, and if it is, what its thoughts are? As Griffin (1984, p. 132) has to admit, 'I do not yet know of any way to ask a beaver whether it contemplates a pond as it drags mud and branches to the middle of a shallow stream'. If only we could find out, by what bounds would our understanding not only of the world of the beaver, but likewise of all other animal worlds, be increased!

The solution to the problem, for Griffin, lies in developing the appropriate mode of communication that would allow an animal lacking the specialized vocal–auditory apparatus used in human speech to deliver an introspective report on its experiences to a human investigator. This has prompted a great deal of experimentation with alternative channels to the vocal–auditory; notably the visual–gestural channel used in sign-language. There are many accounts, both specialized and popular, of attempts to engage gorillas and chimpanzees in conversation with their human investigators, using specially designed sign-languages (these are reviewed by Ristau & Robbins 1982). Various claims have been made regarding the ability of these primate cousins of ours to converse in language, but not one of these claims has remained unchallenged. In many cases of apparent language use, it actually turned out that the animal was merely emitting conditioned responses to covert stimuli of which even the investigator was unaware. This has come to be known as the 'Clever Hans' effect, after a celebrated horse of that name which was believed to be capable of impressive feats of arithmetic multiplication, until it was shown that he could only do it in the presence of someone who already knew the answers (Pfungst 1965)!

A further problem that all investigators into animal language have to face, and which none has satisfactorily resolved, is to explain why animals that are purportedly capable of linguistic communication when reared in a human environment do not manifest this capability under 'natural' conditions. Animals that converse with humans ought to be able to converse among themselves, so why do they not do so? Is it simply that, with small groups of individuals, familiar both with one another and with the country they inhabit, the need just does not arise (Marler 1977)? Do chimpanzees, say, living in their own little communities, have nothing to say to one another? Maybe, but then why should human beings, in similarly small, close-knit communities, have *so much* to say to one another? As

George Steiner has suggested, it is in the intimacy of the small group, and not in the demands of communication with strangers and aliens, that language acquires its primary force and motivation. 'We speak first to ourselves, then to those nearest us in kinship and locale. We turn only gradually to the outsider . . .' (Steiner 1975, p. 231). So why should apes speak to outsiders before speaking to themselves? These questions, compounded with doubts about the validity of the experimental results, make me frankly sceptical of claims that non-human animals converse in language (see also Sebeok & Umiker-Sebeok 1980). I am fairly sure that the answer to whether they possess a linguistic faculty is 'no'.

Let me return to what Griffin has to say on the question of animal awareness. If only we could find an appropriate medium for two-way communication between human and animal, he writes, we would at once have a 'window' into the animals' minds, allowing us to eavesdrop on their mental processes (Griffin 1984, pp. 160–4). Advocating what he calls a 'participatory approach', Griffin likens the problem faced by the ethologist in establishing a dialogue across species boundaries with that faced by anthropologists in making contact with human beings of *other cultures*, and suggests that anthropological methods could well be extended to the study of *other species* (Griffin 1976, pp. 87–90).

Suppose, for example, that I wanted to enter into a dialogue with honeybees. I could not exactly *pretend* to be a bee: readers of Winnie-the-Pooh will know that deception is not easily practised on bees! Perhaps I could instead construct an exquisitely realistic model bee, equipped with radio controls, which I could place in the hive and manipulate at will from a safe distance. Now as is well known from the classic work of von Frisch (1950), honeybees possess a remarkable system for communicating to their co-workers the precise location of a food-source relative to the hive: they do this by repeatedly executing a figure-of-eight movement known as the waggle dance, whose orientation to the vertical indicates the direction of the food-source in relation to that of the Sun. I get my model bee, then, to execute a faultless waggle dance, and sure enough, the other bees are observed to respond in the appropriate fashion, by heading off to find food in the direction indicated by the dance. Yet I would still be doing something no bee has ever done, that is, executing a dance that corresponds to an image in my mind. Moreover, the image need not correspond to reality at all: I could perfectly well direct the bees on a wild-goose chase, towards a non-existent source.

In Figure 7.3 I portray two bees engaged in a dialogue. One has an image in his mind of a food-source, that may or may not exist in reality, and he is advising the other bee of its location, using the specialized 'sign language' of the waggle dance. For the other bee the message has a particular connotation – he thinks: 'so food is over there, I'll go and find it', and off he goes. Now this, of course, is precisely what does *not* happen; or rather, it could only happen between two human beings *pretending* to be bees in the way I have just suggested. We might imagine that in the supposed 'dialogue', one party is a human manipulating a model bee, the other a real bee. At once we can see that human and bee are not interchangeable partners in the dialogue between them. For the real bee the dance has no conceptual connotation at all: if the bee is the dancer, the dance is 'called up' by

Figure 7.3 Two bees engaged in a dialogue.

an internal organic state that was in turn induced by the preceding flight from a food source; in the absence of that source the dance behaviour will not be emitted, thus real bees cannot lie. And if the real bee is witness to the dance, it does not lead it to *conceive* of the presence of food at a particular place (a conception which it might or might not act upon, at its discretion), rather the dance has the direct effect of sending it off to the food source.

The dance, in short, is not a symbol that connotes an idea but a sign that commands action (Langer 1942, pp. 61–3). Hence there can be no *conversation* between humans and bees, or between bees, if by that we mean an intentional exchange of ideas between thinking subjects. Among themselves bees communicate, in that there is an exchange of information, but this information carries what Bronowski (1978, p. 43) has called 'the pre-programmed force of an instruction', and lacks any cognitive content. Since for that reason bees do not converse, participation in the full anthropological sense is out of the question. For the would-be participant observer there is simply nothing to participate in. Thus, although

our fable of the bees may seem far-fetched, it does serve to establish a really fundamental proposition: *conversation across boundaries of culture is absolutely different
from communication across boundaries of species*.

The sociologist Max Weber, writing around the turn of the century, wondered
whether we could understand the thoughts and intentions of non-human animals.
If we could, he argued that it would be possible, in theory, to formulate a sociology
of the relations of humans to animals (Weber 1947, p. 104). While admitting the
real difficulty of determining the subjective states of mind of animals, he did not
altogether rule out the possibility of such a sociology. He even went so far as to
surmise that our ability to understand what he called 'primitive men' might not
be significantly greater than our ability to understand non-human animals! This is
not a view that can still be seriously entertained today. Once more, the issue
hinges on the phenomenon of language. There was a time, in the early days of
anthropological and linguistic study, when it was thought that the languages of
different peoples of the world could be ranked, alongside every other aspect of
their culture, on a scale of development, with those of the West ranking highest
on the scale. Primitive people, it was thought, had primitive languages, inadequate for expressing ideas of any great degree of complexity or abstraction.
Nowadays we recognize that all languages of the world are equally developed,
that there simply do not exist any 'primitive' languages. Nobody knows how
language evolved; but assuming that it *did* evolve, in continuity with pre-human
animal functions, there must long ago have been 'proto-humans' who spoke certain kinds of undeveloped 'proto-language'. Some linguists, such as Lenneberg
(1967), have disputed the possibility of intermediate stages, but even if we infer
their existence in the remote past, nothing remains of them in extant populations
for us to study today. So, far from there being a minor difference between communing with non-human animals and communing with humans, or at least with
'primitive' humans, the gap is in fact a yawning one. As Talcott Parsons notes, in a
critical comment on Weber's text, Weber failed to take account of the fundamental fact that no non-human species has even a primitive form of language;
whereas no human group is known without a fully developed one (in Weber
1947, p. 104, footnote 27).

The words of a language, unlike the components of a communication system
like the honeybees' dance, function primarily as symbols rather than signs. This
means that their reference is to the internal world of concepts rather than the
external world of objects. Attending to concepts, moreover, is what we call
thinking. Thus language is, first and foremost, an *instrument of thought*, and not just
a means for the outward expression or broadcasting of thoughts that are somehow already there, but which – in the absence of a broadcasting medium – would
remain private, known only to the subject. Hence, the crucial difference between
natives of another culture and animals of another species is this: the former
possess a language which enables them to think, the latter do not. To grasp the
natives' thoughts we have but to learn their language, and as Hockett (1963) has
pointed out, one of the specific features of human language is that speakers of one
language can learn to speak and understand another. However, we cannot grasp
the animals' thoughts simply by learning and practising their communicatory
mode, *because the animals have no thoughts, as such, to grasp*.

Morgan, it will be recalled, believed that the beaver had its thoughts, but lacked the means to communicate them – at least to humans. From this point of view the animal is *mute* in just the same way as is a human being who is deaf and dumb. Such an individual is still endowed with the faculties of reason and intellect, and can perfectly well express his or her thoughts if an alternative medium can be devised to overcome the physical impediment. If the fault lies in the mechanism of the vocal–auditory channel, we could replace it with a visual–gestural channel, as in the kinds of sign-language regularly used among people with handicaps of speech or hearing. Experimenters have tried using these same sign-languages, slightly adapted, in the attempt to strike up conversations with apes, but – as already noted – with rather limited success. For the truth is that no amount of searching for alternative channels of communication, or attempts to inculcate human-like communicative modes in animals, will reveal thoughts that just are not there. For my part I would argue that the normal non-human animal is the very opposite of the muted thinker, as originally portrayed by Morgan and reiterated today by Griffin and others. Throughout its waking life the animal continually emits a veritable profusion of signals, but without a reflexive linguistic facility it cannot isolate thoughts as objects of attention. That is, rather than thinking without communicating, the animal *communicates without thinking*; so that the signals it transmits correspond to bodily states and not to concepts.

Thinking, feeling and intending

Perhaps my emphasis on uniquely human intellectual faculties will be considered unduly anthropocentric. To counter this objection, I wish to stress two points. First let me ask of the reader: how many times in the recent past have you stopped to consider possible future outcomes before you acted? Not often, I should imagine. For the most part we no more think before we act than do other animals. As Whitehead (1938 [1926], p. 217) has remarked, 'from the moment of birth we are immersed in action, and can only fitfully guide it by taking thought'. That is, thought interrupts action, breaks it up into fragments; but by no means does it constantly *direct* action. The fact that we can think things out in advance does not imply that we always do. If we did, ordinary life would probably grind to a halt, since its demands would grossly overload our cognitive capacities. As everybody knows, it is impossible to think about everything at once. Consider the allegorical millipede who, when asked how he managed to move all his thousand legs, became paralysed and starved to death. Once he thought about it, he could not do it any more (Koestler 1969, p. 205). So much of what we learn consists of learning *not* to think about what we are doing, so that we can concentrate on other things (Medawar 1957, p. 138). We do not have to think how to ride a bicycle, and so can concentrate on the road ahead. A cyclist who does stop to think is inclined to fall off.

Secondly, I would again ask of the reader: those things that you did spontaneously, without premeditation, did you do them unconsciously? Surely not. You were, after all, responsible for your actions, and you experienced them as things that *you* did. So, by the same token, if we claim that animals do not think before they act, this is not to deny them consciousness or intentionality. It is entirely reasonable to suppose that a great many non-human animals (certainly including all vertebrates), whose nervous systems are organized on rather similar principles to our own, are both purposive and suffering beings, agents and patients. The question of animal *consciousness*, of doing and feeling, must therefore be separated from that of animal *thinking*. Griffin's major error is to have confused the two, though he is certainly on the right track in pointing out that the intentionality of action is indifferent to whether, or to what degree, the procedures for carrying it out are transmitted by instinct or learning; and hence that 'learning is not a reliable criterion of consciousness' (Griffin 1984, pp. 46f., see Ingold 1986b, p. 27). Intuition may tell us that animals are conscious even when their manifest behaviour conforms to a genetically transmitted template, but we cannot infer from this that they necessarily think about what they feel and do.

Recall Griffin's criterion for judging the intentionality of animal actions – that they should be guided by mental images of desired future states. Is it not ironic that we should expect of an animal, as a condition of its being considered conscious and aware, that in all its activities it should proceed in accordance with plans already constructed through rational deliberation, when we ourselves do this but seldom in the course of practical, everyday life? To say that the animal is not conscious because (lacking language) it does not think before it acts, whilst admitting that we are conscious even though (despite language) we usually act before we think, is surely to apply double standards. Animals act as conscious, intentional agents, much as we do; that is, their actions are directed by *practical* consciousness. The difference is simply that we are able to isolate separate intentions from the stream of consciousness, to focus attention on them, and to articulate them in discourse. This corresponds to what Giddens (1979, pp. 24f.) calls the 'reflexive monitoring of conduct', and entails the operation of a *discursive* consciousness that rests upon the linguistic faculty and is uniquely human. Yet it is important to bear in mind that fully articulate, propositional language, such as is printed in books, is *not* the norm of human communication, but only the tip of an iceberg compared with the mass of spontaneous, non-verbal communication which we share with other animals (Midgley 1983, p. 88; Ch. 10, this book).

If it is granted that human conduct is purposive, even when it is not underwritten by a representation in the imagination of an end to be achieved, it must follow that advance planning is not a precondition for the intentionality of action. A distinction has therefore to be introduced, following Searle (1984, p. 65), 'between *prior intentions*, that is, intentions formed before the performance of an action, and *intentions in action*, which are the intentions we have while we are actually performing an action'. Conduct that is spontaneous, carried out without previous thought or reflection, but which we nevertheless experience as issuing from ourselves as agents, rather than being purely involuntary, carries intention in action, but is not motivated by prior intention. Clearly, these two kinds of intentionality correspond to the varieties of consciousness distinguished above, namely practical and discursive. If unplanned human action can be intentional in the former sense, the same must hold for the actions of non-human animals which, we suppose, lack the ability to plan.

To conclude, let me return to Marx's distinction between the works of the bee and the architect, and Kroeber's between those of the beaver and the planning engineer. Morgan in his time, and Griffin in ours, are suggesting that the distinction is not so absolute – that bees and beavers also plan things out, or envisage ends in advance of their realization. I do not think they do; but more than that, I do not think human beings do either, except intermittently, on those occasions when a novel situation demands a response that cannot be met from the existing stock-in-trade of habitual behaviour patterns. On such occasions, when – as Bock (1980, p. 185) puts it – 'the hold of tradition on a people is loosened', behaviour gives way to activity, understood as 'the doing of something new and different'. For Bock, activity is to be distinguished from behaviour as the execution of solutions deliberately designed by the agents themselves to cope with previously unencountered eventualities. In these terms activity implies not just the execution, but the *authorship*, of design.

It is fruitless to enquire whether human beings are unique among animal species. Of course they are unique, having certain capabilities that all other animals lack. The same goes for every species, each of which is unique in its own particular way. *Homo sapiens* is distinguished not by consciousness, but by the extreme elaboration of certain cognitive mechanisms which may be taken to underly both language, as an instrument of planning, and the practical skills by which those plans are executed. Should these mechanisms, constituting the 'capacity for culture' on which anthropology sets such store, be regarded as an evolutionary specialization on a par with other specializations in the animal kingdom? Are we equipped for thinking as beavers are for building dams, or as spiders for spinning webs? Assuredly, if you are a human being, there is a certain adaptive advantage in being able to think, just as there is in being able to construct dams or webs if you are a beaver or a spider. Yet this specialization, since it permits the construction of design, rather than the construction of objects (dams or webs) according to a given design, has made us the most generalized and adaptable animals on Earth. We can, if we will, beat the beaver or the spider at its own game, turning to our own account solutions to technical problems already perfected elsewhere in nature through the long process of evolutionary adaptation (Steadman 1979, p. 159).

All in all, though humans differ but little from other animal species, no more than the latter differ from one another, that difference has mighty consequences for the world we inhabit, since it is a world that, to an ever greater extent, we have made for ourselves, and that confronts us as the artificial product of human activity.

References

Alexander, C. 1964. *Notes on the synthesis of form.* Cambridge, Massachusetts: Harvard University Press.

Beck, B. B. 1982. Chimpocentrism: bias in cognitive ethology. *Journal of Human Evolution* **11**, 3–17.

Bock, K. E. 1980. *Human nature and history: a response to sociobiology*. New York: Columbia University Press.

Bonner, J. T. 1980. *The evolution of culture in animals*. Princeton, New Jersey: Princeton University Press.

Bronowski, J. 1978. *The origins of knowledge and imagination*. New Haven, Connecticut: Yale University Press.

Frisch, K. von 1950. *Bees: their vision, chemical sense and language*. Ithaca, New York: Cornell University Press.

Geertz, C. 1964. The transition to humanity. In *Horizons of anthropology*, S. Tax (ed.), 37–48. Chicago, Illinois: Aldine.

Giddens, A. 1979. *Central problems in social theory*. London: Macmillan.

Griffin, D. R. 1976. *The question of animal awareness: evolutionary continuity of mental experience*. New York: Rockefeller University Press.

Griffin, D. R. 1977. Expanding horizons in animal communication behaviour. In *How animals communicate*, T. A. Sebeok (ed.), 26–32. Bloomington, Indiana: Indiana University Press.

Griffin, D. R. 1984. *Animal thinking*. Cambridge, Massachusetts: Harvard University Press.

Hallowell, A. I. 1962. The protocultural foundations of human adaptation. In *Social life of early man*, S. L. Washburn (ed.), 236–55. London: Methuen.

Harlow, H. F. 1958. The evolution of learning. In *Behaviour and evolution*, A. Roe and G. G. Simpson (eds), 269–90. New Haven, Connecticut: Yale University Press.

Hockett, C. F. 1963. The problem of universals in language. In *Universals of language*, J. H. Greenberg (ed.), 1–22. Cambridge, Massachusetts: MIT Press.

Holloway, R. L. 1969. Culture, a *human* domain. *Current Anthropology* **10**, 395–412.

Ingold, T. 1986a. *Evolution and social life*. Cambridge: Cambridge University Press.

Ingold, T. 1986b. *The appropriation of nature: essays on human ecology and social relations*. Manchester: Manchester University Press.

Koestler, A. 1969. Beyond atomism and holism – the concept of the holon. In *Beyond reductionism: new perspectives in the life sciences*, A. Koestler and J. R. Smythies (eds), 192–232. London: Hutchinson.

Kroeber, A. L. 1952. *The nature of culture*. Chicago, Illinois: University of Chicago Press.

Kroeber, A. L. and C. Kluckhohn. 1952. *Culture: a critical review of concepts and definitions*. Papers of the Peabody Museum of American Archaeology and Ethnology, Harvard University, Vol. XLVII, No. 1. Cambridge, Massachusetts.

Langer, S. K. 1942. *Philosophy in a new key*. Cambridge, Massachusetts: Harvard University Press.

Lenneberg, E. H. 1967. *Biological foundations of language*. New York: Wiley.

Lumsden, C. J. & E. O. Wilson 1981. *Genes, mind and culture*. Cambridge, Massachusetts: Harvard University Press.

Marler, P. 1977. The evolution of communication. In *How animals communicate*, T. A. Sebeok (ed.), 45–70. Bloomington, Indiana: Indiana University Press.

Marx, K. 1930. *Capital*, Vol. I [transl. E. and C. Paul from 4th German edition of *Das Kapital* (1890)]. London: Dent.

Medawar, P. B. 1957. *The uniqueness of the individual*. London: Methuen.

Midgley, M. 1983. *Animals and why they matter*. Harmondsworth: Penguin.

Morgan, L. H. 1868. *The American beaver and his works*. Philadelphia, Pennsylvania: Lippincott.

Morgan, L. H. 1963 [1877]. *Ancient society*, E. B. Leacock (ed.). Cleveland, Ohio: World Publishing.

Pfungst, O. 1965. *Clever Hans (The horse of Mr. von Osten)*, R. Rosenthal (ed.). New York: Holt, Rinehart & Winston.

Reed, E. S. 1982. Darwin's earthworms: a case study in evolutionary psychology. *Behaviourism* **10**, 165–85.

Ristau, C. A. & D. Robbins 1982. Language in the great apes: a critical review. *Advances in the Study of Behaviour* **12**, 142–225.

Searle, J. 1984. *Minds, brains and science*. London: British Broadcasting Corporation.

Sebeok, T. A. and J. Umiker-Sebeok (eds) 1980. *Speaking of apes: a critical anthology of two-way communication with man*. New York: Plenum Press.

Steadman, P. 1979. *The evolution of designs: biological analogy in architecture and the applied arts*. Cambridge: Cambridge University Press.

Steiner, G. 1975. *After Babel: aspects of language and translation*. London: Oxford University Press.

Stocking, G. W. 1968. *Race, culture and evolution*. New York: Free Press.

Thorpe, W. H. 1961. *Bird-song: the biology of vocal comunication and expression in birds*. Cambridge: Cambridge University Press.

Tylor, E. B. 1871. *Primitive culture*, 2 vols. London: John Murray.

Walker, S. 1983. *Animal thought*. London: Routledge & Kegan Paul.

Weber, M. 1947. *The theory of social and economic organization*, T. Parsons (ed.). New York: Free Press.

Whitehead, A. N. 1938 [1926]. *Science and the modern world*. Harmondsworth: Penguin.

8 Organisms and minds: the dialectics of the animal–human interface in biology

BRIAN GOODWIN

The creator and the automaton

Descartes was of the opinion that such is the gulf between humans and animals that the behaviour of the latter could be explained in purely mechanical terms, while humanity is possessed of a creative faculty, irreducible to mechanism, as revealed particularly in language. His definition of creativity was very perceptive. It involved essentially three components: unlimited variety, relevance or appropriateness, and freedom from stimulus control. A competent language-user can generate a virtually unlimited variety of sentences, each of which is relevant or appropriate to the linguistic context, and the particular sentence selected for utterance is not dictated by an external controlling stimulus. Thus, the criterion used by Descartes to distinguish between the human and the animal focused on creativity. Three centuries later, with a highly developed Cartesian science and a theory of evolution that was intended to account for the origin of species (hence of species differences such as speech), how has this criterion been resolved, sharpened or transformed?

In the context of linguistics there is still much support for the view that speech is one of the most important properties by which *Homo sapiens* may be distinguished from other primates, despite the demonstration that the latter (chimpanzees, for example) are perfectly capable of learning a rudimentary sign-language and using it creatively by combining signs in novel and contextually appropriate ways. Nevertheless Chomsky (1979), for one, insists that the extraordinarily rapid acquisition of linguistic competence by human infants and the degree of creativity displayed is so far beyond anything demonstrated by other species that it reveals a qualitatively distinct level of cognitive organization. He thus adopts a Cartesian stance on the issue, and the Cartesian criteria of creative expression in language are clearly elaborated and embraced in his *Cartesian linguistics* (1966) and *Language and mind* (1968).

On the other hand, Descartes' analytical principles for the study of automata, which for him included not only inanimate nature but all the phenomena of biology up to the level of the human mind, have resulted in a biological science dominated by mechanical explanation. Evolution, about which Descartes did not need to bother, is itself regarded as the outcome of a purely mechanical process of variation under natural selection which has generated not only non-human animals, but also human beings, including their brains. So brains must also be mechanisms, and if one accepts the monistic mechanism of contemporary evolutionary theory, then whatever differences there are between humans and non-human animals must be of degree and not of kind. What has Chomsky to say about this? He takes the view (Piattelli-Palmarini 1980) that the human brain is an organ of thought and that, like other organs of the body, it differs from those of non-human animals because of the innate (genetic) differences between species.

Chomsky is fully aware that this innatism explains very little. It is a statement of a problem, not a solution, especially since the genetic differences between humans and chimpanzees amount to no more than about 1 per cent of their genomes (i.e. we are 99 per cent the same, genetically). However, in strictly conceptual terms, Chomsky is perfectly clear about the nature of evolutionary 'explanations' that invoke natural selection to account for the development of differences of form and behaviour between species, as he makes evident in the following: 'It is perfectly safe to attribute this development to "natural selection", so long as we realise that there is no substance to this assertion, that it amounts to nothing more than a belief that there is some naturalistic explanation for these phenomena' (Chomsky 1968, p. 83). Since genes make molecules, genetics is a powerful tool for accounting for differences in the molecular composition of organisms, and for identifying the morphological, behavioural or metabolic consequences of failing to make certain molecules. But genetics does not tell us how the molecules are organized into the dynamic, organized process that is the living organism.

Through the application of Descartes' principles for the quantitative reduction of complex systems to clear and simple elementary processes, it has emerged that animals are not the automata that Descartes believed them to be; and are, in fact, every bit as refractory to scientific understanding as the minds which Descartes singled out as the domain of irreducible creativity. The areas of biology that continue to defy a Cartesian reductionist analysis include brain function, embryonic development, and the evolutionary origins of the major taxonomic groups of organisms. One could argue that these are precisely the areas of biology where creation is most in evidence. However, despite the clarity of Descartes' definition, creativity is perhaps not the best way of characterizing the nature of the problem with which we are presented in these aspects of organic nature. So let us see if we can come to terms with these properties of organisms and minds by a somewhat different approach. Transformation is at times the best way to seek resolution.

The problem of form

The three areas of difficulty identified above, namely brain function, embryonic development and the origins of the major classes of organism, have something in common: they all involve the generation of complex, organized forms. This is perfectly clear in the evolutionary origins of the major taxonomic groups (phylogeny), which are characterized by distinct morphological features; and in embryonic development (ontogeny) wherein organisms of specific form are generated from seeds, buds or eggs. Behaviour and cognition also involve the generation of ordered forms in space and time, whether it be in play, ritualized courtship, pattern recognition or speech. These can all be regarded as the result of generative principles and rules of transformation operating together with the contingencies of context to produce appropriate forms. The problem is to identify the particular types of dynamic order that characterize evolving populations, developing organisms and functioning brains, giving rise to the distinctive forms and patterns that constitute their natural expression.

This is the problem of form in biology. It is that part of the subject that has remained refractory to the analytical, reductionist tradition that Descartes did so much to promulgate, and that has revealed so much about the molecular and cellular properties of organisms and brains. What it has not revealed is their dynamic organization at a level appropriate to the phenomena of form that are such a striking characteristic of the biological realm. In Kuhnian terms, this may simply be a puzzle, something that will eventually be resolved by the progressive accumulation of more detail; or it could be a problem, whose resolution requires a quite fundamental change of perspective and assumptions, amounting to a paradigm shift. Let me now briefly consider these alternatives, whose implications have been discussed in much more detail and from a variety of perspectives in two recent collections of essays (Ho & Saunders 1984, Pollard 1984). Although this may appear to take us on an excursion away from the focus of our enquiry into organisms and minds, it is necessary to clear the biological ground of certain conceptual obstacles. Once this is done, the consequences for an understanding of organized process in biology and the link with creative action should become clearer.

The biological dialogue

The dominant biological view of organisms is that they are complex, self-reproducing systems whose specific properties have evolved by natural selection acting on spontaneous variation arising from gene mutation and genome rearrangement. In this description there are essentially two sets of forces acting on organisms: internal ones coming from the genome, causing variations in organismic properties (including form); and external ones coming from the environment, determining the differential survivorship, and hence adaptedness, of given variants. The organism itself is nowhere defined except as a self-reproducing entity, yet it is in some sense the broker that mediates between the internal, genetic forces and the external, environmental ones, acting so as to optimize the genetic stock. Generally, this mediation is taken to be direct in the sense that phenotypes are assumed to be determined or caused by genotypes, so that selection on the former leads to modification of the latter. Thus, the organism is effectively a transparent shop window with genetic goods displayed directly to the naturally selective shopper, whose selection of appropriate articles ('characters') effectively creates the specific packages of goods we call the members of a species.

There are two fundamental dualisms in this description: between genotype and phenotype, and between organism and environment. I shall return to the second of these in the next section. According to the first, the genotype is considered to contain the essential causes of the phenotype. This is currently expressed by the metaphor of the program, applied to the set of genetic instructions, which directs the construction of the organism during embryonic development by specifying which molecules are produced when, where and in what quantities. The organism is thus held to be reducible to the molecules of which it is composed. Certainly the organism is, in biochemical terms, composed of nothing but molecules. The great achievement of molecular biology is to have elucidated the mechanisms whereby these molecules are made and their quantities controlled. The limitation of this description is that form is not, in general, explicable simply in terms of composition; nor in terms of composition plus a history of the particular conditions obtaining during the generation of the form out of its constituents. Water and ice have the same composition but quite different forms, which are not explicable by the statement that one form appears above zero Celsius and the other below. The explanation of form always requires a theory of organization, of how the constituents are ordered dynamically in space and time. This fact has been recognized at least from the time of Pythagoras, but it is frequently forgotten.

It is because of the absence of such a theory of the organism that both embryonic development and the evolutionary origins of the major taxonomic groups remain unsolved problems. No matter how much we learn about genes and molecules, ontogeny and phylogeny will not be understood until we have an exact description of the type of dynamic organization that characterizes the living state; just as the behaviour of liquids could not be understood in a generative sense until there was a theory of the dynamic space–time order that characterizes the liquid state of matter.

One development in molecular genetics that emphasizes this point rather dramatically is the discovery that there is no correlation between the DNA content of species and their morphological or other complexity. Species of amphibia that are virtually identical morphologically nevertheless have great differences in the DNA content of their chromosomes whereas, as noted earlier, humans and chimpanzees, with very significant morphological and behavioural differences, are very similar in their DNA content. So it is not content or composition that counts, but organization. This point has repeatedly been made in the history of biology (see Russell (1916) for a classical statement; and Goodwin (1985a,b) for recent analyses). However, careers are not made out of wrestling with difficult problems, and the difficulties are most probably of our own making: we are looking at the problem the wrong way, identifying the wrong causes. The causal connections between genotype and phenotype are not simply atomic, Humean, cause-and-effect relations mediated by molecules. This duality, like the mind–body duality, generates confusion and mystification, and it has a similar origin (see Webster & Goodwin (1982) for an analysis of the genetic program as an 'Idea' or a formative 'Soul', and the organism as the 'Body').

Organism and environment

Let me now return to the second dualism on which is based the theory of adaptation under natural selection: that between organism and environment. The scenario is that the environment pre-exists in the form of niches which pose problems for natural selection to solve by promoting organisms with appropriate characters for survival and reproduction in these niches. Spontaneous variations in the genotype result in phenotypic variations which constitute the raw material for this problem-solving exercise. From this perspective, natural selection tends to be seen as the formative or creative agent in the evolutionary process, providing organisms with specific forms and behaviours appropriate to currently prevailing environmental conditions of life. Again, we see that the organism is a mediator of uncertain status between the genes, whose random variations cause random phenotypic variety (random in the sense that it does not correlate with environmental change), and the environment, whose pressures must be accommodated if the species is to survive.

The great insight of evolutionary theory is that organismic life-cycles undergo hereditary changes that depend on a dynamic balance between influences internal and external to organisms, rates of change in populations being dependent on these influences acting on constituent members of the population. The limitations arise again from a failure to recognize the organism as an active agent with its own organizational principles, imposed between the genes and the environment. Organisms both select and alter their environments, and their intrinsic dynamic organization limits the hereditary changes that are possible, so that the variety available for evolution is restricted. There seems to be no other way of understanding the limited set of basic morphological types of organism that constitute the foundation of our systems of classification, nor of explaining why they nearly all appeared within the relatively brief evolutionary period of the Cambrian, with very few fundamental innovations since (see, for example, Arthur 1984, Reid 1985). Furthermore, organisms themselves have the potential for appropriate response to the environment, so that much of the variation that is available for evolutionary change arises not from random genetic mutation, but from the intrinsically regulative and plastic responses of the organism to the environment during its life-cycle. This plasticity can include genetic response, in the sense that environmental stress has been shown to result in adaptive changes in the genome in a number of plant species (Cullis 1984). Thus, the so-called creative power of natural selection is, in fact, very circumscribed (see Ho, in press, for an analysis of these issues).

The extent to which competitive interactions are instrumental in shaping evolutionary changes is a further issue of current debate. Organisms are as co-operative as they are competitive (Bateson 1986), and they make a living in a manner that usually poses no threat to ecological balance. The rather rapacious and territorial images of organismic life-strategies that dominate neo-Darwinist descriptions appear to be largely ideological projections to the biological domain born of a competitive and individualistic society (Lewontin et al. 1984). A more appropriate description for the evolutionary process than natural selection (which was, of course, derived from a comparison with the domestic selection of breeding stocks) is provided by the concept of *dynamic stability*. The environment does not select and shape organisms any more than a bath shapes the spiral form of the water as it flows down the plug-hole. Clearly, if there were no bath there would be no flow and no form; but what generates the details of the spiral pattern is a combination of the intrinsic properties of the liquid state of matter, together with all the contingencies operating on the dynamic process (height of water, size of hole, force of gravity, etc.). Neo-Darwinist descriptions tend greatly to exaggerate the role of the environment, on the one hand, and the role of the genes, on the other. Both of these undergo random (mutually uncorrelated) change. But organisms do not: they change in systematic and ordered ways, which is what makes taxonomy possible.

Thus, in a sense, organisms turn randomness into order by virtue of their own principles of dynamic organization, as Waddington (1957) was fond of emphasizing. The evolutionary process is an exploration of the possibilities inherent in the living state, realized as organisms of specific form and function. 'Adaptation' means no more and no less than the stability of a life-strategy, a dynamic process involving a set of transformations whose generic property is the repetition of a (life) cycle, the period of which is the generation time. There is no organism–environment duality in this process because the dynamic of the life-cycle extends across the boundary between the two. In thermodynamic terms, organisms are open systems. For example, there are developing marine organisms that generate electrical fields due to ion fluxes that extend beyond their structural boundaries, so that dynamically they are continuous with the environment, and similarly with other mass flows. We can, if we wish, separate different states of organization of matter, such as the living and the non-living, liquid and solid. But because one can transform into the other, the boundaries are always fuzzy, and the different states are united under transformation. Thus, duality is replaced by state transition in a unified dynamic, so that there is no more of a duality between organism and environment than there is between bone and muscle in the organism, or between nucleus and cytoplasm in a cell.

The logic of process

The argument of this chapter leads inexorably to the familiar proposition that life is process and transformation. The limitations of the dualities discussed above arise from the attempt to explain stability (of species, or state of adaptation) in terms of something static and stable (genome or environmental niche), rather than something dynamic (organism–environment cycle). The same applies to attempts to explain the stability of behaviour (instinct or habit) or of cognitive activity (recognition or memory) in terms of stable 'representations' or 'internal models'. All of these conceptual dualisms may be derived logically from the Cartesian philosophy of substance in which there are elementary things or objects (molecules, cells, organisms or species) which are acted upon by forces external to them, so that change arises from Humean atomistic cause–effect relationships between hierarchically ordered categories of objects constituted of more-fundamental objects. This has the consequence that these things and the actions in which they are involved are all *dead* mechanisms because they have no life of their own. This was precisely Descartes' view: all such entities are, in fact, machines, automata. However, as we have seen, this view of organisms leads to numerous contradictions and difficulties because of the endless proliferation of dualisms that arise from any attempt to analyse process in static terms. Again, this insight is not new: Zeno instructed us in it many centuries ago. 'There can be no doubt that the Humean conception of Causality . . . must be wrong', write Harré and Madden (1975) in their book *Causal powers*. The alternative is to assert the primacy of process, so that change due to immanent power is of the essence whereas 'things' maintaining stability of state are derived, and require explanation. We are thus led to dialectics, the logic of process.

A fully developed theory of process has some quite startling consequences. If change is taken as primitive, then we must stop thinking about movement as something that happens to things as a consequence of forces from outside themselves acting within a pre-existing space–time framework. Causality becomes immanent rather than transient, and what we call objects and their environments are self-generating complementary forms. There is no figure without a ground, and the only criterion of appropriateness is dynamic stability. Thus, the meaning of a process is to be discovered simply by perception and experience of the complementary relationship between event and context. Space–time is an appropriate descriptive context for localized action connected with particular intentions, but it is generated and maintained by intention and action; it is not a pre-existent given. The same is true of all types of stability: they are actively maintained and held by action which persists as long as the intention (holding in or on) persists, after which there is reversion to change. Thus, everything transforms sooner or later, and all is flux, but it is not chaotic. Process has its own logic. It is not classical two-valued logic, which runs into contradictions as soon as it is faced with processes that have properties of both continuity and transformation. What is required is a logic in which every value is an aspect of all values, by virtue of their primary inner connectedness, and in which there are no absolute and atomic, logical values as in the classical scheme (Jerman, pers. com.). Only thus is it possible to resolve the problem of primary relational order in space–time processes. Russell (1959) showed that classical logic, with the law of the excluded middle, is not compatible with a condition of such inner relation among the components of a dynamic system: for according to such logic, either the relation is a part of the nature of the components, or the relations are identical to the elements themselves. Neither alternative allows for a primary condition of interrelatedness in which every 'part' enfolds the whole (see also Bohm 1980).

Fields and forms

However, relational order is precisely what characterizes the condition of organisms. As we have seen, it is not composition that determines organismic form and transformation, but dynamic organization. Classically, relational space–time order is described by fields, and field equations describe their dynamics. It is the absence of adequate field theories of organismic life-cycles and cognitive processes that accounts for the serious deficiencies in our understanding of organisms and minds, of evolution and cognition. Insofar as they currently exist, such theories of (say) embryonic development do give us some insight into the type of dynamic space–time order that could underlie the generation of biological form (Meinhardt 1982, Murray & Oster 1984, Goodwin & Trainor 1985).

Furthermore, it appears that field descriptions come closest to embodying the logic of process described above. Harré and Madden (1975) have addressed precisely the question of how best to remedy the inadequacies of Cartesian or Humean causality, and conclude that an alternative can be derived from the field concept. They quote Faraday (1857) on the notion of force or power: 'What I mean by the word [force] is the *source* or *sources* of all possible actions of the particles or materials of the universe: these being often called the *powers* of nature when spoken of in relation to the different manners in which their effects are shown'. They then continue: 'The "lines of force" then picture the directional structure of powers or potentials, distributed in space. The fundamental entity then becomes a single, unified field, and in perpetual process of change as its structure modulates from one distribution of potentials of a certain value to another' (Harré & Madden 1975, p. 175).

This vision of a single unified dynamic field, with different qualities and powers, goes well beyond what I have sought to describe in relation to the organic order. However, if we are to take seriously a dialectic of process, then this is where it leads us. It is a far cry from the Cartesian world of mechanism. Whitehead (1929) put the distinction in the following condensed, if cryptic, form: 'Descartes in his philosophy conceives the thinker as creating the occasional thought. The philosophy of organism inverts the order, and conceives the thought as a constituent operation in the creation of the occasional thinker. . . . In this inversion we have the final contrast between a philosophy of substance and a philosophy of organism.'

If I understand it, the message here is that there are not things (e.g. thinkers) that generate thoughts; there are processes that generate complementary forms, such as thinkers and thoughts, together with all of the other aspects appropriate to this dynamic constellation of phenomena. So mind is not in the brain, any more than life is in the organism. These are aspects of ordered processes that exist in the dynamic relationship of thinking and acting, cycling and transforming, generated across the moving, fuzzy boundary between inner and outer, subject and object. Life is relational order lived at the interface, where forms are generated. The developing embryo folds itself into layers that modulate the flux of its dynamic inner–outer order in characteristic ways in different tissues. The brain is a labyrinth of folded surfaces, a complex domain of mappings, projections and transformations which create an unprecedented richness of relational experience between inner and outer; meaningful because of the complementarity of figure and ground, event and context.

So, finally, we are in a position to respond to the question of this book: what is an animal? For Descartes, it was a machine, an automaton. Our scientific culture has tried hard to validate this proposition, but the animal has resisted, just as the mind has resisted. This resistance, together with parallel developments in other sciences, notably recent developments in physics, have pointed strongly towards a very different conclusion. An animal is a centre of immanent, self-generating or creative power, organized in terms of a relational order that results in a periodic pattern of transformation (a life-cycle) involving historical and actual components (genes and environment) and biological universals (the order of the living state). Animals – indeed all living beings – are both cause and effect of themselves, pure self-sustaining activity. They are agents of a 'natura naturans' rather than 'natura naturata', creative rather than created, law-giving rather than lawful, makers rather than doers. However, an organic philosophy of process forces us to the conclusion that, in a certain fundamental sense, much of this description applies as well to other aspects of the world as we know it (Watson 1986). So, in this sense, the world is also an organism, taking us both backwards to an earlier vision of reality as living process, and forward to a new appreciation of that vision. Of course, there are great differences between different aspects of this unified, living field, since there are local state transitions that result in the boundaries we use to distinguish different conditions of order. However, it is all unified under transformation. The current dialectic of the animal–human interface in biology leads to one of those startling changes of cultural viewpoint that brings self-generating power back into fundamental reality and banishes mechanism. The Cartesian dualistic barrier that separated the creator from the automaton has now dissolved, leaving us with a flowing unity, a creative river of life.

References

Arthur, W. 1984. *Mechanisms of morphological evolution: a combined genetic, developmental and ecological approach*. Chichester: Wiley.

Bateson, P. 1986. Sociobiology and human politics. In *Science and beyond*, S. Rose and L. Appignanesi (eds), 79–99. Oxford: Blackwell.

Bohm, D. 1980. *Wholeness and the implicate order*. London: Routledge & Kegan Paul.

Chomsky, N. 1966. *Cartesian linguistics*. New York: Harper & Row.

Chomsky, N. 1968. *Language and mind*. New York: Harcourt, Brace & World.

Chomsky, N. 1979. *Language and responsibility*. Sussex: Harvester Press.

Cullis, C. A. 1984. Environmentally induced DNA changes. In *Evolutionary theory, paths into the future*, J. Pollard (ed.), 203–16. Chichester: Wiley.

Goodwin, B. C. 1985a. What are the causes of morphogenesis? *Bio Essays* **3**, 32–5.

Goodwin, B. C. 1985b. Developing organisms as self-organizing fields. In *Mathematical essays on growth and the emergence of form*, P. L. Antonelli (ed.), 185–200. Edmonton, Alberta: University of Alberta Press.

Goodwin, B. C. & L. E. H. Trainor 1985. Tip and whorl morphogenesis in *Acetabularia* by calcium-regulated strain fields. *Journal of Theoretical Biology* **117**, 79–106.

Harré, R. & E. H. Madden 1975. *Causal powers: a theory of natural necessity*. Oxford: Blackwell.

Ho, M-W. (in press). Genetic fitness and natural selection: myth or metaphor. In *Evolution of social behaviour and integrative levels*. 3rd T. C. Schneirla Conference, New York.

Ho, M-W. & P. T. Saunders 1984. *Beyond neo-Darwinism: an introduction to the new evolutionary paradigm*. London: Academic Press.

Jerman, I. n.d. Some problems and perspectives in a dynamic understanding of life and organisms. Unpublished MS.

Lewontin, R. C., S. P. R. Rose & L. J. Kamin 1984. *Not in our genes*. New York: Pantheon.

Meinhardt, H. 1982. *Models of biological pattern formation*. London: Academic Press.

Murray, J. D. & G. F. Oster 1984. Generation of biological pattern and form. *IMA Journal of Mathematics in Medicine and Biology* **1**, 51–75.

Piatelli-Palmarini, M. 1980. *Language and learning: the debate between Jean Piaget and Noam Chomsky*. London: Routledge & Kegan Paul.

Pollard, J. W. (ed.) 1984. *Evolutionary theory: paths into the future*. Chichester: Wiley.

Reid, R. G. B. 1985. *Evolutionary theory: the unfinished synthesis*. London: Croom Helm.

Russell, B. 1959. *My philosophical development*. London: Allen & Unwin.

Russell, E. S. 1916. *Form and function: a contribution to the history of animal morphology*. London: John Murray.

Waddington, C. H. 1957. *The strategy of the genes*. London: Allen & Unwin.

Watson, A. 1986. The birth of structure: a twentieth-century Copernican revolution. Ph.D. dissertation, University of Sussex.

Webster, G. C. & B. C. Goodwin 1982. The origin of species: a structuralist approach. *Journal of Social and Biological Structures* **5**, 15–47.

Whitehead, A. N. 1929. *Process and reality*. Cambridge: Cambridge University Press.

9 The affordances of the animate environment: social science from the ecological point of view

EDWARD S. REED

The ecological reality of the animate

A frog sees something darting through the air above it. The frog turns and looks carefully. The tiny mite swoops again, its small body pulsing against the air with an incredibly rapid wingbeat, bouncing in an arc over the frog's head, when – in an instant too short for our human eyes to see clearly – the frog's tongue flicks out and snares its prey. This little fable has become a classic and popular story in neurobiology since Maturana *et al.* (1960) first suggested that 'complex cells' in the brain might mediate this remarkable feat of predation. There usually follows a misleading discussion of alleged neural mechanisms of so-called pattern perception; but we would be well advised to ignore this kind of approach. Let us ask not what the frog's eye tells the frog's brain (if, indeed, it communicates anything at all), but how the frog succeeds in feeding. In so doing we will draw on the insights achieved by the new school of ecological psychology, which has developed out of the work of the late James Gibson (see Gibson 1979, Reed & Jones 1982, Reed in press).

It is first instructive to consider what frogs do *not* do. They do not spend their time and energy attacking falling leaves or dust motes floating in the air. The mere fact of something moving in the upper perimeter of a frog's field of vision is not sufficient for it to launch a predatory attack. Secondly, when a bird some distance away stimulates the frog's eye with a flylike speck on its retina, the frog does not act as if an edible object were within range. Thirdly, a sated frog will attack less frequently than a hungry frog, or will not attack at all. Fourthly, our story can be told of many animals besides frogs, including invertebrates such as spiders, which have entirely different neurons and nervous systems. In these cases the objects of interest will, of course, be different. The toad, which looks to an untrained eye not unlike a frog, predates on elongated non-rigid squirming objects, such as worms.

The frog, toad or other predating animal is doing something truly remarkable: co-ordinating and controlling a highly specific mode of action (a 'bout of predation' in the jargon of the animal behaviourists) with respect to a highly specific environmental situation. Not only is the timing and patterning of the frog's tongue-flick precisely geared to the fly's trajectory, it is *specific* to it, since the action does not appear unless the circumstances are appropriate.[1] Frogs and other animals thus routinely distinguish inanimate from animate objects, as a matter of course, in making their living. Moreover, they are equally proficient at distinguishing *kinds* of animate objects. Animals that are preyed upon react in very specific and different ways to predators than to benign creatures. Members of a single species can often distinguish gender markings or behavioural gestures of their conspecifics in ways that are difficult for humans to appreciate, as in the complex competitive flight patterns of male hoverflies intent on mating with a single desired female (Collett & Land 1978).

The typical explanation of how the frog (or any other animal) comes to achieve this discriminatory feat is roughly as follows. The fly causes stimulation at the peripheral sense organs of the frog. This stimulation is coded and communicated into the brain where, as part of a complex feedback cycle, it helps to create a pattern of central nervous activity. Components of this central activity may include the firing of complex cells which are tuned to certain features of the central activity. Especially in humans, the central activity is also the basis for a complex 'interpretation' of the meaning of the stimulus, an interpretation comprising volleys of complex and hypercomplex cell firings, and probably some mysterious 'higher' interpretive processes. In other words, the sensory level of processing is not a source of meaning, but is just the physical fact of stimuli impinging on the nervous system. The higher, perceptual level *infers the causes* of the sensory impingements (e.g. 'this pattern of retinal activity must have been caused by a fly') and thus generates meanings. It is remarkable that this theoretical analysis of perception has persisted from the time of Descartes to the present (Boring 1942, Reed 1982). Despite its popularity, this kind of account spells doom for an autonomous social science.

To argue that there is no meaning in the world that is not inferred or constructed by subjects has long been a popular strategy in social science, and not just in perceptual theory; but we reduce our ontology to 'nothing without us but bodies in motion, nothing within us but organic motions' at great peril (see Burtt 1932, for a brilliant review of the origin and implications of this theory). If such meaningful properties as being animate are not, properly, properties of objects, but only subjective construals of configurations of matter and motion, then there is no *environment* around us. By an environment I mean the surroundings of animals, with the earth below and the sky above, with places filled with useful resources, inanimate and animate objects. To hold that objects have no significant properties for subjects except insofar as those significances are constructed by subjects through the use of symbolic rules is to lose the environment in which we live and replace it with the world of the physicists' imaginations: stimulus prods of energy caused by congeries of elements in motion. For example, in physics there is no such thing as the ground, only packed molecules of carbon, silicon, nitrogen and some other elements. It is the earth on which we walk, and the soil in which we plant, that is relevant for us as perceiving and acting creatures; not the molecules discovered by scientists. Modern psychology, sociology and anthropology have reached for the glittering ring of socially constructed meaningfulness, and have lost their footing on the ground. How can we achieve an ontology that points to meanings without determining them, that denies scientistic physicalism without adopting the sort of pseudo-scientific idealism that has always plagued the social sciences? How can we explain how the frog *sees* animate objects – not how it infers or imagines them, but how it sees them? And how can we achieve all this without losing sight of the reality of socially created meaning? These are the questions Gibson claimed his ecological approach to psychology could help to answer. In the rest of this chapter I shall sketch out precisely how far this ecological point of view succeeds in such a task.

Affordances and information

The key insight for anthropology from ecological psychology is an extension of Gibson's discovery that perception is the awareness of what he called the *affordances* of the objects, places and events surrounding us, through the detection of *ecological information* (Gibson 1979, Reed 1986). The affordances of things that are specified by this information are ecological values for observers, they are opportunities for doing something, for obtaining certain resources, or hindrances such as traps and dangers. In addition, whereas inanimate objects afford actions (to obtain the use values or to avoid the dangers), animate objects afford *interaction*, and socialized objects afford *proper* (as against improper) action and interaction. We cannot interact with the inanimate environment, for it does not act back, nor is it aware of use, as are other animals. To act on an inanimate object is to realize (that is, to make real) one of its affordances, but to act on another animal is to realize the affordances of something that is itself aware of the process of realization. This is why prey hides from predators, and also why predators conceal their acts and intentions from prey as best they can. It is also why walking in the neighbourbood of a rock or a tree is a very different action from walking in the same neighbourhood with a panther on the rock or in the tree. (It is also why we can *learn* that an otherwise innocuous tree may *conceal* a predator, and come to act more cautiously in the woods.) Moreover, while we can interact with any animal that is aware of us, we can only act properly when our partner(s) is *socialized* into the same set of norms and properties of action as we are. All humans smile when happy and most raise their hands and use an open face–body gesture to indicate friendship, but people of different cultures deploy such gestures in different social settings. Thus, even though any human will recognize your friendly gesture, some observers may find the timing and gestural nuances appropriate, whereas others will find them odd, or even objectionable (Ekman 1977, Kendon 1984).

Plants form a special case in ecological psychology. Gibson (1979) treats them as purely inanimate, but that seems unsatisfactory. True, plant action is far more limited than animal, but plants do move and react, as Darwin (1880) showed in great detail, and some plants will prick, poison, and even trap unsuspecting animals. Plants also have a rudimentary awareness of their surroundings, especially their chemical and meteorological properties. Perhaps animate versus inanimate is a dimension, with plants in the middle, or perhaps plants form a separate category altogether (see Ch. 5).

From the point of view of ecological psychology, the task of distinguishing the inanimate, the animate and the social is not simply a question of subjective categorization, but of *ecological* categorization. As the environment of which we are speaking is a *populated* one, we are not simply interested in the objective categorizations of those ecologists who are concerned primarily with the energetics of material transfer in the ecosystem (Reed 1985). On the contrary, we want to discover what distinguishes animate from inanimate objects in ways that are relevant to the animals concerned. Finally, the mere existence of an affordance does not entail awareness of it or the use of it: pointed sticks afford piercing the soil for planting, but the discovery of this affordance was comparatively recent in the history of life, although of profound significance to the bipedal primates who made it. Thus, we need to analyse not only what the affordances of things are, but what kind of information specifies these affordances to observers, and by means of what processes observers might learn to detect the information and thereby come to realize the affordance.

I shall therefore proceed as follows. First, for each of the two distinctions, animate–inanimate and social–non-social, I shall describe in a general way the differences in kinds of affordances. Following this, I shall try to state the evolutionary basis for these differences. Throughout the discussion, I shall assume that the animate and the social are *real* (not physically real, but ecologically real, which is more important). These are not cultural distinctions, but distinctions available in the environment which have been put to use in different ways by different cultures.

Inanimate versus animate

Ecological psychology, Gibson (1979, p. 7) argued, begins with the distinction between the animate and inanimate. Psychology is about the ways of life (the 'habits' or ecological niches) of behaving things, and behaving things are at the very least minimally *aware* of their surroundings. Ecological psychology thus treats the environment not as a world made up of physical elements and properties, but as the habitation of animate creatures – as a meaningful environment. Gibson described at great length the large- and small-scale features of the terrestrial environment in terms of what these afford animals for locomotion, shelter, manipulation and other important activities. Overall, the environment consists of media, substances and surfaces. Media are relatively insubstantial and transparent to information of all sorts (chemical, optical, etc.), and therefore afford both locomotion and perception. Substances are complex aggregates of chemical compounds that are relatively impermeable to locomotion and information; they are more or less rigid, viscous, dense, cohesive, and plastic. All substances except the most evanescent have an interface with the medium (be it air or water), and these interfaces are surfaces whose properties will depend on the properties of their constituent substances. Because all substances are at least somewhat rigid and resistant to deformation, surfaces have determinate shapes and changes of shape, or layouts. Because air and water allow transmission of light, the layout is visible (it is also tangible, and may be audible). In addition to having a characteristic layout, a surface is also resistant to changes of layout (deformation) and dis-integration or disruption. Being substantial, surfaces have a characteristic texture, both in their layout and in their pigmentation; and, again, because of their sub-stantial basis, different surfaces have characteristic spectral absorptions and reflectance properties – simply, they look different.

The inanimate environment consists of places, objects and events, which themselves are made up of substantial surfaces in specific configurations. For terrestrial animals a place is a location within a layout of surfaces, and the ground is the most fundamental surface within and along which other places are situated. A place can, for example, be an enclosure like a cave or hut – a layout of surfaces that surrounds the medium to some degree and may afford shelter, hiding and so on – but it cannot be a detached object, which is a layout of surfaces surrounded by the medium. An attached object is not quite completely surrounded by the medium, having at least one surface portion connected to the larger layout. Ecological events are changes in layout, substance or place of objects.

Because every object is a unique grouping of substantial surfaces, there may literally be a limitless number of differences between particular animate and inanimate objects. However, there is a primary difference in that animals move themselves.

> Animate objects differ from inanimate objects . . . notably in the fact that they move spontaneously. Like all detached objects, animate objects can be pushed and displaced by external forces . . . they can be passively moved – but they also move actively under the influence of internal forces. They are partly composed of visco-elastic substances as well as rigid skeletons, and their movements are always deformations of the surface. Moreover, the style of movement, the mode of deformation, is unique for each animal. These special objects differ in size, shape, texture, color, odor, and in the sounds they emit, but above all they differ in the way they move. Their pos-tures change in specific modes (while their underlying invariants of shape remain constant). That is to say, animals have characteristic behaviors as well as characteristic anatomies. (Gibson 1979; p. 41.)

In this chapter I can hope to give at most a partial elaboration of this profound insight that the distinction between the animate and the inanimate lies largely in the autonomous actions of animals. If the characteristics of animacy lie largely in styles of movement and posture, then the information for animals to perceive and interact with each other has its source in these actions, and social action itself may be distinguished by characteristic activity patterns.

Anthropologists (and many psychologists) who have read this far may be puzzled by the lack of reference to 'animacy' in either developmental or cross-cultural studies. Frankly, this is an intentional omission. The literature on animacy bears at most a tenuous relationship to the issue of the animate versus the inanimate. Lévy-Bruhl, Piaget and their followers seem to me to be arguing about how children and adults from various cultures *explain* occurrences. The researchers then erect a categorization of these explanations (in terms of animacy, sentience, etc.) and *assume* that these concepts are used in the original apprehension of events – an assumption nowhere justified. I am here talking about how things actually *are* in the environment and, below, I shall discuss how they are perceived. Verbal descriptions and explanations – especially those elicited by contrived questions – probably bear little resemblance to the psychological processes involved in the direct perception of animate objects. Whatever resemblance there may be is surely destroyed by the imposition of artificial categories on these utterances by observers who make numerous assumptions about what can and cannot be perceived. Tunner (1985, p. 999) states that 'although many children accepted semantically deviant sentences containing psychological predicates and inanimate subject nouns, they denied that the [things referred to by the] inanimate nouns were alive'. (For more on children's usage of 'living' and 'animal', see Carey 1985.)

Gibson's claim that animacy is rooted in autonomous action has its immediate roots in the research of the Belgian psychologist Albert Michotte, and more-distant roots in Kant. In his *Critique of Judgement*, Kant (1952, p. 371) wrote 'as a provisional statement, I would say that a thing exists as a physical end [i.e. as a living creature, to be treated as an end, not merely as a means] if it is . . . both cause and effect of itself'. It is not unlikely that Kant was here thinking primarily of epigenesis, but his claim was strikingly corroborated for the case of animal movement as well by Michotte (1963) in his research on the visual perception of causality.

Michotte discovered that for an event to be perceived as an instance of a causal relation, there must be an 'ampliation' of the movement; that is, an extension of the movement of the motor object into the motion of the moved object. The characteristics of the motion of the former must be transferred to the latter without being lost by the former. 'Ampliation of movement . . . consists in the dominant movement, that of the active object, appearing to extend itself on to the passive object, while remaining distinct from the change in position which the latter undergoes in its own right' (Michotte 1963, p. 217). Interestingly, perceptions of causality 'are in fact very rare' (*ibid.* p. 183),[2] for it is often the case in nature that causes (like the wind or gravity) go unnoticed. However, as Michotte remarks, 'as soon as we consider human or animal activity . . . examples of causality are extremely numerous'. In fact, in addition to being causes of other effects, animate movements have the property of *being their own causes*. Michotte (*ibid.* p. 194) speaks of a 'double representation' where the causality embodied in 'the movement performed by the passive object belongs to the active object'. In his terminology, self-ampliation characterizes animate movement. The changes of posture or movement of an animal are effects caused by that animal. Animal bodies 'are subject to the laws of mechanics and yet not subject to the laws of mechanics, for they are not governed by these laws' (Gibson 1979, p. 135). Biologists often claim in a loose way that animals are 'sensitive to motion', meaning they respond quickly and effectively to perceived patterns of motion, but I suspect that what both predator and prey are most aware of is self-ampliated motion.

Michotte was able to show that ampliation of movement is directly perceived, provided certain information is present. Further analysis, especially that of Runeson (1983), has clarified Michotte's findings. If optical information for the transference of motion between two objects is displayed, then not only is a causal event seen, but properties of the objects (e.g. elasticity) are also seen. Moreover, in a series of ingenious experiments, Michotte (1963, ch. 12) showed that *animacy* is a visible property. If a single visual object changes its shape and/or motion with no external cause and in a cyclic fashion, so that a 'self-ampliation' (both transference and maintenance of the motion within a single object) is specified, observers see an object they describe as living and 'moving of its own accord' (*ibid*. 1963, p. 185). Michotte used rectangular figures with a 'head' and a 'tail' end, with the 'head' moving non-rigidly while the tail was still, and vice versa. His subjects all saw a moving 'worm' or 'caterpillar'. He was also able to simulate swimming and other movements.

To summarize: although there are many differences between animate and inanimate objects, a fundamental difference is the ability of animate objects to move autonomously. This 'self-ampliation' is specific to animals, but it can be simulated by optical displays (using shadowcasters, cinematography, etc.), and such simulations are perceived as being alive. Hence, the ecological distinction between animate and inanimate would seem to be conveyed, at least through optical information. No doubt there are other sources of information for animacy – especially acoustic, tactile and chemical – but I have been unable to find research bearing directly on these questions.

The characteristics of the animate, and the information for perceiving them

The affordances of animate objects are different from those of inanimate objects largely because the former are autonomous. Because other animals are *aware* of their surroundings (including us) and because they *act* on those surroundings (including us), we perceive them and act with regard to them in ways very different from our perceptions of and actions towards inanimate objects: 'When touched [animals] touch back, when struck they strike back; in short, they *interact* with the observer and with one another. Behavior affords behavior, and the whole subject matter of psychology and the social sciences can be thought of as an elaboration of this basic fact. Sexual behavior, nurturing behavior, fighting behavior, cooperative behavior, economic behavior, political behavior – all depend on the perceiving of what another person or persons afford, or sometimes on the misperceiving of it' (Gibson 1979, p. 135). We are only just beginning to understand the processes and principles underlying the perception and realization of such mutual affordances. Moreover, not only do animate objects afford special things in their own right (these mutual or interactive affordances), but also – as we become aware of others as animate and aware – we become aware of the fact that the environment affords things to them as well as to us. We live in a shared environment: some objects, events and places have affordances for others as well as for ourselves. In some cases the affordances are the same, but they may also differ. In any event, 'it is only when each child perceives the values of things for others as well as for herself [that] she begin[s] to be socialized' (Gibson 1979, p. 141). Socialization is thus a *natural* consequence of our living in a populated, animate environment, full of various affordances. However, I shall reserve discussion of the social for the next section.

In addition to being autonomous agents, animate objects have a number of other properties that are perceptible and of considerable importance to observers. Perhaps most importantly, unlike machines or other inanimate objects, the activity of animate objects is never perfectly repetitive. Even learning to perform a skill involves what Bernstein called 'practice without repetition' (see Whiting 1984). In all animate movement the determining factor is the goal or intention, and the means of achieving this may vary. Not only do animals persist in action when trying to accomplish something, but they also select and modify their postures and movements in order to achieve their aim, a phenomenon Tolman (1932) labelled 'docility'. The importance of this property of cyclic non-repetition for the perception of animacy has been demonstrated indirectly in two different ways. The first was Heider and Simmel's (1944) classic animation study of 'apparent behavior'. Using geometrical shapes and patterns of docile motion (repetitions of intentions without precise repetition of motor patterns), they were able to simulate a social encounter that was perceived in a similar way by more than 90 per cent of their subjects.

The second indirect proof of the salience of information about docility for perceiving animacy comes from Johansson's (1973, 1975) justly famous studies of biological motion. Johansson attaches lights (or reflecting tape, and shines a light on the tape) to the major joints of a person. A film or video is then made in which only the dozen or so joints are visible as mere spots of light. Observers of these spot-light displays thus get no information about the figural properties of the person. Viewed in freeze frame, these displays look like a random collection of spots. The instant the film rolls, however, observers perceive a person walking, skipping, dancing or whatever. Even 6-month-old babies perceive these displays as representing animate movements (Bertenthal *et al.* 1985). It is known from biomechanical studies of human gait that there are many complex perturbations of the oscillatory motion of the joints in walking. These can be analysed as complexes of harmonics in the Fourier spectrum of the gait pattern. Johansson has shown that, if one synthesizes a display of a spot-light walker using only the fundamental Fourier component (so that the swinging of the lights is a perfectly repetitive sinewave), then the display is seen as 'very different from a human walking style. It looks very mechanical and floating and totally devoid of force. Adding, say, three of the subsequent higher harmonics [which modifies the overall repetitive cycle] makes the style of walking humanlike but relaxed . . .' (Johansson 1985, pp. 49f.)[3] As many different kinds of actions can be displayed using Johansson's technique, it would be worthwhile to find out if the animateness of actions other than walking is similarly destroyed by eliminating the docility in the pattern.

A further variant of the Johansson experiment indirectly proves Michotte's hypothesis that the perception of animacy is related to the perception of causality. If a computer-generated synthesis of a spot-light walker display is made, the pattern of light motions is close to that of the normal case (although more regular) except for the interposition of the lights. When one films a person walking with lights attached to the joints, every time the person's body or limbs are interposed between light and camera the light will temporarily 'blink out'. The exact pattern of blinking-out is somewhat difficult to simulate. When displays without accurate interposition are shown they are often not seen as a person walking, or even as something animate. Observers frequently report seeing a complex rather than a unitary event, often describing anomalous causal relations, such as lights 'bouncing off of each other' (Bertenthal et al. 1985). The self-ampliation is lost, and an inanimate causal relation is seen instead of an animate action. Even when interposition is approximately simulated, the displays do not generate the same vivid perception of animate motion that an authentic display does. Apparently, either a lack of self-ampliation or an absence of docility (as with the overly regularized patterns of simulation) can block the effect of perceiving an animate event.

A further characteristic of the animate is growth. All animate objects grow not just in size, but with specific changes in morphology as well. Long ago D'Arcy Thompson (1942) discovered a number of principles of growth that he was able to express geometrically – to describe, as it were, the transformations of shapes that mean growth. Shaw and his colleagues have developed Thompson's ideas further by testing very specific predictions about human cranio-facial growth; first, against actual growth records and, secondly, using their hypothesized transformations to make visual displays. Observers accurately regard as instances of growth each class of transformations classed by Shaw and colleagues as representing growth. For example, a series of profiles generated by the correct transformation is preferred as an illustration of ageing. Moreover, when a non-living object is appropriately transformed (in this case a Volkswagen 'beetle' was used) it, too, is seen as growing and ageing (Pittenger et al. 1979).

There is, in general, a remarkable specificity in perception of the animate. Although animate objects are complex and display many properties, although each is usually unique in some ways, and although animate movements are never fully repetitive, identification and discrimination of animate objects is especially keen. It is well known, for example, that an observer who has seen up to 1000 pictures of faces can still recognize whether a newly presented portrait is familiar. Bassilli (1978) has modified Johansson's spot-light technique for studying the perception of facial expressions (he uses a large number of spots placed all over the face and filmed so that only the lights are visible). He has shown that observers will not confuse the non-rigid movements of a spot-lighted foam sponge (squeezed and contracted by hand) with facial movements, purely on the basis of motion pattern – but many observers do see his non-rigid motions as 'alive', perhaps detecting the self-ampliation of the hand movements through the sponge display.

There are many other cases of remarkably complex animate properties and interactions that seem to give rise to perceptual specificity. For example, Laver (1980) has been able to distinguish 21 different 'phonation types': falsettos, creaky voices, whispers, harsh voices and various mixtures. These can be used to characterize speakers quite specifically, but they nevertheless are subject to transformation as speakers interact. Even children modulate their voice loudness and quality, for instance, to fit to different interpersonal distances (Johnson *et al.* 1981). It is likely that the very complexity of animate action allows for the accurate discrimination and identification of individuals and their actions. The complex group of properties that constitutes any animate object allows precise identification of the actor, and the unique transformations of these properties allow precise identification of the action. In any event, there is certainly good evidence to show that animate objects and actions are directly perceived by most mammals and birds that have been studied. Human acculturation is likely to lead to a selection and differentiation of certain kinds of information for animacy, but it seems unlikely (*pace* Tapper in Ch. 4, this book) that the category is a cultural invention.

From the animate to the social environment

Nowhere does the ecological approach to psychology show its value more than in explaining the transition from merely animate interaction to socialized inter-action. Traditional psychology treats categories such as 'animate', 'sentient' or 'intentional' as *mental* constructs, as subjective interpretations of the objective world. Following this line of thought, sociality can arise only *after* comunication, for social interaction of any sort can occur only when two or more subjectivities are somehow linked. This linkage can only be effected by the objectification of feelings and ideas that are embodied in various social signals. The question naturally arises as to how communication could precede sociality – why should two or more animals' subjective interpretations of reality have enough in common for communication to begin? I do not believe that this question can be answered. It seems to me that the assumptions which give rise to the view of sociality as objectified subjectivity as simply wrong, and that we need to reject these assumptions and replace them with more-fruitful ones.

The animate environment is every bit as real as the physical world, and neither needs to be socially constructed, although both need to be perceived to be appreciated and used, and both can be appropriated for a whole host of social purposes. Is it not possible that all animate interaction is based on the perceiving of a shared environment? Perception of the self in the environment is *already* a social act if that self is a social creature, with an appreciation of the environment to be *shared* with others – friend and foe, predator and prey, mate and child, and so on. In other words, subjects are not private, but public and shared – even in the kind of wordless sociality that is found in birds and mammals, and certainly in human social relationships. 'It is often believed that perceiving is a private affair, unique to the individual, whereas knowing is shared with others because of the common language. But this assumption of private perception and public knowledge is quite mistaken. Even the direct perception of objects and surfaces is shared over time because of common points of observation and the ability to see from other points than the one now occupied' (Gibson, in Reed & Jones 1982, p. 412).

Gibson and Pick (1963) have shown one way in which visual perception is basic to human social interaction. They studied how people see where others are looking (and hence, what others are seeing). They found that this was a matter not of simply detecting where the eyes were pointed, but of seeing the relationship between eye and head postures: 'there is an invariant reciprocal relationship between compensatory eye turning and head turning. Hence, in the stimulus-array there will be an invariant reciprocal relationship between the projected form of the iris in the eye and that of the face for any fixed direction of gaze' (Gibson & Pick 1963, p. 389). This means that I can tell whether you are looking at me (or at someone or something else), regardless of how your head is oriented at the moment. For mobile observers such as ourselves, not only is the ability to see the environment not restricted to a particular point of view, but also our ability to see what another is looking at is independent of their point of view. Perception need not be considered as such a completely private matter at all.

In a series of ingenious experiments, Menzel (1978) showed that chimpanzees are aware of what other chimpanzees see, and that they are aware of both what those things afford, and what each chimp affords its partners as well. Food items were hidden in a variety of caches, and the hiding places were then shown to a single chimp. He or she can easily remember even a complex series of hiding places, and so can subsequently find the food, often by a much more direct path than the one used to show where the caches were (for what chimps see and remember are the invariant relationships in the environment). These knowledge-able chimps can and do indicate the position of foods to their fellows, through a variety of gestural signals. However, when a 'bully' is around – a chimp that the first chimp knows will take the food by force – then the chimp which knows where the caches are will go to considerable efforts to distract or mislead him. Even though these efforts frequently fail, they reveal a mutual awareness of the affordances of the hidden objects and of the social grouping of chimps.

The literature on animal communication is replete with studies showing that mammals and birds (at least) are aware of the animate environment in a social way, that they can and do share information about its affordances. Vervet monkeys, to mention one example, have an intricate system of alarm calls, distinguishing aerial from terrestrial predators, and distinguishing between several kinds of terrestrial predators as well. Perceptual learning is required to acquire this communicative skill. Whereas adult calls are quite specific to the different kinds of prey, infants may give a 'leopard alarm' or 'python alarm' or 'eagle alarm' to a host of similar creatures. Baboon alarms are the exception, and are specific even in infancy, though probably no animal is as easily confused with a baboon as a hawk is with an eagle (Seyfarth & Cheney 1980, Seyfarth et al. 1980). Such social sharing of perception for the purpose of communication is not limited to primates. Other animals, such as ground squirrels, are also known to have a highly specific system of predator alarms (Owings & Leger 1980).

Must we conclude from these studies that each species has its own 'worldview' which is inaccessible to outsiders? I think not. If one vervet monkey can communicate about the danger of pythons to another, why are we humans debarred from appreciating the warning? If we can appreciate the communicative intentions of other species because we share their perception of the same environment, surely we can appreciate what our fellow humans are aware of. 'If you see a head-on view of a bounding tiger and I see a side view, you are in greater danger than I am; but we both see the same tiger. We also see the same event: you see him approaching you and I see him approaching you' (Gibson, in Reed & Jones 1982, p. 412). Certainly there is room for error in sharing perception: thus, an infant vervet might mistake a non-predatory bird for a dangerous eagle. However, one can detect errors by looking for oneself. According to Reynolds (1975), even chimps are aware of this and learn to ignore the alarm signals of 'nervous Nellies'. Chimpanzees know that one can understand what another says and yet still disbelieve or ignore it. Why cannot anthropologists and other social scientists heed this ages-old wisdom?

Socialization, I am claiming, is a consequence of the fact that social animals are aware of the affordances around them in a *shared* way, in a way that recognizes both commonalities and differences for different observers in the values of objects, places and events. Where there exists such awareness, social norms will develop out of animate interactions. For example, it is well known that human postures have a cultural as well as a biomechanical meaning (Hewes 1955). There are poses of deference, ostentation, respect, communicative intention, aggressiveness, and more. These vary from culture to culture, but always within certain basic constraints. There are biological and ecological limits to the ways in which people can sit and stand. Only if the various postures could have acquired specific perceptible meanings could such a system have emerged. Yet, unless one is willing to embrace the doctrine of a 'social contract' for each culture, the only explanations of such cultural proprieties would seem to be rooted in our human ability to share our perceptions as well as our environment.[4] Such norms can emerge even in biologically constrained cases. For instance, it appears that approximately six emotional expressions (e.g. happiness–smile; sadness–frown; disgust–raised upper lip) are universal among humans. When a person is happy, she smiles, it is as simple as that. However, social norms ensure that the timing, intensity and occasional masking of these expressions is varied in different situations (Ekman 1977).

We can thus distinguish animate from social interaction by reference to *propriety*. Animate action is the awareness and realization of the affordances of the environment by an agent. Interaction occurs when two or more agents realize affordances in a *mutual* way, so that each presents acceptable affordances to the other (predator hides from prey, and vice versa; potential mates look attractive to each other; etc.), but in socialized interaction the agents' relations are further constrained by the perceived need to present *proper* affordances to the other. There are many ways to eat one's food, but all humans follow at least some social norms in what is eaten, the timing of meals, with whom one eats, the postures adopted during eating, the utensils used, and more (Farb & Armelagos 1980).

Social proprieties are constraints on the use of affordances. 'An affordance is neither an objective property nor a subjective property; or it is both if you like.

An affordance cuts across the dichotomy of subject–object and helps us to understand its inadequacies. It is equally a fact of the environment and a fact of behaviour. It is both physical and psychical yet neither. An affordance points both ways, to the environment and to the observer, (Gibson 1979, p. 129). A propriety is like an affordance, in that it is neither subjective nor objective, neither social nor biological – or it can be considered both. It points to a cultural group and to the group's environment. For example, well-defined subcultures (lorry-drivers, skindivers and others) have evolved their own gestural systems. These are social creations which involve aspects of our environment of which these groups are especially aware. Such gestural systems are embodiments of a socially shared environment, of relationships between a group of people, their environment, their skills and their perceptions.[5]

Conclusion: social affordances and shared affordances

From an ecological point of view, to be socialized involves above all two things. First, the awareness of what I can afford you; that is the observers' awarenesses of their own affordances for others. This can become highly differentiated, as it is in humans who are aware of how what they offer others differs depending on diverse social factors, such as complex kinship or economic relations. However, the fundamental ability to perceive oneself as having specific affordances for conspecifics (protection, copulation, grooming, play, etc.) is widespread in mammals and birds. Secondly, there is the 'socialized awareness' of the environment – my being aware of what things afford to you, independently of what they afford to me. I cannot undertake to help you unless I perceive what it is that you need, what affordance would satisfy your present intentions. This kind of mutual affordance has not been studied for its own sake, but its existence can to some degree be inferred from studies of animal communication systems. If a group of animals uses a set of signals that includes specific indications of various affordances (e.g. different kinds of danger, different kinds of places or objects), then it is reasonable to suppose that the perception of these affordances can be shared among members of that group. Such specificity of communication is relatively widespread in birds and mammals, and it is plausible that shared perception of affordances is also found in many of these instances. To the best of my knowledge the relation between these two kinds of socialized perception has not been studied, so we have no way of knowing whether one precedes the other, or whether both evolved from a common skill.

   In this chapter I have focused on relatively simple forms of social perception and action, in order to emphasize the evolutionary continuity of social affordances and shared awareness (and at least to hint at the need to consider the phylogeny of socialization, as well as its linear development in the evolution of *Homo sapiens*). Even the breathtakingly intricate articulations of social propriety in humans have their roots in these two modes of awareness. Mintz (1985, p. 157) – and the majority of social scientists who would agree on this point – is simply wrong when he asserts that 'We are able to perceive and interpret the world only in terms of pre-existing, culture-specific systems for endowing reality with meaning'. This perspective puts the cognitive order between us and the world itself – we must *think* the world to be able to *see* (classify) it, rather than the other way around. We perceive independently of interpreting (and we often interpret independently of perceiving). No doubt we often interpret what we see, but we also see it. Seeing is *not* classifying, it is a prerequisite for categorization. Seeing is one of our basic forms of contact with the environment – the real world – including the social environment. Observers see the affordances of things around them, and the affordances of themselves, and also the affordances of things surrounding others. This provides them with both social awareness and knowledge, which may then be used to categorize and interpret things. Socialized awareness and activities *precede* the ability to label and refer to socially constructed categories of objects. Human sociality is in this sense *natural*, having evolved as a refinement of our perception of, and action in, the environment.

The widespread presence of socialized action and awareness among mammals and birds indicates the inadequacy of the time-worn concepts of modern social science, concepts that divide subject from object, observer from environment, individual from group, and nature from culture. The concept of affordances and the information that specifies them to purposeful observers suggests a new way to conceive of the differences among the inanimate, animate and social, that allows us to see both the continuities and discontinuities in evolution. To argue, as I have done, that the rudiments of socialization lie in forms of awareness and action found in many of the higher animals is not to neglect the remarkable specificity and specialization of human history and cultural diversity. Instead, I would hope that the ecological approach suggested here could be used to begin the much-needed project of articulating precisely in what that transformation lies. Instead of taking refuge in metaphysical manoeuvres that lift the realm of intersubjectivity from its foundations in reality to an ontologically ambiguous level of representation, the ecological approach provides just the right tools to bring the human sciences back down to earth. What are the affordances and ecological information that different peoples have appropriated and transformed, via language, gesture and other symbolic means, into cultural realities? This is the kind of fruitful question that promises to reunite not only human beings with the natural environment, but also the diverse human sciences into a coherent understanding of our various ways of being in the world.

Notes

The research and writing of this paper were supported in part by a Fellowship from the National Endowment for the Humanities No. FA 24240–84, by a Drexel University Mini-Grant and by a Drexel University Research Fellowship. I thank Gunnar Johansson and Sverker Runeson for a number of helpful comments, and Tim Ingold for a superb editing job, for which all readers should be grateful.

1   As the 'circumstances' in this case involve visual information, it is possible for an experimenter to 'fool' the frog by displaying information specifying a fly. This does

not detract from my point, since only specific information succeeds in eliciting the desired behaviour. See Gibson (1960).

2   One of the greatest confusions in the study of animacy comes from the peculiar status of mechanisms as partially inanimate and partially animate. The animacy of a machine is, as the evolutionists say, secondary or derived; it is given to them by their animate creators. The category 'mechanical' will thus only be understood *after* those of the animate and inanimate are sorted out, hence the absurdity of a mechanistic biology or psychology. Mechanically driven displays, such as simulated flies or worms, can 'fool' animals (e.g. frogs or toads) into predating, but in all cases the mechanism used must capture some of the information for animacy. The evidence certainly suggests this, although the issue has not been explored experimentally in a systematic manner.

3   It is interesting to speculate whether acoustic information for animacy is also based on docility. Whereas inanimate and mechanical sounds are often tones or complexes of tones varying primarily in loudness, this is almost never the case with animal sounds. Animal sounds are usually spectrally complex, with patterning involving mixtures of changing frequency, intensity and duration, not to mention characteristic onsets and endings. Bright (1984) and Jenkins (1985) both emphasize the specificity of pattern despite the complexity of animal sounds. Schafer (1977) points out that some insect sounds are exceptions to this rule.

4   Note that I am *not* saying that we share our 'perceived environments' with one another – that is just the view I am rejecting. Culture is *not* based on the 'objectification' of 'subjective' ideas, and the perceived environment is simply a portion of the actual environment, not something separate from it. It is a biological fact that there are perceiving observers who can share not only the affordances of their surroundings, but also their awarenesses of these affordances. This sharing does not require the observers to objectify their awareness, because perceiving is not subjective in the first place. I can perceive the affordances of things for you as well as the affordances of things for me.

5   For gesture systems and a review of gestural communication in humans, see Kendon (1984). Kendon's approach is close to the present one: 'the communicative value of gesticulation has been very little studied. Most of the recent work has looked upon gesticulation as a kind of symptom of inner processes. I am arguing that we also try an approach that looks upon gesturing as part of the individual's communicative resources' (p. 88). Communicative resources are as much social as they are individual.

References

Bassilli, J. 1978. Facial motion in the perception of faces and of emotional expression. *Journal of Experimental Psychology: Human Perception and Performance* **4**, 373–9.

Bertenthal, B., D. Proffitt, N. Spetner & M. Thomas 1985. The development of infant sensitivity to biomechanical motions. *Child Development* **56**, 531–43.

Boring, E. G. 1942. *Sensation and perception in the history of experimental psychology*. New York: Appleton-Century-Crofts.

Bright, M. 1984. *Animal language*. Ithaca, New York: Cornell University Press.

Burtt, E. 1932. *The metaphysical foundations of modern physical science*. London: Routledge & Kegan Paul.

Carey, S. 1985. *Conceptual change in childhood*. Cambridge, Massachusetts: MIT Press.

Collett, T. & M. Land 1978. How hoverflies compute interception courses. *Journal of Comparative Physiology* **A125**, 191–204.

Darwin, C. 1880. *The power of movement in plants*. London: John Murray.

Ekman, P. 1977. Biological and cultural contributions to bodily and facial movement. In *The anthropology of the body*, J. Blacking (ed.), 39–84. London: Academic Press.

Farb, P. & G. Armelagos 1980. *Consuming passions*. Boston, Massachusetts: Houghton-Mifflin.

Gibson, J. 1960. The information contained in light. *Acta Psychologica* **17**, 23–30.

Gibson, J. 1979. *The ecological approach to visual perception*. Boston, Massachusetts: Houghton-Mifflin.

Gibson, J. & A. Pick 1963. Perception of another person's looking behavior. *American Journal of Psychology* **76**, 386–94.

Heider, F. & M. Simmel 1944. An experimental study of apparent behavior. *American Journal of Psychology* **57**, 243–59.

Hewes, G. 1955. World distribution of certain postural habits. *American Anthropologist* **57**, 231–43.

Jenkins, J. 1985. Acoustic information for objects, places, and events. In *Persistence and change*, W. Warren & R. Shaw (eds), 115–38. Hillsdale, New Jersey: Lawrence Erlbaum.

Johansson, G. 1973. Visual perception of biological motion and a model for its analysis. *Perception & Psychophysics* **14**, 201–11.

Johansson, G. 1975. Visual motion perception. *Scientific American* (June), 76–88.

Johansson, G. 1985. About visual event perception. In *Persistence and change*. W. Warren & R. Shaw (eds), 29–54. Hillsdale, New Jersey: Lawrence Erlbaum.

Johnson, C., H. Pick, G. Siegel, A. Cicciarelli & S. Garber 1981. Effects of interpersonal distance on children's vocal intensity. *Child Development* **52**, 721–3.

Kant, I. 1952. *The critique of judgment* (Meredith translation). Oxford: Oxford University Press.

Kendon, A. 1984. Did gesture have the happiness to escape the curse of the confusion of Babel? In *Nonverbal behavior*, A. Wolfgang (ed.). Toronto: Hofgref.

Laver, J. 1980. *The phonetic description of voice equality*. Cambridge: Cambridge University Press.

Maturana, H. J. Lettvin, W. McCulloch & W. Pitts 1960. Anatomy and physiology of vision in the frog. *Journal of General Physiology* **43**, 129–75.

Menzel, E. 1978. Cognitive mapping in chimpanzees. In *Cognitive processes in animal behavior*, S. Hulse, H. Fowler & W. Honig (eds), 375–422. Hillsdale, New Jersey: Lawrence Erlbaum.

Michotte, A. 1963. *The perception of causality*. New York: Basic Books.

Mintz, S. 1985. *Sweetness and power*. New York: Viking.

Owings, D. & D. Leger 1980. Chatter vocalizations of California ground squirrels. *Zeitschrift für Tierpsychologie* **54**, 163–84.

Pittenger, J., R. Shaw & L. Mark 1979. Perceptual information for the age level of faces as a higher order invariant of growth. *Journal of Experimental Psychology: Human Perception & Performance* **5**, 478–93.

Reed, E. 1982. The corporeal ideas hypothesis and the evolution of scientific psychology. *Review of Metaphysics* **35**, 731–52.

Reed, E. 1985. An ecological approach to the evolution of behavior. In *Issues in the ecological study of learning*, T. Johnston & A. Pietrewicz (eds), 357–83. Hillsdale, New Jersey: Lawrence Erlbaum.

Reed, E. 1986. Why do things look as they do? and An ecological approach to cognition.

Both in *Against cognitivism*. A. Costall & A. Still (eds). Brighton: Harvester Press.

Reed, E. (in press). *Revolution in perception: The ecological psychology of James Gibson*. New Haven, Connecticut: Yale University Press.

Reed, E. & R. Jones (eds) 1982. *Reasons for realism: selected essays of James J. Gibson*. Hillsdale, New Jersey: Lawrence Erlbaum.

Reynolds, P. 1975. Comments on Marler's paper. In *The role of speech in language*, J. Kavanagh & J. Cutting (eds), 38–40. Cambridge, Massachusetts: MIT Press.

Runeson, S. 1983. *On visual perception of dynamic events*. Acta Universitas Upsaliensis: Studia Psychologica Upsaliensia. Serial No. 9 (first published 1977).

Schafer, R. 1977, *The tuning of the world*. Philadelphia, Pennsylvania: University of Pennsylvania Press.

Seyfarth, R. & P. Cheney 1980. The ontogeny of vervet monkey alarm calling behavior. *Zeitschrift für Tierpsychologie* **54**, 37–56.

Seyfarth, R., P. Cheney & P. Marler 1980. Monkey responses to three different alarm calls. *Science* **210**, 801–3.

Thompson, D'Arcy W. 1942. *On growth and form*. Cambridge: Cambridge University Press.

Tolman, E. 1932. *Purposive behavior in animals and men*. New York: Century.

Tunner, W. 1985.The acquisition of the sentient-nonsentient distinction. *Child Development* **56**, 989–1000.

Whiting, H. T. A. (ed.) 1984. *Human motor actions: Berstein re-assessed*. Amsterdam: North Holland.

10 *Becoming human, our links with our past*

NANCY MAKEPEACE TANNER

One of the most significant facts about us may finally be that we all begin with the natural equipment to live a thousand kinds of life but end in the end having lived only one. (C. Geertz 1973, p. 45.)

Similarities and differences

In our society the question of what an animal is has been, and probably shall continue to be, largely a question of how we humans can differentiate ourselves from the rest of the animals on Earth. There are many ways to do this, but they fall into two broad categories: those supported by evidence produced by several disciplines, and those that are supported by faith and politics with only some of the evidence thrown in to make them sound scientific. Unfortunately, the history of theories of hominid evolution has often been dominated by those of the latter kind. The implicit question asked by such theories is: 'How did *we* get to be where *we* are?'. This is rather analogous to the question posed by Darwin's opponents: 'Why were *we* chosen?'. 'We' got to where 'we' are step by step, not by great and sudden leaps – it was a gradual change. What many evolutionary scientists forget to ask is, 'Who are *we*?'.

In human evolution the constituent steps of physical and cultural change were *not* taken with an end in sight, or with the idea of advancing to the next rung of a ladder leading to the angels (with us, of course, already situated near the top). Each step worked while it was being used, and each expanded rather than replaced the repertoire of behaviours. Gathering with tools did not completely replace foraging for plants or predation without tools; pirating meat from carnivores did not replace either gathering, forging or predation; hunting did not replace any of these behaviours; and even horticulture, agriculture and the domestication of animals did not entirely replace gathering and foraging of plants, hunting and trapping for meat, or fishing. When we use Darwin's basic concepts of natural *and* sexual selection, combined with data on a total population (females and children as well as males), and acknowledge that the process of evolution is a stepwise one, we see that human evolution is not 'a major biological mystery' (Tooby & DeVore 1987), nor does it require a 'special moment' (as creationists also believe) to separate us from our close relatives, the apes.

It must be stressed that there was, during the period of divergence from the apes, very little difference between us and our relatives. Even today, as we can see when studying chimpanzees, the differences between what we do and what they do are largely of degree rather than kind. Chimpanzees utilize a range of environments, though not so great a range as ours; they use tools, though not so often or as sophisticated as ours; they form flexible small groups or 'parties' within larger communities or unit groups, though not so variable as ours; and they are more omnivorous than other apes, though not so omnivorous as we are. This has made the chimpanzee a prime exemplar in the behavioural reconstruction of our distant ape ancestor – that stem ape which was ancestral to both the African apes and the earliest hominids. Since what we do is necessarily described in human terms, we often claim a difference in kind, but these claims merely attempt to shade the strong relationship we have with our ape relatives. Surely we use incredibly more-complex tools, but they are *not fundamentally different* from those used by chimpanzees. Both are, when described in a broad and basic way, physical objects used to obtain a goal.

Perhaps more than any other characteristic, language may be regarded as unique to humans, but only if we define language in strictly human terms. In our total communication system both non-verbal and verbal forms are essential. Non-verbal communication, very similar to the kind we employ – using body movement, expression, gestures and sounds to convey our wishes – is also used by chimpanzees (and many other animals), not just in the laboratory with training, but also in the wild. For other animals to learn to use human symbols, laboratory training *is* necessary; however, extensive training is also required for human children to use human language. Criticisms of ape-language studies that dwell on the need for extensive training of the apes in order to get them to use our symbols ignore the fact that human children receive large amounts of the most outrageous coaching and reward in their learning of human symbols. The verbal aspects of human communication – the employment of words and syntax – are not so far as we know found in animals other than ourselves. If we then define language as '*only* that portion of human communication which uses symbols in the form of words and syntax' we can say that humans alone use language itself. But human communication also includes smiles, nods, grunts, sighs, handshakes, tears and stares. In communication as in tool use, only an artificially restrictive definition of human activities can fully separate us from our ape relatives. Yet we are different, different in degree, but obviously a very large degree. How did those differences that do exist arise?

The Chimpanzee Model and the Gathering Hypothesis

In my book *On becoming human* (Tanner 1981) I addressed the specific question: What theory can explain the data if, unlike previous theories, the behaviour of females and offspring is taken into account, and if actually existing fossil and archaeological material, rather than what one assumes will someday be found, is assembled to explore the transition from ape to human? The behaviour of our fossilized ancestors can be reconstructed by combining information on our close ape kin and from living humans who gather and hunt with the results of fossil and archaeological analyses, such as microwear studies of teeth and tools. I used the chimpanzee model, the gathering hypothesis, natural selection which is primarily concerned with survival of the young, plus sexual selection – all of which remain important in my thinking (Tanner 1987) – to delineate a model of our ape ancestors, to hypothesize about how the transition from ape to earliest human occurred, and to reconstruct the behaviour of the earliest hominid, *Australopithecus*. I proposed that the major anatomical shifts, apparent in very early fossils in the transition from ape to earliest hominid – first bipedalism, then gradually decreasing canine tooth sizes, and increased manual dexterity through change in use and form of a hand which had been freed by bipedalism – could be correlated with plant gathering with tools by females and with female sexual selection of males.

Many evolutionary theories today centre around the invention of stone tools, linking it with the increase in brain size roughly 1.8 Ma (million years ago) seen in *Australopithecus/Homo habilis*. The problem with this linkage is that stone tools are evident more than half a million years before evidence of increased brain size, both in the Hadar formation about 2.5 Ma and at Omo about 2.25 Ma.[1] It is also common in these theories to link evidence of possibly increased meat-eating (through butchery) with the invention of stone tools. Now that the evidence is clearer than ever that the earliest hominids ate mostly plants, and that the initial changes in lifestyle and technology that separated us from our ape relatives were rooted in plant gathering (see below), there is a strong desire to see some time *other* than the divergence from our ape ancestor as 'the moment' when we *really* became human.

This need to see a remarkable break rather than a slow and very unremarkable change separating us from all other animals leads many scientists to ignore the time gaps they often leave in evolutionary theory. Thus evidence from about 1.8 Ma (of the appearance of *Australopithecus/Homo habilis*), from between 1.5 and 1.9 Ma (for the butchery of animals using tools), and from 2.25–2.5 Ma (for the first stone tools) is melded, despite the large gaps in time between these periods.[2] The result is the development of theory regarding human origins that only works if evidence which *currently exists* is ignored.

The present dispute over whether meat was scavenged, hunted or pirated is actually a side issue in the study of human evolution. Hominids had been developing the path which we now recognize as the line to humans for well over a million years *before* the period in which stone tools are found, and even that was long before we find evidence of increased meat-eating.

The diets of ancestral apes and of transitional and early hominids, around which their social life developed, were *very heavily* biased towards plants (Linton 1971). This was so even *after* butchery of large carcasses was developed. Social traditions regarding tool use and technical knowledge were developed earlier, probably within and between chimpanzee-like[3] mother-centred social groups. Such matrifocal groups were based on relations between mother and offspring, siblings, mothers' siblings, mothers' siblings and mothers' offspring, and occasional unrelated companions (both male and female).[4] As among chimpanzees, together they probably made up the cores of the ape ancestors' and of early hominids' social groups. Making and use of tools (of unmodified stone or fashioned from organic materials), cognitive recognition or knowledge of hidden resources (often buried or seasonal plant foods), non-verbal communication (both gestural and vocal, and using body movements and facial expression) and especially the teaching and learning carried on mostly between mothers and off-spring as part of their normal social life and food-sharing activities, were all developed initially, and later accentuated into the beginnings of the hominid–human pattern, within the context of plant food gathering.

A process-oriented model of a total population, a population of females, males and young followed through the millions of years from the divergence from our ape ancestors, gives us a much better picture than a static model or series of models of discrete populations, in limited periods of time and space, which 'characterize each hominid species at a given point in time' and 'require that hominid evolution be regarded as a discrete series of branches and stages' (Tooby & DeVore 1987, pp. 200, 203). According to my evolutionary model, though later hominids may have begun to utilize large meat sources by butchering with stone tools (though probably they did so by pirating meat from carnivores rather than by scavenging carrion), the social co-operation, technology and learning ability for doing so were developed earlier, mostly by females with young, while gathering.

Studies of wild, unprovisioned chimpanzees confirm previous studies in provisioned areas, showing that female chimpanzees use tools *far* more often, for longer periods of time, and even in less social settings than do males – something surprising to see in these normally gregarious animals (Boesch & Boesch 1981, 1983, 1984, McGrew 1981, McGrew & Collins 1985, McGrew *et al.* 1979). The mothers, using tools, also reward their daughters for attempting tool use, marking a rudimentary system of transmission of social tradition. This is not surprising since certain chimpanzee tool usages, such as cracking nuts with stones, are done and have been reported (for more than a century) from only certain areas (Boesch & Boesch 1981, 1983, 1984, Struhsaker & Hunkeler 1971, Beatty 1951, Savage & Wyman 1843–4). This example of ape 'teaching and learning' for a food-getting skill provides a significant clue as to how the transitional population between our ape ancestors and the earliest humans may have *begun* to rely on social traditions, the rudimentary learning of cultural guidelines, for life-sustaining skills.

Chimpanzee data on tool use suggest what sorts of tools, used in what sorts of ways, may have been involved in transitional ape-hominid and very early hominid food-getting. Chimpanzees have been observed using sticks and unaltered rocks to crack open fruit and nuts, crumpled leaves to obtain water and baboon brains, as well as sticks, twigs, strips of bark, stems and grasses to obtain honey and to collect several species of ants and termites.[5] With regard to the interpretation of the fossil and archaeological record, the single most important feature of chimpanzee tool use is that most of the objects they utilize would not leave readily recognizable archaeological remains.

When we look at gathering–hunting humans today, we find that plant food makes up most of the diet wherever it is sufficiently available. All apes eat mostly plants[6]; even chimpanzees, which are more omnivorous than other apes, obtain 95 per cent of their food from plants (Teleki 1981). Tooth wear in pre-hominid

Sivapithecus/Ramapithecus and in australopithecines shows evidence of very heavily plant-biased diets (Walker 1981, Grine 1981). Now, if we find that all modern horses are quadrupeds, and that all known fossil horses are also quadrupeds, it is true that they *could* have run around on their hind legs for half a million years of so and not have left relevant fossils, but we find it reasonable to assume that any unknown fossils in between will also be quadrupedal. So it is, shall we say, *likely* that the diverging ape-hominid population ate mostly plants. Moreover, since we know that the common plant-obtaining implement among humans today is the digging stick, that all known chimpanzee tools are either of organic materials or unmodified rocks, and that microwear analysis of early *stone* tools shows them to have been frequently used on plant materials (probably for preparation of both food and better organic tools; see Toth 1982, 1985, Keeley & Toth 1981), it is *likely* that plant food gathering was the medium which inspired early technological development.

Why was it females who carried out this development? Because they had to. As I have mentioned, we find that chimpanzee females use tools far more than males. The males do not have to. Modern scholars are generally overworked, busy people, always looking for ways to work as much as possible and yet have more leisure time. That is the crucible which gives rise to theories such as 'optimal foraging', which expect to find all animals living their lives in an endless quest for time off. Time off from what? 'Optimal foraging' theory expects that any given animal will not expend energy searching for food over more than a minimum distance unless the more distant food provides a higher energy concentration than that nearby. This assumes for the animal that reasons for preferring certain foods, such as liking the taste, are either absent or adaptive. 'Optimal foraging' also assumes that the animal's environment and diet do not allow it to leave a large surplus of never-eaten food; in other words, it assumes that no animals live in non-marginal environments. When you eat raw fruits, nuts and termites, however, a non-marginal environment is not hard to find. The food quest in such an environment is not so much akin to a workday in an urban–industrial society as it is to going out to the refrigerator for a sandwich after watching television. By and large, foraging is 'adequate' rather than 'optimal', with each animal doing only as efficient a job as its environment and its dietary needs and preferences demand.

For pre-hominids and early hominids, as for chimpanzees, there was little benefit to be gained from using tools when they could forage adequately without them. Only those who were most nutritionally stressed, namely females who were pregnant, nursing or sharing with offspring, had need for gathering technology. Initially, therefore, these females were the likely first users of modified organic tools and unmodified stone tools for obtaining, collecting, carrying and opening plants, whereas the males were engaged in their still-effective plant foraging and small-animal predation without tools. The new gathering with regular tool use was built on an ancestral ape behavioural base of plant foraging with occasional tool use, while the method of predation by pre-hominids and hominids remained essentially the same for several million years. Plants continued to provide most of the food for early hominids on the savanna.

Early gathering – characterized by inventions of tools, development of skills, cognitive mapping of where to find desired plants and in what seasons, an understanding of which skill and tool was useful for obtaining which type of plant (for example, a fruit or nut high in a tree required different efforts and tools than an underground root), together with transmission of this knowledge to the next generation – helps us to comprehend how a series of incremental changes could forge the beginning of larger brains for humans than among apes. Most significant, it helps us to understand how learning and cultural transmission came to be central to the way in which the human line developed.

Testing the model

Field studies of primates and of diverse human cultures provide anthropology with a very special resource. Comparative primate field studies *and* cross-cultural fieldwork are both extremely important for interpreting the fossil and archaeological record of human evolution, as are laboratory studies of primates. So-called 'strategic modelling' (Tooby & DeVore 1987, Pilbeam 1986) is no sub- stitute *either* for the examination and synthesis of existing field and laboratory research, *or* for attending to evolutionary models and hypotheses that assist the comprehension and interpretation of the data that such research provides.

I constructed my model using information available in the mid-1970s: data from chimpanzee studies showing greater female involvement in tool use for food procurement and female choice in sex; data from molecular studies indicating very great genetic similarity between humans and African apes and a likely divergence date of between 4–8 Ma rather than 10–20 Ma, as was previously thought; and data showing that chimpanzees had a diet consisting mostly of plant food supplemented by some small animals, but less-specialized than that of the other African ape, the gorilla (Tanner 1981, Tanner & Zihlman 1976, Zihlman & Tanner 1978). The Gathering Hypothesis, resting on the Chimpanzee Model, has been tested and re-examined in terms of even more recent research (Tanner 1982, 1984, 1987). New information on chimpanzee tool use has since come from studies by Boesch and Boesch (1981, 1983, 1984) in the Tai National Park; they have documented even more fully the much greater use of tools for food-getting by females compared with males. Microwear analysis of hominid and pre- hominid teeth shows a diet heavily biased towards plants (Walker 1981, Grine 1981). Similar microwear analysis of stone tools shows that they, too, were often used on plant materials: of nine 1.5-million-year-old stone tools (postdating 'increased meat-eating' by hominids) which allowed analysis, five were shown to have been used on plant materials (Toth 1982, 1985, Keeley & Toth 1981). Much further molecular information on primate phylogeny has appeared. The exten- sive work by Sibley and Ahlquist (1984) is notable, and complements and extends a great deal of work by other researchers. The primary importance of molecular studies lies in their demonstration of the phylogenetic proximity of humans and African apes, especially chimpanzees. The 'molecular clock' aspect is less import- ant, though still valuable; and despite worries and continuing criticism of its accuracy it actually has changed the minds of most evolutionary biologists. Even those who do not accept the idea of divergence at 4–8 Ma may now wish only to push it back to 10–12 Ma, and not to 20 Ma as before.

Similarly, the role of plant food gathering as an initial step in hominid evolution is being accepted even by those who ignore the aforementioned evidence of greater female tool use. Some people still attempt to go back to outmoded theories of social interaction which treat females as goods or commodities, or try to create alternative theories (Lovejoy 1981) which keep males in a role which gives them 'control' (a concept which is of dubious relevance for small groups – whether ape or human). Others are realizing that the active roles of females and offspring cannot be ignored.

Sexual choice and the evolution of communication

To explore the process of becoming human we have to ask: How did we enter the long route of producing a body which can live in many environments, with only very minor physical adaptations to each? What sort of links with our past do we have? Specifically, how did the earliest known hominid, *Australopithecus*, evolve from the same ancestral ape population as did chimpanzees? The Gathering Hypothesis provides many of the answers. Darwin's often-neglected theory of sexual selection and the role of sexual choice by females provides others.

Although chimpanzee females exercise considerable, perhaps total, sexual selection (Tutin 1980, de Waal 1982), the change to human bipedalism was especially important. Bipedalism removed from ready male view the signs of oestrus which non-human primate males use to spot potential sexual partners. This encouraged females to use other signals of sexual interest. Female sexual selection was thereby reaffirmed among early hominids, but in a context which encouraged increasing non-verbal communication about sex. Extensive non-verbal communication about sexual activity has already been reported for chimpanzees. For example, female pygmy chimpanzees have been observed gesturing about positioning in sexual activity at Yerkes National Laboratory (Savage-Rumbaugh *et al.* 1977).

Freud (1953 [1929]) long ago suggested that some human ideas regarding attractiveness might be related to the experience of sexual pleasure. Hominid females may have found males walking upright with erect penises sexually attractive. Similarly those males with reduced canine sizes (a feature also conducive to increase of molar sizes to handle a changing diet) and with greater manual dexterity may have been more attractive; these would be males who could thereby smile, kiss, embrace and caress more effectively than their ape ancestors, whose big canine teeth were more appropriate to growling and threat activities than to smiling, kissing and other arousal-inducing behaviours. Of course, these behaviours also involve more-subtle communication skills than bluff and threat and, like tool-using, they operate in a feedback relationship with the brain for both males and females, with immediate and long-term benefits encouraging their use and embellishment.

Thus, initially, natural selection for bipedalism and hand use during the transition from ape to human anatomy could be correlated with the development of gathering among females, while the concept of sexual selection (Andersson 1982) is useful to explain similar early physical changes among transitional males for whom foraging and predation still provided sufficient food. We have sex to thank for a lot more than our own pleasure, and for more than just being here today. Our evolutionary path was partially created by it.

Sex has influenced who and what we are. We are who and what we are because we like each other far more than we dislike each other – that is, threat and fighting are far less common than peaceful interaction, even if the fights grab most of the headlines in the newpapers and many of the lines in primate researchers' notebooks.

Observational bias

Whenever the people of one society think about their own past, ideas are liable to be influenced by the myths, beliefs and common conceptions of their culture. This often occurs in scientific thought as well, even though it is generally unintentional and usually unrealized. Extensive knowledge of another widely differing human social group – especially of the sort that comes from long-term fieldwork involving participant observation – can help to dispel ethnocentric assumptions. Here anthropology as a discipline, with its wide use and high evaluation of fieldwork, is in a much more fortunate position than many other disciplines. However, even anthropologists can sometimes find themselves bound to Western cultural assumptions. Nowhere has this been more evident than in the almost total omission of females and children from most reasoning about the past right up until the 1970s. The 'evolution of man' was what was explored.

After Darwin (1859, 1871), and for at least the following century, theories of human evolution largely omitted women and children. The generic masculine of the English language took its toll. When people said 'man' they believed they were talking about total populations. Until roughly a generation ago women were also often ignored in social anthropological theories, except as goods to barter or exchange (Lévi-Strauss 1963). This omission even characterized a great deal of actual research on living peoples for some time. Currently, however, although present socio-cultural theories have not yet fully assimilated the extensive data, a great deal of information does already exist on both sexes and for all ages for many contemporary societies employing a variety of food-getting techniques, living within different ecological settings, of various sizes, and whose beliefs and values differ widely from each other's and from our own.[7]

Data from primate studies are crucial for evolutionary work, but such studies are presently still largely, though certainly not completely, flawed by two major problems. First, most studies continue to adopt an old conceptual framework according to which social interaction is characterized by hierarchical *dominance* and *control* of group members (a framework unfortunately still common even in socio-cultural anthropology). These concepts are more appropriate to studies of nation-states than to small-group interaction, where the benefits of such 'dominance' are fleeting, if present at all. The second problem is the emphasis on primate study methods involving feeding by observers; such provisioning creates unusual concentrations of animals wherein 'abnormal conditions may elicit interesting but otherwise rare behaviours such as begging, aggression, and interspecific interactions' (Wrangham 1974, p. 83).

Unfortunately, observations of often shy, always intelligent, and potentially highly mobile primates such as chimpanzees are difficult even with artificial feeding. But provisioning does alter observed behaviour – the researchers involved know it and sometimes comment on it, but often do not take account of it in their conclusions. Observations in long-term study areas which utilize provisioning still need to be adequately balanced by observations under more natural conditions. However, all types of primate studies, with or without artificial feeding, in the wild or in zoos or laboratories, can give valuable information about primate behaviour. We simply need to bear in mind that the frequency and intensity of observed behaviour such as aggression is greatly heightened when artificial feeding is employed, even in otherwise wild conditions.

Our characteristically Western tendency to think in dichotomies also causes problems in the recording and selection of data. Action, of course, is contrasted with inaction; physical movement with sitting still; something happening with nothing happening. If something is happening while you are observing, you write it down. If 'nothing' is happening, you often do not. Dualistic concepts unconsciously bias us to write down observations of highly charged physical action and not the more placid times ('inaction'). Behaviour that is important, but not highly physical, is easy to miss and, even when observed and noted, can be hard to extract from raw data files when the keys used to file that data are biased in the same way.

Among apes and other primates, including humans, greatly active periods are less frequent and of shorter duration than less-active periods. This makes them far easier to record and quantify. In addition, their very nature as unusual events leads us to feel they must also have an unusual importance. However dramatic unusual events may be, it is in the ordinary, everyday activities and relationships discovered by examining both sexes and all ages that one finds the small, exciting things that made us human.

The integration of information from several anthropological specialties – in particular, socio-cultural anthropology (especially field studies of gathering–hunting peoples), physical anthropology (especially primate field studies and comparisons of hominid fossils) and archaeology (particularly data on early stone tools) – makes it possible to hypothesize that the gathering innovation was central in the transition from ape to human. On an ape base of plant foraging and predation, gathering with predation developed for transitional ape-hominids. Gathering, with its regular use of tools, greater reliance on regional cognitive mapping in the new and more-arid savanna mosaic environment, and transmission of skills and knowledge from one generation to the next, formed a basis for culture to become the human adaptation.

Culture is the human adaptation

I have suggested that the Gathering Hypothesis, with mothers as gathering tool-users and socializers, could explain how learning and transmission of skills to the next generation began to set us on the even more uniquely human route entailed in the physical expansion of the brain. Clifford Geertz (1973, p. 64) has pointed out that 'as the *Homo sapiens* brain is about three times as large as that of the Australopithecines, the greater part of human cortical expansion has followed, not preceded, the "beginning" of culture'. Over the long span of human evolution this growth of the brain and evolution of the mind has been linked in a feedback manner with the continuous elaboration of tools and customs which, in turn, have been combined with an ever-increasing reliance on learning about these tools, skills and specific lifeways (Geertz, *op. cit.*).

Cultural guidelines, which in some instances can be similar over broad regions of the world but in others can differ widely among neighbouring societies or among different ethnic groups within the same society, are the primary means which each human generation uses to pass on its experience and concepts of how to deal with the world. The human body is not highly specialized for particular environments, yet we live in many ways and places. We are even beginning to think about how we can live in these environments in ways that will make it possible for our grandchildren still to utilize them – although admittedly Westerners are still novices in this matter, and have much to learn from other peoples whose cultures provide means of living for long periods in various regions with much less destruction of the natural environment. We are also studying and practising how to live in space and on other planets.

Cultural innovation and change, like physical evolution, builds on what exists, without necessarily replacing it. The sequence of change is critical in studying human evolution, since later behavioural innovations – such as increased meat-eating through pirating and butchery, and later through hunting, fishing, and still later with animal domestication – could come about *because previous behaviour allowed it to develop*. Gathering was undoubtedly important to our diet whenever plant food was available, from the earliest days of the transition from ape to human, to that period millions of years later when technical innovation produced horticulture ('hoe agriculture') in small human societies. Even after 'plough agriculture', indeed even after industrialization, many people in farming or industrial societies use gathering, hunting, trapping and fishing to augment their larder.

In conclusion, let me return to my initial point that human biological evolution and cultural change occur step by step. Each step not only worked while it was being used, but also expanded the repertoire of human behaviours. No one step was 'the moment' that created us – however, there was a *first* step, a small step by a small near-hominid. That step was gathering plants with tools, and that soon-to-be hominid was female.

Notes

1 For evidence of the first stone tools, see Howell (1976, 1978), Merrick & Merrick (1976), Chavaillon (1976), Guilmet (1977), Roche & Tiercellin (1977), Johanson *et al.* (1980) and Johanson & Edey (1981).

2 On the appearance of *Australopithecus/Homo habilis*, see Tobias (1976) and Leakey *et al.* (1978). Early evidence for butchery with tools is presented by Bunn (1981, 1982) and by Potts & Shipman (1981). For references regarding the first stone tools, see note 1.

3 For early development of tools by chimpanzee-like females, see Boesch & Boesch (1981, 1983, 1984).

4 For descriptions of chimpanzee social groups, see van Lawick-Goodall (1975), Teleki (1973), Teleki *et al.* (1976).

5 See Suzuki (1966), van Lawick-Goodall (1967, 1973), Struhsaker & Hunkeler (1971), Rahm (1971), Nishida (1973), Teleki (1973), Sabater-Pi (1974), Kortlandt (1966, 1984, 1986), McGrew *et al.* (1979), McGrew (1981), McGrew & Collins (1985), Boesch & Boesch (1981, 1983, 1984).

6 See Kortlandt (1966), Nishida (1968), Wrangham (1977), Chivers (1977), Rodman (1977), Hladik (1977), Riss & Busse (1977), Chivers & Hladik(1980), McGrew (1981).

7 For a recent effort to survey and begin to interpret some aspects of this material, see Ross (1986).

References

Andersson, M. 1982. Female choice selects for extreme tail length in a widow bird. *Nature* **299**, 818–20.

Beatty, H. 1951. A note on the behavior of the chimpanzee. *Journal of Mammalogy* **32**, 118.

Boesch, C. & H. Boesch 1981. Sex differences in the use of natural hammers by wild chimpanzees: a preliminary report. *Journal of Human Evolution* **10**, 585–93.

Boesch, C. & H. Boesch 1983. Optimisation of nut cracking with natural hammers by wild chimpanzees. *Behaviour* **83**, 265–86.

Boesch, C. & H. Boesch 1984. Mental map in wild chimpanzees: an analysis of hammer transports for nut cracking. *Primates* **25** (2), 160–70.

Bunn, H. T. 1981. Archaeological evidence for meat-eating by Plio-Pleistocene hominids from Koobi Fora and Olduvai Gorge. *Nature* **291**, 574–7.

Bunn, H. T. 1982. Meat-eating and human evolution: studies on the diet and subsistence patterns of Plio-Pleistocene hominids in East Africa. Ph.D. dissertation. University of California, Berkeley.

Chavaillon, J. 1976. Evidence for the technical practices of early Pleistocene hominids. In *Earliest man and environments in the Lake Rudolf Basin*, Y. Coppens, F. C. Howell, G. L. Isaac & R. E. F. Leakey (eds), 565–73. Chicago, Illinois: University of Chicago Press.

Chivers, D. J. 1977. The feeding behaviour of the siamang (*Symphalangus syndactylus*). In *Primate ecology*, T. H. Clutton-Brock (ed.) 355–83. London: Academic Press.

Chivers, D. J. and C. M. Hladik 1980. Morphology of the gastrointestinal tract in primates. *Journal of Morphology* **166**, 337–86.

Darwin, C. 1859. *The origin of species by means of natural selection*. London: John Murray.

Darwin, C. 1871. *The descent of man and selection in relation to sex*. London: John Murray.

Freud, S. 1953 [1929]. Civilization and its discontents. In *Civilization, war and death*, J. Rickman (ed.). Psycho-analytical epitomes, no. 4. London: Hogarth Press.

Geertz, C. 1973. *The interpretation of cultures: selected essays*. New York: Basic Books.

Grine, F. E. 1981. Trophic differences between 'gracile' and 'robust' australopithecines: a scanning electron microscope analysis of occlusal events. *South African Journal of Science* **77**, 203–30.

Guilmet, G. M. 1977. The evolution of tool-using and tool-making behaviour. *Man (New Series)* **12**, 33–47.

Hladik, C. M. 1977. Chimpanzees of Gabon and chimpanzees of Gombe: some comparative data on the diet. In *Primate ecology*, T. H. Clutton-Brock (ed.), 481–503. London: Academic Press.

Howell, F. C. 1976. An overview of the Pliocene and earlier Pleistocene of the Lower Omo Basin, southern Ethiopia. In *Human origins: Louis Leakey and the East African evidence*, G. L. Isaac & E. R. McCown (eds), 227–68. Menlo Park, California: Benjamin.

Howell, F. C. 1978. Hominidae. In *Evolution of African mammals*, V. J. Maglio & H. B. S. Cooke (eds), 154–248. Cambridge, Massachusetts: Harvard University Press.

Johanson, D. C. & M. A. Edey 1981. *Lucy: the beginnings of humankind*. New York: Simon & Schuster.

Johanson, D. C., M. Taieb, Y. Coppens & H. Roche 1980. New discoveries of Pliocene hominids and artifacts in Hadar: International Afar Research Expedition to Ethiopia (Fourth and fifth field seasons, 1975–77). *Journal of Human Evolution* **9**(8), 583–5.

Keeley, L. H. & N. Toth 1981. Microwear polishes on early stone tools from Koobi Fora, Kenya. *Nature* **293**, 464–5.

Kortlandt, A. 1966. Experimentation with chimpanzees in the wild. In *Progress in primatology*, D. Stark, R. Schneider & H. J. Kuhn (eds), 208–24. Stuttgart: Gustav Fischer.

Kortlandt, A. 1984. Habitat richness, foraging range and diet in chimpanzees and some other primates. In *Food acquisition and processing in primates*, D. J. Chivers, B. A. Wood & A. Bilsborough (eds), 119–60. New York: Plenum Press.

Kortlandt, A. 1986. The use of stone tools by wild chimpanzees and earliest hominids. *Journal of Human Evolution* **15**, 77–132.

Leakey, R. E. F., M. G. Leakey & A. K. Behrensmeyer 1978. The hominid catalogue. In *Koobi Fora Research Project, I: The fossil hominids and an introduction to their context, 1968–1974*, M. G. Leakey & R. E. F. Leakey (eds), 86–182. Oxford: Clarendon Press.

Lévi-Strauss, C. 1963. *Structural anthropology*. New York: Basic Books.

Linton, S. 1971. Woman the gatherer: male bias in anthropology. In *Women in cross-cultural perspective, a preliminary sourcebook*, S. E. Jacobs (ed.), 9–21. Champaign: University of Illinois Press.

Lovejoy, O. C. 1981. The origin of man. *Science* **211**, 341–50.

McGrew, W. C. 1981. The female chimpanzee as a human evolutionary prototype. In *Woman the gatherer*, F. Dahlberg (ed.), 35–73. New Haven, Connecticut: Yale University Press.

McGrew, W. C. & D. A. Collins 1985. Tool use by wild chimpanzees (*Pan troglodytes*) to obtain termites (*Macrotermes herus*) in the Mahale Mountains, Tanzania. *American Journal of Primatology* **9**, 47–62.

McGrew, W. C., C. E. G. Tutin & P. J. Baldwin 1979. Chimpanzees, tools and termites:

cross-cultural comparisons of Senegal, Tanzania and Rio Muni. *Man (New Series)* **14**, 185–214.

Merrick, H. V. & J. P. S. Merrick 1976. Archaeological occurrences of earlier Pleistocene age, from the Shungura formation. In *Earliest man and environments in the Lake Rudolf Basin*, Y. Coppens, F. C. Howell, G. L. Isaac and R. E. F. Leakey (eds), 574–85. Chicago, Illinois: University of Chicago Press.

Nishida, T. 1968. The social group of wild chimpanzees in the Mahali Mountains. *Primates* **9**, 167–224.

Nishida, T. 1973. The ant-gathering behaviour by the use of tools among wild chimpanzees of the Mahali Mountains. *Journal of Human Evolution* **2**, 357–70.

Pilbeam, D. 1986. Human origins. The David Skomp Distinguished Lecture in Anthropology. Indiana University.

Potts, R. & P. Shipman 1981. Cutmarks made by stone tools on bones from Olduvai Gorge, Tanzania. *Nature* **291**, 577–80.

Rahm, U. 1971. L'emploi d'outils par les chimpanzees de l'ouest de la Côte d'Ivoire. *Terre et la Vie* **25**, 506–9.

Riss, D. C. & C. D. Busse 1977. Fifty-day observation of a free-ranging adult male chimpanzee. *Folia Primatologica* **28**, 283–97.

Roche, H. & J-J. Tiercellin 1977. Géologie-préhistoire – decouverte d'une industrie lithique ancienne *in situ* dans la formation d'Hadar, Afar Central, Ethiopie. *Comptes Rendus des Séances de l'Académie des Sciences, Série D* **284**, 1871–4.

Rodman, P. S. 1977. Feeding behaviour of orang-utans of the Kutai nature reserve, East Kalimantan. In *Primate ecology*, T. H. Clutton-Brock (ed.), 384–414. London: Academic Press.

Ross, M. H. 1986. Female political participation: a cross-cultural explanation. *American Anthropologist* **88**(4), 843–58.

Sabater-Pi, J. 1974. An elementary industry of the chimpanzees in the Okorobiko Mountains, Rio Muni (Republic of Equatorial Guinea), West Africa. *Primates* **15**(4), 351–64.

Savage, T. S. & J. Wyman 1843–4. Observations of the external characteristics, habits and organization of the *Troglodytes niger. Boston Journal of Natural History* **4**, 362–86.

Savage-Rumbaugh, E. S., B. J. Wilkerson & R. Bakeman 1977. Spontaneous gestural communication among conspecifics in the pygmy chimpanzee. In *Progress in ape research*, G. H. Bourne (ed.), 97–116. New York: Academic Press.

Sibley, C. G. & J. E. Ahlquist 1984. The phylogeny of the hominoid primates, as indicated by DNA–DNA hybridization. *Journal of Molecular Evolution* **20**, 2–15.

Struhsaker, T. T. & P. Hunkeler 1971. Evidence of tool-using by chimpanzees in the Ivory Coast. *Folia Primatologica* **15**, 212–19.

Suzuki, A. 1966. On the insect-eating habits among wild chimpanzees living in the savanna woodlands of Western Tanzania. *Primates* **7**, 481–3.

Tanner, N. M. 1981. *On becoming human: a model of the transition from ape to human and the reconstruction of early human social life*. New York: Cambridge University Press.

Tanner, N. M. 1982. Review of *woman the gatherer*, F. Dahlberg (ed.). *Man (New Series)* **17**, 809–10.

Tanner, N. M. 1984. Comment on A. B. Stahl: 'Hominid dietary selection before fire'. *Current Anthropology* **25**(2), 151–68.

Tanner, N. M. 1987. The chimpanzee model revisited and the gathering hypothesis. In *The evolution of human behaviour: primate models*, W. G. Kinzey (ed.), 3–27. Albany, New York: State University of New York Press.

Tanner, N. M. & A. Zihlman 1976. Women in evolution: innovation and selection in human origins. *Signs: Journal of Women in Culture and Society* **1**(3), 585–608.

Teleki, G. 1973. *The predatory behavior of wild chimpanzees*. Lewisburg: Bucknell University Press.

Teleki, G. 1981. The omnivorous diet and eclectic feeding habits of chimpanzees in Gombe National Park, Tanzania. In *Omnivorous primates: gathering and hunting in human evolution*, R. S. O. Harding & G. Teleki (eds), 303–43. New York: Columbia University Press.

Teleki, G., E. E. Hunt Jr. & J. H. Pfifferling 1976. Demographic observations (1963–73) on the chimpanzees of Gombe National Park, Tanzania. *Journal of Human Evolution* **5**, 559–98.

Tobias, P. V. 1976. African hominids: dating and phylogeny. In *Human origins: Louis Leakey and the East African evidence*. G. L. Isaac & E. R. McCown (eds), 377–402. Menlo Park, California: Benjamin.

Tooby, J. & I. DeVore 1987. The reconstruction of hominid behavioral evolution through strategic modeling. In *The evolution of human behavior: primate models*, W. G. Kinzey (ed.), 183–237. Albany, New York: State University of New York Press.

Toth, N. 1982. The stone technologies of early hominids at Koobi Fora, Kenya: an experimental approach. Ph.D. dissertation, University of California, Berkeley.

Toth, N. 1985. The Oldowan reassessed: a close look at early stone artifacts. *Journal of Archaeological Science* **12**, 101–20.

Tutin, C. E. G. 1980. Reproductive behaviour of wild chimpanzees in the Gombe National Park, Tanzania. *Journal of Reproduction and Fertility* **28**, 43–57.

van Lawick-Goodall, J. 1967. *My friends the wild chimpanzees*. Washington, DC: National Geographic Society.

van Lawick-Goodall, J. 1973. Cultural elements in a chimpanzee community. In *Precultural behavior*. Symposia of the Fourth International Congress of Primatology. Vol. I, E. W. Menzel, Jr (ed.), 144–85. Basel: Karger.

van Lawick-Goodall, J. 1975. The behavior of the chimpanzee. In *Hominisation and behavior*, G. Kurth & I. Eibl-Eibesfeldt (eds), 74–136. Stuttgart: Gustav Fischer.

de Waal, F. 1982. *Chimpanzee politics*. New York: Harper & Row.

Walker, A. 1981. Diet and teeth. Dietary hypothesis and human evolution. *Philosophical Transactions of the Royal Society of London* **292**, 57–64.

Wrangham, R. W. 1974. Artificial feeding of chimpanzees and baboons in their natural habitat. *Animal Behaviour* **22**(1), 83–93.

Wrangham, R. W. 1977. Feeding behaviour of chimpanzees in Gombe National Park, Tanzania. In *Primate ecology*, T. H. Clutton-Brock (ed.), 504–38. London: Academic Press.

Zihlman, A. & N. M. Tanner 1978. Gathering and the hominid adaptation. In *Female hierarchies*, L. Tiger & H. M. Fowler (eds), 163–94. Chicago, Illinois: Beresford Book Service.

11 *Human animality, the mental imagery of fear, and religiosity*

BALAJI MUNDKUR

On choosing a viewpoint

'The *instinct* of religion – religiosity as it has been called – is inborn to man', the orientalist Zénaïde Ragozin asserted in 1886. 'The human race with all its varieties', she added, 'has all that animals have, and two things which they have not – speech and religiosity, which assume a faculty of abstract thinking, observing and drawing general conclusions solely and distinctively human'. Preceding scholars – Charles DeBrosses, Herbert Spencer, Edward Tylor and a few others whose influences on anthropological studies of religion are summarized by Evans-Pritchard (1965) and van Baal (1971) – had also remarked on speech and religion as distinctively human traits. However, we know from science that monkeys communicate with each other by semantically nuanced gestures and oral calls and that, in mental agility, anthropoids, especially chimpanzees, easily endure comparison with a young child's powers of observation and inference. However, Ragozin was tracing the antecedents of Assyrio-Babylonian deities, and her explicit concern was to explain 'the awakening and development of religiosity', rather than religion itself. Religiosity, she believed (1891, pp. 149–52), was eons ago elicited by the natural environment and arose from 'fear and loathing', primarily of 'powerful animals . . . whose numbers and fierceness threatened [primordial man] at every turn with destruction, from which his only escape would seem to have been constant cowering and hiding'.

The word 'instinct' has very precise ethological significances as well as limitations. Stimuli may trigger instinctive reactions, but instincts do not necessarily guide an animal, most especially anthropoids and man, through an *entire* pattern of normally predictable behaviours, for these are liable to be modified by external influences. Ragozin erred in linking the concept of instinct with religion, whose overt practices and avowals are wholly related to, and vary endlessly with, the economic and cultural histories of different societies. On the other hand, who will deny that she quite properly infuses the notions of basic emotional urge and cause-and-effect into her explanatory word 'religiosity', while categorizing this phenomenon as universal?

As these remarks suggest, I am concerned with the fundamental nature and genesis of the impulses provoking raw sentiments about the supernatural; not with religion *per se* or the influences (if any) of natural selection upon beliefs, practices and moral codes. These are only accretions of secondary importance.

By contrast, man's animal nature encompasses both ecological and intuitive (i.e. cognitive) sensitivities which, in evolutionary terms, are far more crucial in the psychobiological expressions of social groups wherein animals from time immemorial have given shape to myth, ritual and the symbolic imagery of cults. We know the latter aspects well enough, but not the interrelationships of the many factors that contribute to the emotional outpourings constituting religiosity. In this respect the psychobiological aspects of reverential fear or awe, aggravated by stress-related anxiety and depression, have far-reaching implications that deserve closer attention than they have so far received.

'Long ago, in the days of [the divinity] Waptokwá', according to one of the animal- and tension-laden myths of the Gê (Rio Tocantins, Brazil), 'all animals were still human. . . . He transformed some into animals, and let others remain human. Since then the latter no longer eat human flesh, but hunt game animals' (Wilbert & Simoneau 1984, p. 260). Apparently irrational beliefs and rituals surrounding death, burials and fear of the spirits of ancestors have all too often commanded more attention than questions of *what* the nature of the physiological mechanisms underlying elementary fear is, and how this is channelled into submissive religious attitudes. For example, Evans-Pritchard (1965, p. 44) belittled enquiry into emotion in these naive terms:

> If we were to classify and explain social behaviour by supposed psychological states, we would indeed get some strange results. If religion is characterized by the emotion of fear, then a man fleeing in terror from a charging buffalo might be said to be performing a religious act; and if magic is characterized by its cathartic function, then a medical practitioner who relieves a patient's anxiety, on entirely clinical grounds, might be said to be performing a magical one.

Objections of this kind do not lessen the actual significance of fear.

In the first place, why do humans attribute awe-inspiring qualities to animals, and adopt them selectively as symbols of their deepest secular and religious emotions irrespective of the ferocity or innocuity of the species? Bridging the distance between the humanities and the biology of protocultural behaviour necessitates expatiation on complex details that are hard to accommodate in this chapter. Treatises on the nature of religiosity are vanishingly few; on religion, they are innumerable, because, as a phenomenon, religion is pliant to unfettered theological speculation, as well as more detached but narrowly focused anthropological interpretation. By contrast, mere enquiry into the universal features of religiosity – not to mention its causes – calls for breadth of knowledge, eclecticism and discriminative judgement hard to muster in these days of narrow specialization. Sociologists admit that their basic criteria for a questionnaire on the subject are so complexly interwoven and liable to elicit undependable avowals of faith and belief that clear understanding of the 'religiosity' of even contemporary agrarian and industrialized peoples is difficult (Budd 1973, Cardwell 1980, Hood 1985, Opatiya Conference 1971).

Anthropological definitions of 'religion', though diverse enough, leave little room for quibbling; after all, in our bones we know what the word means. However, even my simple working definition of 'religiosity' – as a state of mind prompted by belief in the supernatural and its numinous power – introduces an initial uncertainty as to the true nature of the overt behaviour we term 'religious'. I agree with Byrnes (1984, p. 194) that Allport's (1960, pp. 257, 264–6) differentiation between intrinsic and extrinsic religiosity in modern societies is the most important single advance in all of the sociopsychological research based on fulfilment theory. 'Intrinsics' are genuinely dedicated, prayerful and self-giving persons whose faith is devoid of ulterior motives. 'Extrinsics' follow social conventions either unquestioningly or hypocritically under the influence of family or communal customs, political expedience or the demands of social rank. The difficulties of choosing accurate criteria for identifying members of each class are severe (Baker & Gorsuch 1982, pp. 119–22, Hood 1985) and worsen in the case of 'primitive' (i.e. small-scale, pre-literate, pre-industrial) societies whose traditional practices provide, much as in advanced societies, ample room for both intrinsics and extrinsics to flourish. However, what I shall discuss are a few of the basic behavioural characteristics innate in all higher animals, with special reference to man's sensitivities to other species as an important part of his tendency to be *intrinsically* religiose.

In recent years sociologists focusing on human group behaviours have proposed new theories of emotion (reviewed by Armon-Jones 1985), which they refer to as 'constructivist'. According to this view emotions are explicable as socially constructed responses to 'happenings in the environment', which are presented through specific modes of social organization, normative expectations, beliefs and values. However, these are responses, not causes, and while Armon-Jones (1985, pp. 10–13) emphasizes their functional significance in the sociocultural system of guilt as an important moral correlate embedded in fear, the causes and neurologically passive manifestations of the latter receive no attention in terms of natural 'happenings in the environment'. On the contrary, 'it is essential to constructivism', writes Armon-Jones (emphasis added), 'that emotions be understood *not as natural, passive states* but as socially determined patterns of ritual action'. Important though the social determinants are (despite their capriciousness), how much more understandable these patterns would be if the biologically universal, and therefore fundamental, determinants were identified and made part of the picture!

Thus, a chasm exists between the theories of socioreligious psychology and the empirical outlook of the numerous subdisciplines of biology. The chasm between the latter and sociocultural anthropology is just as deplorable. Preoccupied with refining theories built around myths, rituals and symbols, this discipline has forsaken much of its earlier interest in the incipience of superstitious attitudes as conjoint products of the human psyche and the natural environment. Tylor (1871, 2, pp. 208–23), Durkheim (1915, pp. 118, 224, 234) and Lévy-Bruhl (1966, pp. 36–55), for instance, gave far more weight to the mystique of animals and the fear that they incite in primitive societies than is given in modern theoretical (as opposed to parochial) ethnological approaches. Yet Durkheim, for one, explicitly discounted the fearsome aspects of animals as the force that incites cult. 'The beings of the totemic species are', he believed, '[the cultist's] friends, kindred or natural protectors. . . . The sentiments at the root of totemism are those of happy confidence rather than of terror and compression'.

Spiro (1966) correctly states that theoreticians all too frequently deal not with explanations of religion, but with the role of religion in explanations of society, and that the roots of religious, *motivational* behaviour must ultimately be sought in the sciences. It is therefore regrettable that he seeks answers not from the 'harder' subdisciplines of biology and experimental psychology, but from the inevitably idiosyncratic, speculative 'insights' which psychoanalysis and depth-psychology offer on the subjects of painful drives and motives. These, in his view, include 'castration anxiety', 'cataclysmic fantasies', 'Oedipal sexuality' and the like. Because they are culturally forbidden, he thinks, they arouse 'moral anxiety'. Spiro insists that any definition of religion ought to include belief in *superhuman* beings. Nowhere does he consider the religious significance of animals *vis-à-vis* human animality. However, this is a consequence of his preoccupation with modern high religions such as Burmese Buddhism and Judeo-Christianity to the exclusion of their early archaeological and scriptural backgrounds. In their ancestral regions, India and the Near East, there is abundant evidence for the involvement of animals in prehistoric symbols, cults and myths. The superhuman divine beings of popular Hinduism still maintain their ancient superzooic attributes.

Thus, there is merit in Geertz's (1966, p. 1) implied recommendation of approaches that transcend the limits of cultural anthropology, though in practice[1] he overlooks the 'harder sciences': 'Virtually no one', he writes, 'thinks of looking elsewhere – to philosophy, history, law, literature, or the "harder sciences" . . . for analytical ideas . . . the anthropological study of religion is in a state of stagnation'; and ' . . . anthropologists are, like theologians, firmly dedicated to proving the indubitable'.

The reasons for this impasse are summed up in Leach's (1982, pp. 86–121) views on humanity and animality. He states that sociocultural anthropologists do not need to be expert anatomists or geneticists or experts in biology, but they are likely to talk a lot of nonsense if they do not take into account what experts in those fields have been able to discover. Correspondingly, studies in the biological aspects of human adaptation need to be supplemented by ethnographic and sociocultural investigations of various kinds. However, he adds that since biologists operate within the quantitative framework of statistically-based natural science, whereas sociocultural anthropologists mostly argue on the basis of intuition, communication between the two sides is very difficult.

I have tried to overcome this difficulty eclectically, with extensive data from social studies, art, biology and the humanities, in a book on emotionality and the veneration of animals of various species, with particular reference to the place of fear in the genesis of serpent cults (Mundkur 1983). It is heartening that philosophers, too, have tried to achieve interdisciplinary communication by including a neurobiologist, an ethologist–psychologist and a psychiatrist in an anthology on the subject of emotions (Rorty 1980). Although in her fleeting remarks on religion the philosopher Midgley (1978) is unconcerned about fear and religiosity, and animals as sacred symbols, she promotes scholarly enquiries in two admirable ways: first, by explaining in plain language the biological aspects of human behavioural potentials and, secondly, by discussing the strengths and excesses of certain sociobiological claims that impinge on cultural phenomena. This is important because the weaker claims have been rejected outright in some anthropological quarters, whereas the sociocultural implications of other, quite reasonable ideas, with a sound basis in biology, seem destined to encounter continued opposition from those who hold that 'the human condition' has little in common with that of species ranking lower in evolution. A succinctly sceptical estimate of certain sociobiological interpretations of cultural traits has been presented by Washburn (1980), and is all the more valuable because it comes from a primatologist.[2]

Ultimately, it is the data from psychology and biology that we must reckon with in cross-cultural studies of emotion in relation to animal cults and religiosity. Historians of religion recognize the need to seek significant new ideas from professional partnerships with 'behavioral psychologists . . . artists and aestheticians, physicists, biologists and physicians – people whose religious interests and insights historians of religion have all too often failed to take seriously' (Alles & Kitagawa 1985, pp. 162f., see also Brown 1985, Rudolph 1985, p. 110). I cannot envisage how historians of religion stand to gain from psychobiological information, and I doubt that it can alter their research directions significantly. On the other hand, psychobiologists have far more to gain from the history of religions, a field which, despite its occasional psychoanalytical forays into primitive religions, has traditionally been concerned with the religious life and sacred literature of the world's great civilizations. Anthropologists, distracted by structuralist, cultural–relativist and other theories of primitive religion, have largely avoided this literature in addition to that of behavioural psychology. Thus, they have missed many opportunities of connecting the unambiguous scriptural evidences of animal-centred emotion with the semiologically often obscure expressions of it in non-literate societies.

Last, but not least, I am gratified by the eclecticism of the historian Toynbee (1956, pp. 1–20). He begins his thesis on religion with a firm theoretical base in evolution and the biology of survival, as he traces the rise of primitive societies to powerful civilized States rejuvenated by old rivalries based on the worship of zoomorphized or anthropomorphized spirits representing Nature. These few extracts will suffice for our purposes:

> Self-centeredness is evidently of the essence of Terrestrial Life. A living creature might, indeed, be defined as a minor and subordinate piece of the Universe which, by a *tour de force*, has partially disengaged itself from the rest and has set itself up as an autonomous power that strives, up to the limits of its capacities, to make the rest of the Universe minister to its selfish purposes to make itself into a centre of the Universe, in the act entering into rivalry with every other living creature . . . for every living creature this self-centeredness is . . . indispensable for [its] existence. [Moreover,] the first aspect in which Nature presents herself to Man's intellect and will is as a monster who is creating and destroying perpetually, prodigally, aimlessly,

senselessly, ruthlessly . . . bestial Nature does not seem even to be aware of there being a difference between right and wrong.

The salient aspects of 'bestial Nature' and human animality are identical. Most experimentalists in the pure sciences, especially biologists, probably agree that nature is all-pervading, and that even her impalpable manifestations ultimately fall within the purview of the inflexible laws of physics and chemistry, whereas concepts of the supernatural are highly protean because they are of necessity based on idiosyncratic assumptions. However, scientific advance has rarely been fatal to the spread of vehement belief in the existence – beyond the pale of science – of a mysterious, intelligent and purposeful force or forces that regulate all Creation, but to which only human beings are bound to render final account. A majority of people in technologically advanced but conservatively religious societies see this as man's special destiny, even though their civilized forbears invested mythological animals with the human qualities of speech and craftiness just as people in contemporary non-literate societies do.

If we are to understand man's urge to venerate an animal or use it as a symbol of his deep sentiments, then we cannot exempt our species from the evolutionary forces that affected the sensory systems and produced patterns of nervous behaviour in the phylogeny of all vertebrate species, especially the primates. The peculiarities of excitation of the human mind have fortuitous origins in the evolution of the genus *Homo* during countless millennia of environmental pressures and natural selection. In Nature's scheme, which is amoral and tolerant of catastrophe, primordial hominids were entirely dispensable. So, too, are populations of modern species, including our own. Let us therefore reject anthropocentricity and consider the alternatives biocentrically. Let us acknowledge that individuals differ from each other in the intensities of their inborn impulses and that, collectively, these impulses lead to *social* behaviour. This, of course, is distinctive of every vertebrate species. Man's uniqueness rests largely on the power of speech, and speech alone has stirred up the multifarious belief-systems that form so important a part of human societal compulsions. Thus, I fully endorse the ethnographer Tokarev's (1979, pp. 3f.) separation of outspokenly atheistic from theistic and 'neutral' interpretations of religion as a social phenomenon. The task of understanding the essence of religious imagery and its roots ultimately resolves, in his view, to this question: How did concepts of things with no real existence arise in human consciousness?

I submit that fear of supernatural forces is a normal human fear that makes most of us undiscerning enough to glorify subjectively constructed 'realities'. In this respect a few select species in every fauna are bound to have induced primeval man's hallucinatory imageries and intrinsically religiose sentiments eons before ritual and cult gave form or distinctiveness to his religions.

The many faces of elementary fear

The vast majority of human behavioural traits, including moral and ethical rules, altruism, religious beliefs and cult practices, merely reflect the vagaries of societal influence. Therefore, one can make inferences about them only within circumscribed, predominantly socio-economic and historic contexts. Yet they remain pliant to psychoanalytic, structuralist, and occasionally even biological, speculation. Now, unless it is transparently groundless, we ought not to spurn speculation, for this has an important role in refining the formulations of science. However, these traits are too remote from the empirical findings of the biological sciences and experimental psychology to be regarded as innate, even if one concedes that they have tenuous roots in the exigencies of environmental adaptation and natural selection of ancestral human groups.

By contrast, individuals – as well as groups of human and non-human primates – share certain broad emotional tendencies originating in genetic mutations affecting the biochemistry of the neuromuscular and hormonal systems. These in turn generate tendencies that, early in primate evolution, were apt to have been associated with certain overt behaviours, some of which were excrescential, as I prefer to call them (and will deal with later), whereas other behaviours were clearly adaptive. The origins of both these classes of behaviour are, however, inseparable from unmitigated 'self-centredness', in Toynbee's sense, inasmuch as natural selection favours those neuromuscular responses ('emotional behaviours') which have the potential of enhancing survival – primarily that of the individual and ultimately of the social group. It was surely within tightly-knit social groups that the typical characteristics of almost all existing primate species evolved, including foraging behaviour, aggression against competitors for food and mates and, above all, avoidance of personal harm, especially from predators. Every vertebrate species has its own *active* pattern of adaptive behaviour. In particular, the mammals have better-developed propensities for aggressive self-defence when cornered by predators or challenged by rivals in sexual partnerships. These 'fight-or-flight' behaviours are automatic. They only occur under specific conditions of visual, auditory and olfactory stimulation that instantaneously and inexorably produce sharp, qualitative and quantitative physicochemical changes in the body.

It is important to remember that susceptibility to a specific stimulus, the internal physiological changes and the consequent overt patterns of behaviour have a genetic basis: they are not learned but are hereditary, instinctive responses marked by muscular tension and severe nervous agitation. Overt patterns of response are, therefore, the net result of the co-ordinated functions of various organs under the influence of nervous impulses and hormones secreted into the bloodstream. Thus, in a mammal shocked by the sight, sound or smell of its natural predator, the hormone epinephrine is produced by the adrenal medulla and transported to the liver, where it binds to a specific membrane receptor of liver cells so as to activate a membrane-bound adenyl cyclase, producing 3',5'-cyclic adenine mononucleotide phosphate. The latter compound in turn activates a protein kinase, which activates the enzyme glycogen phosphorylase, which, by immediately hydrolysing glycogen stored in the liver, releases glucose into the blood to serve as the source of energy fortifying the body's muscular response to the shock. The heart beats faster and more vigorously to transport oxygen quickly; the spleen contracts, releasing more blood cells so as to enhance muscular activity and blood supply to the brain, skin and viscera; pupils dilate, enhancing visual acuity in poor light; bronchi distend to take in more oxygen; and the coagulative capacity of blood and lymphocytes (for the repair of any wounds) is augmented. All of these changes occur swiftly, within minutes or seconds and, evolutionarily speaking, their survival value stems from their capacity to mobilize the body's resources for flight from the agent of the shock. Violent last-minute defensive aggression ('fight') with a predator is characterized by a comparable syndrome involving the specific hormone norepinephrine, which is chemically related to epinephrine. Less violent, though no less emotion-charged, aggressive forms of behaviour ('anger') of one primate towards another of the same species have the same underlying mechanisms. For our purposes these are an animal's essential qualities when it exhibits shock from elementary adaptive fear (or aggression, as the case may be).

Most human beings are conscious of their few, if often severe, fears of the natural world. Actually, these fears are firmly embedded in our *unconsciousness* –at least to the extent that we instinctively recoil from realistic dangers such as the edge of a cliff, swelling darkness, lonely places, thunderclaps or certain formidable animals. Environmentally provoked fears are typically strong but transient, i.e. they last only as long as the cause is experienced, though the unusually sensitive may show distress for somewhat longer. Anxiety, the persistent or recurrent dread or apprehension of realistic or imaginary things, can prove to be an equally strong, distress-laden emotion. Thus, we may distinguish between anxiety and fear as emotions provoked by spontaneous internal stimuli and actual external dangers, respectively, although the feelings are almost identical. It is more difficult to define depression, which is a prolonged, but etiologically vaguer, form of anxiety. The qualitative physiological correlates of these three emotional states are well documented (Gale & Edwards 1983, Zuckerman & Spielberger 1976).

The remarkable fact common to elementary (adaptive) fear, anxiety and depression is that predisposition to all three has a genetic basis, and that the two sexes are affected differently with respect to frequency and intensity, i.e. they are sex-linked emotions. Anxiety and depression normally afflict people in all cultures in considerably high frequencies (Chkili *et al.* 1981, Dealy 1981, Kalunta 1981, O'Nell & Rubel 1980). Furthermore, the physiological arousal of severely anxious or depressed people, especially in hormonal respects, is identical with that of persons displaying elementary fear (Mathew 1982, Marzillier *et al.* 1977, Robertoux 1981, Leshner 1978, Boulenger & Uhde 1982).

How far may we descend the schematic ladder of evolution and still use the descriptive words 'emotion', 'fear', 'anxiety' and 'depression' for overt, adaptive responses of animals whose intelligence and level of 'conscious' premeditation of behaviour are rudimentary compared with man's? This is a moot question, for Mitchell (1979, pp. 389–422) argues that many non-human primate species closely resemble humans with respect to sex-linked differences. In either case the females display more fear than males, whereas the males are more susceptible to the effects of early deprivation, and to the stress and depression of early social separation than are females. The fact remains that electrochemical transmission of impulses causing ('motivating') sensory responses to the environment occurs in the nervous system via mechanisms that are virtually identical from fish to man (Changeux 1985, pp. 38–66). Comparative neurology has given rise to a new subdiscipline of biology – vertebrate neuroethology – which focuses on sensory and motivational aspects by unifying neurophysiological knowledge with that gained from careful behavioural observations of animals in their natural habitats (Ewart 1980, Hoyle 1984).

Now, to turn to certain psychobiologically impalpable tendencies, natural selection may not readily suggest itself as the only parsimonious explanation for the origin of the class of behaviours I call 'excrescential': Hebb (1972, pp. 203–205, 215, 278, 281) lists numerous perfectly innocuous objects, such as an apple with a worm in it, mechanical toys or a plaster model of a chimpanzee's face with a movable jaw, which agitate, even terrify, chimpanzees confronted with them. Since none of the objects eliciting these tantrums occurs in the chimpanzee's habitat, this is an extraordinary form of idiosyncratic sensitivity in that, *prima facie*, it may seem to have conferred no clear evolutionary advantage in the natural selection of fears and associated behaviours of the kind that predators elicit. Nevertheless, the complex aetiology of excrescential behaviours is dissociable neither from the environmental selection pressures that produced the superior intelligence and adaptive radiation of mammals, nor from the susceptibility to emotional pressures that higher primates exhibit more markedly than other mammals. Excrescential behaviours have an indistinct, if clearly genetic (polygenic?) basis in that, like inborn predisposition to elementary fear, they are quite widespread, sex-linked and vary sharply in intensity from individual to individual, depending on the stimulant. They may appear to be morbid, but it is difficult to account for them except as peculiarities incidental to the progressive anatomical differentiation of the mammalian brain, culminating in the tremendous expansion of the neocortex in anthropoids and, much more so, in man. Their power over one's emotional well-being is by itself sufficient grounds for the view, clarified below, that these mental traits are not comparable with vestiges of organic evolution such as the human vermiform appendix and hair. Rather, they seem to have exerted their psychomotor potentials positively; eventually leading to refined structural–functional relationships and the co-ordination of specialized regions of the brain. The survival values of all varieties of severe nervous agitation were subject to natural tests and approval long before man scrutinized their overt expressions at the social level.

In short, human excrescential fears are abnormal only in the sense that a minority of otherwise emotionally self-possessed individuals harbour them in unusual form or conspicuously high degree, and thereby acquire the epithets 'odd', 'phobic', 'neurotic', 'dysthymic', etc. All the same, everyone's emotional outpourings follow identical pathways: via the limbic system (a group of primitive brain structures crucial in the control of both covert biochemical changes and overt emotional behaviour) acting in concert with cognized images, memories or other neural messages impressed upon the *association* and *sensory* areas of the cortex. Clearly, the word 'fear' embraces a varied set of triggering mechanisms and causal factors whose levels of effectiveness are not always easy to estimate. Archer (1979) considers its several naunces.

Though in most respects 'normal', human beings have always carried their share of mild-to-intense dysthymic sensitivities, neurotic tensions and phobias about natural phenomena and objects, in much the same way as Hebb's chimpanzees. There are strong foundations for these correspondences. The elementary patterns of the body's physicochemical responses to mental perturbations are similar in chimpanzee and man – a not unexpected consequence of the extremely close correspondences (involving blood groups, DNA and amino acid sequences) at the molecular and cytogenetic levels in man, chimpanzee, gorilla and orang-utan (Mitchell & Gosden 1978). The complete amino acid sequence of six proteins, including the alpha- and beta-chains of haemoglobin, is exactly the same in man and chimpanzee. Changeaux (1985, p. 254), pointing out that the mean difference between amino acid sequences in 44 proteins does not exceed 0.8%, estimates that the genetic distance between humans and chimpanzees is 'only twenty-five to sixty times greater than that between human populations of Caucasians, Africans, and Japanese!'.

In the final analysis, short- and long-term memory, learning and intelligence have a cellular and molecular basis. Emotions, as a rule, are triggered by a complex set of preprogrammed, interconnected neural mechanisms and pathways developed in early mammalian evolution. It is important to remember that, in man, panic attacks of anxiety (marked by increased levels of 17-hydroxy-ketosteroids in the blood) at times occur suddenly, without an apparent trigger, and, unlike elementary fear, are not under obvious external stimulus control (Kandel 1983). Yet, anxiety can be adaptive in the sense that it prepares us for potential danger, and can contribute to the mastery of disturbing circumstances. However, for reasons not clearly understood, it can also become pathologically dysfunctional in individuals who are inappropriately tense about neutral events or objects that are neither dangerous nor portend danger.

The electrochemical characteristics of the limbic–cortical system's 'dissonance' and 'resonance' effects, which tip the delicate balance from neutrality to either fearful or pleasant emotion, are complex. To be brief, dissonance leads to fear or depressive effects (and resonance to elation, so to speak). The value of dissonance in adaptive behaviour is clear from Struhsaker's (1967) studies of vervet monkeys in natural surroundings. Their alarm calls have acoustic differences that function in a semantic fashion, particularly to announce the proximity of specific animals – especially predators – to other members of the troop. Man not only resembles the anthropoids in the essential features of neural circuitry and transmission of impulses but, despite his unique trait of speech, also retains remnants of a simian system of gestural communication. Concluding his discussion of the working of man's brain, Changeaux (1985, p. 161) observes that one can understand 'how a single word could evoke resonance or dissonance with a memory image, thus provoking joy or distress'. Thus, one can hardly over-estimate the role of auditory and gestural communication in the coherence of primate societies, nor indeed in the incipience of protocultural expressions of man's innermost, emotive tensions. The latter are apt to be transmitted across *social generations* of human and non-human primates in remarkably similar ways that hinge on the efficacy of 'the single word' or an emotion-rousing event conducive to dissonance: when stalked by a leopard or threatened by other dangers, foraging baboons instinctively – without wasting time to verify – flee for cover instantaneously at a single warning cry from an alert member of the troop. This is a mechanism of survival fostered automatically in these gregarious animals because, while the laggards risk elimination, natural selection is also a creative force. A baboon that survives the attack not only learns something of the speed and tactics of the leopard, but also acts more efficiently on the next occasion by emitting the same cries of distress. Understood by all members of the troop, different distress signals are imitated and passed on from generation to generation when an individual is under sudden emotional stress caused by one stimulus or another.

Similarly, emotion-rousing speech or precept, whether justifiable or baseless, can instantaneously put human beings on the alert via the same involuntary mechanisms that are part of the innate pattern of emotional response developed during primate evolution.[3] Porteus (1931, p. 48) describes panic-stricken, frantically weeping Australian aboriginal men, women and children rushing for cover to a local mission building because someone, late in the night, had cried 'kurdaitcha!'. Regarded as one of the most vicious of the many protean, zoo-anthropomorphic evil spirits inhabiting their world of imaginary fears, kurdaitcha reputedly works in league with the medicine man, making itself invisible in order to steal upon and kill hapless tribesmen in horrendous ways. The latent belief that one's own clansman could in subjective reality be kurdaitcha only enhances the tensions of the aborigine's workaday world. Elkin's Aboriginal men of high degree (1977) cannot fail to impress its readers by his account of the variety and depth of fears in the Australian aborigine's mind, his veneration of the landscape's natural features and the 'dangerous' animals dwelling there, and the sorceror's power of aggravating the fears of his tribesmen to the extent of causing their 'psychic' death. The physiological degeneration preceding this entirely psychosomatic crisis is well attested in medical studies of diverse peoples (Cannon 1942, Marmot 1984, Steptoe 1983).

At a less dramatic level, Bibeau (1981) describes the virtually epidemic onset of depressions and anxieties engendered by belief in witchcraft and malevolent agencies such as ngbundu and bé (or their equivalents) that are part of the African spirit world. Beliefs like these are nursed limitlessly, world-wide – and not only in tribal societies. Fantastic predatory animals such as the basilisk pervade the décor of medieval churches and cathedrals; and European peoples still attribute bizarre qualities to certain animals that inspire visual images of rapacious semihuman monsters (Debidour 1961, Farson 1975, Mehring 1925). The common bases of the subjective 'realities' of sorcery, myth and the precepts of the higher religions are discussed from a cognitive, psychiatric viewpoint by Zeldine (1977). May we not conclude that the urge to envisage and glorify the supernatural arose primevally, in all mankind, from practically identical, innate sensitivities?

To sum up: physiological sensitivity to specific environmental stimuli is innate in individuals of even the lowest animal species. It is the fundamental factor enhancing self-preservation through adaptation, and from it flow myriad patterns of overt, purely instinctive animal behaviour. These patterns vary from one species to another, and may be impelled by many causes. In the higher vertebrates physiological arousal (except in relation to reproductive and combative drives) is brought about chiefly by specific predators, and the behaviour patterns they have impelled in the prey species during its evolution are, as Russell (1979) shows in detail, wholly fear-mediated responses that enhance escape.

Anthropoids and humans generally evolved under rather low pressure from predators. Nevertheless, their brains are endowed with neuronal circuits that enable an individual to cope with emotional pressures rooted not only in elementary fears but, as is clearly the case in humans, anxiety as well. Almost as a rule, the responses are idiosyncratic, and when the causes are imaginary, inexplicable except as excrescences whose only adaptive value may be that they prepare an individual to forestall situations that he or she perceives as menacing. In any event psychic processes are directly and simultaneously controlled by the sensory organs and the neuronal and hormonal systems from the instant these are activated by an appropriate stimulus. In anthropoids and humans they also determine an individual's (actually the brain's) potential ability to circumvent inimical situations 'intelligently' – by 'suppressing' the tendency to yield to instinctive urges. This is an unpredictable balancing process, as it involves a sifting of neuronal impulses registered in two different parts of the brain: (1) the 'thinking' frontal cortex, which processes and mixes information about transiently cognized events with information often subconsciously retrieved from the memory bank; and (2) the anatomically primitive limbic components whose functions are closely tied to an individual's genetically programmed tendencies.

Obviously, the initial stimuli are visual, olfactory or auditory. The imageries they provoke, no matter how fleetingly, may be experienced either consciously or – as in dreams, nightmares and hallucinations – subconsciously. The neurophysiological pathways and cellular bases of memory, learning and innate higher functions of the brain, as Izard (1984) and Woody (1982) explain in detail, are interrelated in a complex manner. That subconsciously stimulated neuroendocrinological and muscular effects accompany deeply meditative (and probably deeply prayerful) attitudes is known from biochemical and electromyogram data on the remarkable therapeutic efficacy of the practice known as 'transcendental meditation' (TM). The remarkable experimental revelations are that – rather like anxiolytic and antidepressant drugs acting on the brain – TM restores self-control and normal poise of anxiety-prone patients by inhibiting their pituitary–adrenal psychophysiologic activity, and that TM practitioners display a significantly greater level of clinical improvement than a matched sample of psychiatric in-patients. In addition, their rate of attrition is lower (Mathew 1982, p. 176, Jevning et al. 1978).

Whether by purposeful, intense concentration (as in TM) or by following a normal pace of life, the end-products of the brain's activities are mental images whose repercussions on decisions prompted by fear or anxiety can be far-reaching. Because of speech and superior intelligence, individual men and women are better equipped than anthropoids to respond to mental imageries and stressful moods. We do so by 'reasoning' and venting our instinctive emotional tendences in far more versatile ways. That is, we have the potential of subduing these tendencies either fully or partially, or sometimes not at all. Thus, 'intelligent' actions or thought can also ensue from poorly developed discriminative abilities that could worsen a person's mental tensions.

These, then, are some of the principal factors whose interaction produces the human urge to sublimate emotion through appeals to mental images perceived as supernatural forces. They form the core of intrinsic religiosity manifest in beliefs such as *kurdaitcha* and *ngbundu*, for from time immemorial religiosity has been exacerbated by symbolic associations and the peculiarities of group psychology that ultimately aid an individual's resistence to life's stresses. Thus, cult practices are merely outlets for fear and the anxiety drive. Modern experimental psychology recognizes an important characteristic of this drive – the tendency of a person to generalize his or her sharp susceptibility to one specific stimulus, i.e. to transfer responses to other, quite unrelated, even imaginary, stimuli. This characteristic of otherwise normal persons has been corroborated through the use of animals, such as reptiles, as objects of fear (Buss *et al*. 1968). Extreme psychiatric cases are not uncommon (Mundkur 1983, p. 234).

What is the symbolic significance of animals and zoomorphic monsters in both normal and aberrant mental imageries flowing from emotional stress? Semiotics alone can explain very little. For more-decisive answers, I shall consider the interplay of innate tendencies and cultural influences that aggravate the normal fantasies of the juvenile mind.

The ontogeny of supernatural and zoomorphic imageries

Interest in animals and love of pets, including (sometimes) serpents and fierce dogs, is ubiquitous in children. Freud (1913, p. 126), whose theories I reject, remarked accurately that:

> There is a great deal of resemblance between the relations of children and of primitive men towards animals. Children show no trace of the arrogance which urges modern adult civilized men to draw a hard-and-fast line between their own nature and that of all other animals. Children have no scruples over allowing animals to rank as their full equals. Uninhibited as they are in the avowal of their bodily needs, they no doubt feel themselves more akin to animals than to their elders, who may well be a puzzle to them.

In addition, children betray an attitude common in the myths of 'primitive' as well as 'civilized' peoples everywhere; ambivalence about a few selected species of animals whose appearance and habits invite both amity and wariness. The cultic and secular expressions of ambivalent awe of the serpent, the bear, the wolf and the lion, and even innocuous species such as the pangolin and the land otter, are well documented with respect to adults. However, anthropology tells us little about why children are emotionally predisposed to nurse a particular category of symbolic associations more easily than another. Enquiries such as Du Bois' (1944, pp. 170, 365, 417, 567–9), on Alorese children, are rare. Research in cognitive development from infancy to adolescence, stemming from Jean Piaget's pioneering discoveries 50 years ago, is still overwhelmingly directed towards children in 'Western' societies. This is regrettable, but not nearly so serious an imbalance as it may seem.

Basically, emotions are *unconditioned* neurosensory responses, i.e. they are independent of cultural history, though (especially in older children) culture, habituation or an individual's assertiveness could effectively modify or prevent normal overt reactions to a stimulus, particularly a weak one, from running their full course. The younger the individual is, the more sharply we can delineate innate behavioural patterns and the smaller the variations are bound to be between children born in different cultures.

Biologically, parental seeds carry the genetic determinants of emotional sensitivities; and modern embryology reveals that they germinate in the womb. Thus, a child's development of visual–mental cognition is intimately connected with the biology of cells and tissues. Proneness to anxiety – of the generalized, 'normal' kind as well as the frequent disorders that persist into adulthood – is partly the product of a variety of prenatal stresses on the pregnant mother. Herrenkohl (1982) discusses these in lucid detail with reference to experiments on laboratory animals and the implications for human embryonic and later mental developments. Prenatally, the mammalian mother is the virtual host-mediator, via the placenta, between the foetus and the external environment, because circulating blood ensures that her metabolism and that of the foetus are integrated. Under duress, from which few pregnant women are exempt, her pituitary and adrenal hormones interact in positive and negative feedback loops to modulate and regulate the amount of stress hormones she produces. Moreover, as Herrenkohl (1982, p. 53) explains, the foetal system has a life and dynamic of its own. Its brain–pituitary–adrenal gland axis is *active early in foetal development*. The foetal system also undergoes positive and negative feedback influences unto itself and the blood flowing across the placenta makes the mother and foetus respond to each other's physiological changes. The foetus is therefore exposed to epinephrine, corticosteroids and adrenocorticotropin – hormones produced during maternal stress – as well as to its own hormones, produced during feedback. We have noted that epinephrine is a prime factor in anxious or fearful behaviours. The direct effects of its increment in the foetus are, of course, imperceptible. Nevertheless, their potential is latent and bears comparison with experimental injections of epinephrine into adult humans. The consequence of this has been described as an almost immediate change of mood to a 'cold' emotion which, when aggravated by an additional stimulus (auditory or visual), gives way to more intense and genuine fear-like states much like those experienced naturally (Leshner 1978, pp. 288–308).

Preconditioned during the foetal stage to respond hormonally to sensory stimuli affecting the pregnant mother, the human infant from the moment of birth faces a constantly changing physical environment. Many emotional responses to specific classes of stimuli are dormant at birth but develop gradually after an infant is weaned away. Yet, even at 12 months of age, or less, infants are extraordinarily sensitive not only to situations that demand cognitive appraisal and adaptive behavioural response, but also to cues from an adult's (especially the mother's) facial expressions and gestures. Cross-cultural observations reveal that signals of happiness, anger, fear, disapproval and surprise produce clear-cut responses. The efficacy of the interaction of cognition and facial gestural communication is exemplified by the 'visual cliff', a laboratory device that simulates a dangerous situation in order to test an infant's avoidance behaviour at an age when its cautiousness is not markedly developed: when a visual cliff is adjusted to a height that produces no clear avoidance but requires much referencing to the mother, most 12-month-old infants will cross the deep side if the mother feigns joy or interest. By contrast, very few attempt to cross it if she feigns fear or anger (Ekman et al. 1969, Hiatt et al. 1979, Sorce et al. 1985). That natural facial expressions of emotion evoke responses among chimpanzee infants, too, is clear from observations in the wild (van Lawick-Goodall 1967).

However, in human child development the specific functional relationships between early experiences and later cognitive skills or personality traits are not easy to estimate. Many circumstances complicate the factors of maternal foetal conditioning. For instance, the left hemisphere of the foetal brain matures later than the right, and abnormal variations in maternal testosterone (the hormone which influences foetal brain differentiation) can affect the electrophysiological co-ordination of the two hemispheres. Impairment of the posterior areas, particularly of the right hemisphere, may reduce the efficiency of memory, viz. the retrieval and processing of stored information, while also affecting the generation and perceptual qualities of visual–mental imageries conducive to hallucinations (Paivio & de Linde 1982, pp. 265–8). Cerebral asymmetry of the frontal region can influence electrical activity and the expression of positive versus negative emotions (Davidson 1984). The repercussions may be felt in learning disabilities and medical–psychological problems, including proclivity to be abnormally anxious or depressed. Even borderline, elevated blood pressure (inherited by about 30 per cent of all adults) may take its toll. 'Early . . . during the borderline phase, patients tend to be emotionally labile . . . show the physiological correlates of anxiety . . . evidence covert aggressive tendencies they imagine to be dangerous and [in sustained cases] maintain hostile trends expressed somewhat more frankly in fantasy' (Weiner 1983, pp. 205, 222). Furthermore, there is a link between personality (somatic anxiety, psychic anxiety, muscular tension, impulsivity, obsessive–compulsive reaction of psychasthenia, irritability, suspicion, guilt, and other traits) and the inherited biochemical parameters of activity of the enzyme monoamine oxidase. Blood platelets show a correlation between this activity and one or another personality trait in depressed patients as well as emotionally wholesome volunteers, irrespective of their sex, but there is a distinct and significantly higher coefficient of correlation between all of the traits and depression in female patients (Perris et al. 1984, table 3). In short, every individual's brain is heir to two environments: the physicochemical internal environment genetically foisted upon one by one's parents and the cognizable external environment that demands reaction from the moment of birth. Questions of environmental reference in behavioural genetics and child development, as Plomin (1983) and Scarr and McCartney (1983) explain, are inseparable from questions concerning emotionality.

The ability of the 12-month-old child accurately to respond to the mother's cues in the visual cliff test is the measure of its early cognitive sensitivities. Autonomic avoidance of bodily harm progressively becomes independent and sharpens as the interplay of innate visual cognition and learning (whether spontaneous or acquired by social contact) gathers efficiency. Sensitivities increase in variety, may change periodically, become generalized (fear of animals, darkness, sounds, strangers), and are normally intertwined with anxieties. These are often severe and irrational but, as I have pointed out, in social psychology anxieties are regarded as adaptive in that they prepare an individual for an emergency. Cognitive behaviours involving wariness are innate in all higher animals. It is important to remember that behaviour patterns evolved adaptively in the context of predator–prey relationships and that, through communication, social groups constantly refine those patterns as individual members gain experience.

Live animals or their models, so far as I know, have not been utilized in enquiries comparable with the visual cliff test, but experiments with non-human primate infants (Mundkur 1983, Rosenblum 1978) do clarify the evolutionary bases of the growing human child's spontaneous fears and mental tensions. Both normal and excessive stresses have the potential of causing a child to clothe the underlying visionary associations with 'meaning' – i.e. subjective reality, the raw material of supernaturalism. That the boundary between 'normal' fears and those labelled 'excessive' or 'pathological' is obscure is not disputed by experts on childhood fears, who confirm that there is a strong correlation between fears (or anxieties) and age, and between sex and susceptibility to particular fears. Younger children are more likely than older ones to fear situations involving environmental factors such as noises (especially thunder), lightning and, in addition, unfamiliar faces or objects. The tendency to fear a specific animal or animals peaks at about 4–5 years of age and may (or may not) diminish in intensity subsequently. The older child is more likely to fear darkness, death, the pressures of school, ridicule, robbers and, especially, imaginary creatures. Younger children express a wider variety of fears than older children; the tendency to shed a particular fear and embrace a new one is typical of both sexes. Remnants of some of these sensitivities often remain dormant in adults or are apparent in neurotic or psychotic displays.

There is little room for doubt either about the intrinsic nature of the broad characteristics noted so far or about their cross-cultural demonstrability. Childhood fears and anxieties, it would appear, relate to the ability to comprehend, and cope with, the environment. Displaced or generalized anxiety neuroses may, in fact, merely represent a more vigorous level of (usually irrational) coping behaviour that enables the child to be on the ready for anticipated emergencies. However, we can only conjecture about the relative extent of involvement of truly adaptive fears, excrescential fears and prenatal stresses in expressions of irrational anxieties, whether normal or excessive.

The percentage frequencies of broad categories of childhood fears (deduced from details of the fear first mentioned by a child during an interview) are shown in Table 11.1. The high frequencies of fear of darkness, of being bitten, swallowed or scared by animals, and of the supernatural (including fantasized hybrid animals and animal–human monsters), is remarkable, given that the sample of children for this survey was drawn from New York city schools. It is noteworthy that the data are from an era (about 1930) considerably before the advent of 'monster' films or television. The questions and the manner of questioning were designed to encourage spontaneous answers. Unrestrainedly bizarre mental imageries are inordinately frequent in all age groups up to 12 years, despite some divergences that correlate with the economic background and intelligence quotients of the children. Younger children show fear of animals a great deal more frequently than do older ones (27.3% of the 5- and 6-year old children, compared with 11.1% of the 11- and 12-year olds). The supernatural (witches, giants, ghosts, mysterious deaths, monster men, etc.) haunts children of all age groups somewhat more uniformly and to an appreciably greater extent than fears of animals. The broad findings seem unimpeachable. However, the compilers of Table 11.1 do not specify the animals that children mention most often. In addition, differences correlatable to sex are not as sharp as in more-recent surveys.

A pronounced fear of animals in general has been noted in several surveys. Maurer's (1965) study of 500 American schoolchildren aged between 5½ and 14 years reveals that they do not fear the things they have been taught to be careful about: street traffic and germs. 'The strange truth', she observes, 'is that they fear an unrealistic source of danger in our urban civilization: wild animals'. This was the *sole* category mentioned by the children (in the course of the Wechsler test) in 64% of responses to the question 'What are the things to be afraid of?' asked in a neutral tone to forestall defensive answers to other forms of questioning. In the replies of 5- and 6-year-olds (who also named other fears such as darkness and ghosts), 80% named one or more wild animals, with the serpent 'the most unpopular' of these, predominating (30%); followed in order of fearsomeness by the lion (25.8%), the tiger (12.5%), the bear (8%) and 34 other, less-frequently mentioned animals. It is possible that these fears in some cases were sheer fantasies augmented or nurtured by the child's social upbringing, especially picture books, television and visits to zoos. However, chimpanzees are free from such artificial aggravations, and so it is remarkable that the chronological development of at least one specific fear, ophidiophobia, is closely similar in chimpanzee and human youngsters. Maurer's finding that the serpent was the most disliked animal (supported by Rachman's (1974) European surveys, which classify fear of the serpent as generally 'acute'), is important because the fear of wild animals in general declines steadily from a frequency of about 80% in 5–6-year-old children to 73, 68, 61 and 23% in 7–8-, 9–10-, 11–12- and 13–14-year-old children, respectively. Despite the general decline among older children of neurotic fears of practically all other animals, the intensity of ophidiophobia shows a precisely opposite ontogenetic tendency. Very young chimpanzees and humans are alike in that they are devoid of ophidiophobia but acquire it naturally at about the age of 5 years. Other surveys (especially Zlotowicz 1974, Poznanski 1973) yield essentially the same results.

Table 11.1 Percentage distribution of the fears first mentioned by children under the general headings I–XVIII.

Type of fear	All children	Age group (years)				Sex group		School group		IQ group			School groups matched in age, sex, IQ			
		5–6	7–8	9–10	11–12	Boys	Girls	Private	Public	120 and above	100–119	80–99	IQ 100–119 Private	IQ 100–119 Public	IQ 120 and above Private	IQ 120 and above Public
I Bodily injury and physical danger	9.6	5.1	4.0	14.0	15.2	12.1	7.0	12.0	8.0	9.5	11.4	6.3	15.1	9.4	11.6	7.7
II Animals	17.8	27.3	22.0	11.0	11.1	18.1	17.6	13.2	20.9	15.7	19.4	17.7	9.4	17.0	7.7	15.4
III Bad people, robbers, etc.	7.3	12.1	6.0	6.0	5.1	6.5	7.1	2.5	10.5	3.9	6.9	12.5	1.9	3.8	3.9	7.7
IV Supernatural events and beings, mystery	21.1	20.2	26.0	18.0	20.2	19.6	22.6	15.7	24.7	15.0	24.0	24.0	18.9	34.0	7.9	19.2
V The dark, being alone, strange sights, deformities	14.1	11.1	11.0	14.0	20.2	11.1	17.1	18.2	11.3	18.9	9.1	16.7	18.9	1.9	23.1	23.1
VI Nightmares and apparitions	8.8	6.1	15.0	8.0	6.1	8.1	9.6	8.8	8.8	11.0	7.4	8.3	5.7	11.3	7.7	11.5
VII Scolding, guilt, failure	2.0	0.0	0.0	4.0	4.0	1.0	3.0	0.6	2.9	1.6	1.7	3.1	0.0	3.8	0.0	3.9
VIII Loss of property	0.3	0.0	0.0	0.0	1.0	0.5	0.0	0.0	0.4	0.0	0.6	0.0	0.0	0.0	0.0	0.0
IX Illness, injury, death of relative	1.8	0.0	1.0	3.0	3.0	2.0	1.5	2.6	1.3	3.1	1.7	0.0	1.9	0.0	7.7	3.9
X Loss of parent or other relative*	0.0	0.0	0.0	0.0	0.0	0.0	0.0	0.0	0.0	0.0	0.0	0.0	0.0	0.0	0.0	0.0
XI Others injured, fighting	1.3	2.0	0.0	2.0	1.0	2.0	0.5	1.9	0.8	2.4	0.6	1.0	0.0	1.9	3.9	0.0
XII Startling events and noises	2.8	1.0	4.0	3.0	3.0	3.0	2.5	5.0	1.3	4.7	1.7	2.1	1.9	1.9	7.7	0.0
XIII Frightening gestures, noises, tales	6.8	5.1	7.0	10.0	5.1	7.5	6.0	8.2	5.9	4.7	8.6	6.3	15.1	7.6	0.0	7.7
XIV Scary games	0.8	1.0	0.0	2.0	0.0	0.0	1.5	1.3	0.4	1.6	0.6	0.0	0.0	1.9	0.0	0.0
XV Certain persons and objects	0.8	1.0	0.0	1.0	1.0	1.5	0.0	1.9	0.0	1.6	0.6	0.0	1.9	0.0	7.7	0.0
XVI Marriage*	0.0	0.0	0.0	0.0	0.0	0.0	0.0	0.0	0.0	0.0	0.0	0.0	0.0	0.0	0.0	0.0
XVII Nothing	4.8	8.1	3.0	4.0	4.0	6.5	3.0	7.5	2.9	5.5	5.7	2.1	9.4	5.7	11.6	0.0
XVIII Don't know; can't remember	0.3	0.0	1.0	0.0	0.0	0.5	0.0	0.6	0.0	0.8	0.0	0.0	0.0	0.0	0.0	0.0
Number of children questioned	398	99	100	100	99	199	199	159	239	127	175	96	53	53	26	26
Number of items reported	398	99	100	100	99	199	199	159	239	127	175	96	53	53	26	26

* Did not occur as a first-mentioned fear.

(*Source:* Jersild *et al.* 1933.)

Several holocultural studies disclose a clear and consistent relationship between child-rearing practices and perceptions of supernatural beings (Rohner 1975, Spiro & D'Andrade 1967). Table 11.2 (in which the supernatural is implicit in some of the categories) represents a part of Lapouse and Monk's (1959) very extensive work with urban American children. Their survey confirms clear-cut sex-linked differences and high incidences of fears and worries about animals (about 44%), chiefly the serpent, while also suggesting how differences in social backgrounds (and presumably domestic pressures) impinge on children's fears.

To compare different statistical results too rigidly would be unwise, since wider than normal deviations are inevitable when forms of questioning and sampling methods vary. Nevertheless, the reliability of these studies is borne out by an important factor – the stability of children's fears and anxieties over at least a year, as gauged in investigations that adhere to one and the same form of questioning. Eme and Schmidt (1978), for instance, wrote down and coded children's responses according to the 18 categories of Jersild et al. (1933), and found practically the same high frequencies of fear of animals. In addition, they found that the three most common fears and anxieties repeatedly expressed by over 40% of children (83% stability) fall into three categories: (a) bodily harm, threat of injury apart from falling, or a pain event; (b) robbers, kidnappers or death; and (c) animals. It is noteworthy that normal urban children harbour more fears than disturbed (but not psychotic or physically handicapped) children studied by Pinkus and Clary (1962). Both groups, they state, reported 'fear of getting hurt more than any other single fear and had about the same [40 versus 30%] high degree of unrealistic fear of unfamiliar animals'.

The major points about children's deep-seated fears and anxieties are: (a) they are sex-linked and their intensity varies between individuals of the same sex; (b) in ontogeny, they are induced (and sometimes shed) because of largely inexorable psychophysiological drives; (c) their expressivity depends conjointly on genetic determinants, conditioning of the foetus by maternal stress hormones and, after birth, the demands of the environment; and (d) they are practically stable from early childhood onward. Bayley's (1978) longitudinal study of 54 men and women, from their birth to the age of 36 years, is remarkably detailed. She reveals that a variety of emotional tendencies are correlatable to sex as well as mental growth, and that their stability pattern in each case is the same before and after the age of 18 years. Studies such as these reveal how individuals react consciously to an infinitely variable range of fear- or anxiety-mediated mental imageries.

The brain's activity is none the less revealing at the subconscious level of dreams, nightmares and hallucinations. In these, too, mechanisms of memory retrieval and image formation play their part – except that the 'thinking' frontal cortex appears to be far more quiescent than the evolutionarily primeval, emotion-engendering limbic components of the brain. Animals have a noteworthy place in many tension-laden dreams. A large cross-cultural sample of dreams indicates that 40% of the emotions that they arouse subconsciously can be

Table 11.2 Significant differences in prevalence by sex, age, race and economic status: fears and worries in a weighted representative sample of 482 children aged 6 to 12 years, as reported by mothers*.

Fears and Worries	Percentage	
(a) *By sex*	Males	Females
Snakes	25	61
Bugs	12	40
Strangers	9	20
Dirt	8	22
Animals	7	16
(b) *By age*	6–8 years	9–12 years
Little cuts and bruises	47	29
Thunder and lightning	46	31
Blood	44	27
Staying alone at home	31	18
The dark	30	19
Animals	16	7
Tests or examinations at school	15	25
(c) *By race*	White	Negro
Using other people's glasses, dishes, silver or towels	46	68
Snakes	41	59
Thunder and lightning	35	60
Going to the doctor or dentist	32	49
Germs	23	43
Dirt	12	31
Animals	8	32
Going into the water	5	25
People like postmen, policemen, teachers, tradesmen	1	13
(d) *By economic status*	White, upper half	White, lower half
Using other people's glasses, dishes, silver or towels	41	54
School marks	29	47
What happens in the world, such as wars, floods, hurricanes, murders	29	44

Fires breaking out	20	36
Being kidnapped	9	22
People because they are of different nationality, race or skin colour	3	10

* Only differences significant at or below the 5% level are included.
(*Source:* Lapouse & Monk 1959.)

characterized as apprehensive (or fearful or nightmarish), 18% as angry and 6% as sad. Another 18% are classifiable as neutral excitement or surprise and 18% as happiness (D'Andrade 1973). The figure for apprehensive dreams is consistent with detailed analysis of dreams of the Mehinaku, a practically unacculturated central Brazilian people ideally suited for research because its members have a penchant for the recall and immediate verbalization of dreams to family and housemates. In 55% of Mehinaku men's dreams and 42% of the women's there were tense scenes. Women experience a higher level of tension, though their frequency of dreams is lower. The single major source of anxiety to both sexes is dreams of animals. These account for 30% of apprehensive dreams, and are considered to be the most distressing because they generally include visions of assaults by venomous insects, serpents (especially anacondas) and jaguars (Gregor 1981). An analysis of 250 adult dreams of Australian Aborigines, South Pacific Islanders, and North American Indians (Van de Castle 1969, p. 190), reveals 'exceedingly high' percentages of animal dreams, ranging from 23 to 51%, with the highest figure prevailing among the Australian Yir Yoront.

Animal dreams among urban adult Americans, too, are quite remarkable: of 1170 objects envisioned in the dreams of 1000 persons surveyed by Hall & Van de Castle (1966), the serpent figured considerably more often than any other animal except the familiar dog. Animals seem to occur in dreams of men and women with about the same frequency (7.5%) – a figure not too distant from that of Jersild et al. (1933) for children's bad and recurrent dreams of *attack* by animals. Griffith et al. (1958), who isolated 'typical, universal' imageries in the dreams of Japanese and American college students, reported quite high total frequencies of unrealistic situations involving 'creatures, part human, part animal (15.2%)', 'wild, violent beasts (35.7%)', 'snakes (49.3%)', 'falling, with fear (63.6%)' and 'being frozen with fright (71.7%)' compared with 'sexual experiences (67.2%)' and 'loved person's death (50.1%)'. In British (London) schoolchildren aged up to 14 years studied by Kimmins (1973), the milder dreams waned in frequency after the age of 10 years, but fear as the 'manifest content' persisted strongly – with animals named as the cause in 20% of the dreams. Dogs, rats, mice and serpents were the animals most often envisioned by girls, but boys' dreams were primarily of lions, tigers and bulls.

On balance, if dreams mean anything, then recurrent dreams apparently have a special meaning. Robbins and Houshi (1983) conclude that only one type of recurrent dream – the anxiety dream, in which the dreamer flees for safety from threatening situations – is conspicuous in coded data. The threats in the dream imageries, in the order given by these authors, were from wild animals, monsters, burglars or natural forces such as storms, fires and floods. This is a remarkable list, for the dreamers were urban American undergraduates, and 43% reported that these particular threats were recurrent. Males and females did not differ significantly in this respect though, of the 60% who experienced recurrent dreams in general, 73% were female and 47% male, and many commented spontaneously that their recurrent dreams began in childhood. The broad trends of emotion-laden dreams are clear enough. Cross-culturally the differences appear to be small, despite the divergent sampling methods of all these surveys.

Evidently, the subconscious mind is under considerable tension, and, especially when its imagery involves fearsome animals, sex or food, a large segment of one's brain's activity may only be reflecting basic sensitivities imprinted during the psychological evolution of primates. In every essential respect the neurophysiology of sleep is precisely identical in monkeys, apes and humans to the extent that experimental evidence of dreaming (though, of course, not dream contents) has been obtained from behavioural responses of rhesus monkeys (Vaughn 1964, Adey et al. 1963).

In short, because of complexly interrelated neural impulses, men, women and children tend to harbour – and sometimes cannot repress – sentiments about natural phenomena that they look upon as hostile. They vent their (often unrealistic) concerns through dreams, and consciously through hallucinatory beliefs and actions in order to pacify normal, or sometimes abnormal, mental tensions. The question remains: how do individuals and groups sublimate fears and anxieties embedded in naive mental constructions of the supernatural?

Visual hallucinations and supernatural animals

Notwithstanding one's ability to reason and inhibit (or yield to) instinctual impulses, at the *social* level humans selectively reify certain mental imageries into artistic symbols and beliefs. I agree with Kirk (1973) that structural anthropological interpretations of the deeper significances of these unstable traditions are largely speculative. Throughout the immeasurably long periods of its development, every society has nurtured religious arcana with expedient imagination. The emotions that gave rise to the precursors of current beliefs about the supernatural qualities of merely natural phenomena are, after all, far older than our species.

Prehistoric art, too, is replete with fantasy rooted in the artist's mental imagery, whose motifs are at least visually concrete and subtly self-revealing in contrast with ancient superstitious beliefs, about whose meanings we can only surmise. The clues to the strongly emotional origins of the motifs of cultic art lie in the hazy zone between discriminative ('intelligent') thought and fantasy. Crossing it readily in the direction of fantasy is tantamount to hallucinatory behaviour; it would be arrogant to deny that educated modern people differ from their remote forebears in this respect. However, it is an odd fact that (with no compunction at all) we are apt to consign a primitive society's spirit world of animals to the sphere of hallucinations while elevating our own 'wiser' convictions about the supernatural to the realms of theology and mysticism.

I do not use the word 'hallucination' pejoratively. Visual hallucination (termed eidetic imagery) is perfectly normal, and occurs frequently in children and adults of all societies. Johnson (1978, pp. 163–85) explains its neuroanatomical basis in much detail, indicating that:

> the memory image is externalized on a surface and is clear. . . . Visual thinking is the voluntary act of producing an image in an eye. . . . Acoustic hallucinations can simulate a cortical reflex of visual or auditory hallucination, a response producing sounds and visions. . . . A hallucination (unlike the dream experience) takes shape and acquires significance and direction. . . . Various agents or drugs [and also oppressive, remembered dreams] can cause visual hallucinations.

The purposeful use of narcotics and hallucinogens to invoke animal spirit assistants or divinities with animal attributes is well attested in sorcery, shamanistic and other ritual contexts in quite unrelated cultures (Noll 1985, Harner 1973). Artistic implements for sniffing drugs are known, for example, from Valdivia, Ecuador, 3rd millennium BC.

Spontaneous hallucinations spurred by drumming, chanting or even simple mental concentration are probably more common than those induced by drugs. Australian Aborigines chew mild narcotics from plants of the Solanaceae family, but are not known to use chemical stimulants of any kind that produce subconscious mental states; yet their medicine men hallucinate during trances and verbalize dream and other 'experiences' that are inseparable from their cultural and physical milieux (Elkin 1977, pp. xi, 14, Peterson 1979, p. 178). World-wide, children verbalize their 'experiences' no less fancifully. Like the 'medicine men', who out of hostility, vengefulness or fear use their reputedly death-dealing pointing bones or other charms, children also act out their hallucinatory tensions – partly to terrify friends by impersonating the zoomorphic monster or spook they all fear. Psychiatrists specializing in normally and excessively anxiety-prone children interpret this as a 'neutralizing' tendency aimed at gaining self-confidence through 'identification with the aggressor' (Bregar 1971). Anxiety, mingled with eidetic imagery, is often evident in young children's drawings of human shapes that are modified slightly (subconsciously?) to represent an animal alter-ego. Humans and animals are often virtually indistinguishable in normal drawings – the shape may be humanoid, but in the child's mind it explicitly represents an animal (for instance a cat, modified from a 'human formula' for portraying a 'lady'). By contrast, intentional renditions of 'lizard in hat', 'tiger', 'tiger in hat', 'bull', 'gorilla' and 'elephant' may each be quite humanoid in appearance. George, a very disturbed 9-year-old, tended to draw human figures with long fangs or 'tusks' and 'a policeman with two poisonous snakes; they bit off his arms', as he described his drawings (Koppitz 1968, pp. 154f., Goodnow

1977, pp. 123, 126). Du Bois' (1944) study of the Papuanoid tribes of Alor reveals that adults and children are terrified by certain animals, chiefly walking-stick insects, snails and serpents. She singles out the latter ('the most unpopular'), but mentions no other species in her tabulations of rank order of preferred items in pencilled sketches made by 6–16-year-old Alorese children.

My point is that patterns of childhood fears and anxieties transcend time and cultural differences and, therefore, are a truly universal characteristic of our species. I have shown that they tend to persist in adults, albeit with changes, and now submit that the incipient urge to foster – and glorify – emotion-charged imageries involving animals (visualized in dreams, nightmares and hallucinations) through surrealistic art and myth, was a major protocultural behavioural development tantamount to intrinsic religiosity. We cannot know when this happened.

About a million years ago *Homo erectus*, the precursor of modern man, possessed a quite well-developed system of gestural and auditory communication, if not rudimentary speech. In this hominid's conscious psyche, as well as in the subconscious imagery of memories and dreams, lay all the neuronal, cognitive apparatus needed to arouse emotions rooted in his hallucinatory perceptions of the phenomenal world. Nevertheless, we do not know whether or not *H. erectus* projected his environment-related fears on to notions of animals (or trees or stones) as the powerful numina of cults, i.e. systems of religious worship in the modern sense. I doubt that he found solace in the numinous any more than do chimpanzees. What consistently enhanced his survival and propagation were crude bifacial (Acheulean) stone tools, the fire-drill and other stratagems answering to basic needs such as foraging, the safety of his social group, sexuality and, occasionally, protection from the climatic rigours of the Pleistocene era. Could the hominid species evolving from *H. erectus* have differed much in these respects? I hesitate to opine that the genetic and mental qualities of his early descendants – *H. sapiens* and *H. neanderthalensis* – were markedly superior.[4] However, by the beginning of the Middle Pleistocene all of the major biobehavioural and neuroanatomical transformations necessary to produce humanity had already taken place, conditioned, according to Brace (1979, p. 287), 'literally by a milieu of its own manufacture – the cultural ecological niche. The creator and consequence of this happening we recognize in a formal sense as a member of the genus *Homo* specifically designated *erectus*'.

How, then, did innate hominid cognitive faculties and psychic tensions transform into *reverential* fears, i.e. into an awe of animals and incipient rituals? We can only surmise: we know that the Middle Pleistocene fauna was at least as abundant as that of the Mesolithic, but that clearer details of animal symbols and cult practices emerge chiefly during the Neolithic period. Suffice to say that at various stages in the Pleistocene what are now subtropical deserts or northern temperate forests were extensive grasslands that supported large numbers of herbivores. Populations of *H. erectus* about 350 000 to 1 million years ago were sparse and faced little difficulty in obtaining small game. Their rudimentary tools seem to have served better in skinning and dressing their quarry than as lethal weapons, but we do not know how or why these early hunters killed the large species found in campsites as far apart as Africa and China. They may have corralled them with fire, driving them to death in bogs or over cliffs. The debris includes bones of giant baboons, elephants, cervids, rhinoceroses, bears and hippopotamuses – species formidable enough to agitate man's imagination. The history of the deification of tropical animals such as the baboon, the lion and the hippopotamus (exemplified by the ancient Egyptian god Thoth and the goddesses Sekhmet and Thoueris, respectively) is a long one, paralleling the extraordinary veneration of cervids and the bear by aboriginal cultures of northern Eurasia and North America.

Archaeological relics portraying animals are increasingly rare the farther back one goes in time. Even comparatively recent relics often provide few clues as to why a particular species is included or excluded from artistic compositions representing groups of animals, or which amongst them were objects of a cult.

Excavated in Namibia and radiocarbon dated to between 25 500 and 27 500 BP, the stone slab in Figure 11.1 is one of six reputedly oldest examples of mobiliary art. The painted form on this one has been described as 'basically feline

Figure 11.1   Stone slab, bearing a painting of a quadruped with human hind legs, bovine body, feline (?) head and an antelope's horns, Namibia, *ca.* 27 000 BP (after Wendt 1974).

in appearance'. However, this is moot. To quote Wendt (1974), it possesses 'a pair of obviously human legs which seem to have been drawn at a later date in place of the original bent hind legs'. The head is clearly not human, for 'there are two slightly curved horns visible which – together with a certain feature possibly representing male genitals – add some bovine traits to this [motif]'. Only one of the other five slabs depicts a clear animal form (a striped zebra-like species), whereas the third and fourth have the vague outlines of a rhinoceros and an antelope, respectively. The paint on the remaining two slabs is so badly eroded that the motifs are unrecognizable. From so meagre a sample no conclusion is possible other than that hallucinatory notions were important enough that they were expressed graphically.

To estimate the significance of the bizarre hybrid in Figure 11.1 we are obliged to make a tremendous leap in time and rely on ethnographic analogy and the archaeological sequences of southern Africa. The Khoisan-speaking people of this region have deep prehistoric ties to sacred areas, and until quite recent times have pursued their traditional hunting way of life. According to Phillipson (1985, pp. 7170–78) archaeological sequences of mode 3 (represented in Figure 11.1) and mode 5 industries are considerably long and complex, and the rock-shelter paintings of this region can only be interpreted with reference to the belief systems of the artists. The eland, a large antelope, occurs most frequently in this art, though strangely not in the food debris represented by faunal remains in occupation sites. A large number of species is represented in these paintings, almost always naturalistically. In Ndedema Gorge and its environs, for instance, paintings of mythological creatures constitute only 1.7 per cent of the very large total of animals in rock art. Naturalistic depictions of the eland predominate. Yet, the only clearly identifiable, fantasized and mythologized species are the serpent (3%), bristle-bulls (2%) and the baboon (1%), the rest being imaginary zoomorphs (7%), ceremonial human figures (5%), anthropomorphs with an antelope's head or limbs (42%) and winged antelope-men (40%). Pager (1972, pp. 2, 153, 338–9, 358), who describes these paintings, comments on the great importance of super-natural serpents (rather than supernatural birds) all over Africa, adding that the poor representation of serpents at Ndedema suggests that their portrayal, strangely enough, was not a matter of major concern to the painters. What is highly significant, however, is that some of the mythologized serpents at Ndedema have a serpent's body, eland's head and human shoulders, with arms holding a bow or stick (Figure 11.2). The serpent is ambivalently respected and feared in San traditions. Eland and serpents seen in the vicinity of San graves are viewed as spirits of the dead and held in high esteem. 'A special snake lives between the horns of all eland, and before eland meat can be consumed, it has to be purified of the venomous juices it contains' (Vinnicombe 1976, p. 233).

At least some of the San rock-shelter paintings, writes Lewis-Williams (1983, pp. 6, 11), 'clearly depict trance hallucinations which were the product of and which contributed to these beliefs about medicine men'. The mantis is a key metaphor in San and /Xam myths, and during dances that involve the eland and the medicine-man's 'dying' in a trance, but is not often seen in art. In fact, 'after

Figure 11.2   Rock shelter paintings of serpents with antelope heads, post-first millennium AD, Ndedema Gorge, South Africa (after Pager 1972).

careful study of all aspects of paintings labelled mantis-like creatures', Pager (1972, p. 338) 'found none of them to resemble even remotely the insect *Mantis religiosa*'. Dreams and sorcery are central in San beliefs. The rain is addressed as 'O beast of prey'; the rain's chief animals are the cobra, the puff adder and the tortoise, all three of which San by their own admission 'fear greatly . . . these [animals] the rain puts aside as its meat . . . [and] with them, pelts us, because it is a strong thing'. Sorcerors, in San belief, 'resemble lions', Their 'lion's eyes' gaze at persons doomed 'to get ill and die' (Bleek 1933, p. 303, 1935, p. 7). Yet felines are not at all a popular motif in San rock-shelter paintings (Lee & Woodhouse 1970, fig. 36). Data such as these show that while several species are accorded great importance in myth and ritual, only a very few inspire art motifs. The rest are subordinated or ignored for no obvious reason. The merits of opposing views about frequency counts and the social contexts of San art notwithstanding (cf. Woodhouse 1984, and Lewis-Williams' reply), the motives that impel artists to depict a species preferentially are extremely complex in every hunting and gathering society. Clearly, the primitive artist's emotions are difficult to fathom if we analyse his subject matter without appreciating the psychobiological factors that determine not only an individual's hallucinatory preferences but also their social appeal.

Australian Aboriginal ideas about numinous animals are like those of the San, in that a few species, and one in particular, command preferential attention or veneration or both. Though Australian Aboriginal metaphors illuminate a different kind of problem, partly because their paintings are not naturalistic, their relationship to the tensions of a hunter–gatherer social life is no different. Throughout tribal Australia these tensions crystallize as respect for the medicine man's occult powers and their source, the mythical Rainbow Serpent, from whose mouth the 'man of high degree' obtains *kimba* (quartz crystals) for his mantic paraphernalia. Tales about his psychic displays – such as his control over, and transformation into, animals, inanimate objects and the elements – abound alongside beliefs in the efficacy of rituals to neutralize the Rainbow Serpent's easily provoked wrath. Elkin (1977) and Maddock (1978, pp. 1–21), among many others, have discussed this creature's symbolism. Its concrete zoomorphic renderings embody a variety of aboriginal concepts of the 'Dream Time', 'the fundamentals of existence', the 'totemic essence', the 'life principle', 'spirit' and 'divinity'. The commonest form of 'familiar' or 'assistant' of the medicine man – the tribal 'custodian of religious conscience' – is a serpent, and sometimes a lace lizard. Nevertheless, unlike the eland in San art, depictions of the Rainbow Serpent are sporadic in Australian Aboriginal paintings at sacred sites, and reptiles in general may be outnumbered by representations of harmless or mythically and economically less-significant species. How can this be reconciled with my statement that the numinous reputation of an animal derives merely from its formidableness?

According to Mountford (1978, pp. 30–3, 69f.), Australian Aboriginal tribes far removed from each other believed in a class of mythical beings known collectively as *bunyip* (or other names), which they described as vengeful, horrendous death-dealing monsters possessing scales, fur or feathers. Examples of *bunyip* are the *myndie*, an immense human-headed venomous serpent with a three-pronged tongue, the huge dingo *turudun*, the emu *gourke* or human–emu-spirit *gurugudji* and the kangaroo-woman *ngaljod* (Figs 11.3–6, respectively). Myth eloquently attests to the hallucinatory transformation of *bunyip* into various zoo-anthropomorphic spirit-beings, all of which are but aspects of the Rainbow Serpent. The latter's coiled form is evident within the 'X-rayed' body of *turudun* and only implicit in the human–emu. In Figure 11.6 the kangaroo-woman is shown as a celestial being whose urine is rain, but in subjective reality she is the incarnation of the bisexual Rainbow Serpent and rain-making is this wrathful animal's normal function. However, not all Aboriginal paintings on bark cloth or at sacred sites are in the X-ray style or suggest aspects of transformation. In sum, we cannot be certain whether important hallucination-inspired societal anxieties can be assessed solely via an artist's mind's eye.

The designs are not sacred in themselves, but only when applied to or in association with a place which is sacred. This is apparent from Davidson's (1936) exhaustive lists of sites and index to the rock carvings, paintings and Wondjina galleries throughout Australia. Birds, especially emus, are depicted quite often, but the frequency of serpents is no more impressive than that of birds and other totemic animals such as the kangaroo, dingo, fish, insects, lizards, opossum and platypus. By contrast, mythical beings 'seem to be lacking in the area' of three

Figures 11.3–11.6   Australian Aboriginal paintings of the protean, bisexual Rainbow Serpent as *bunyip* (after Mountford 1978).

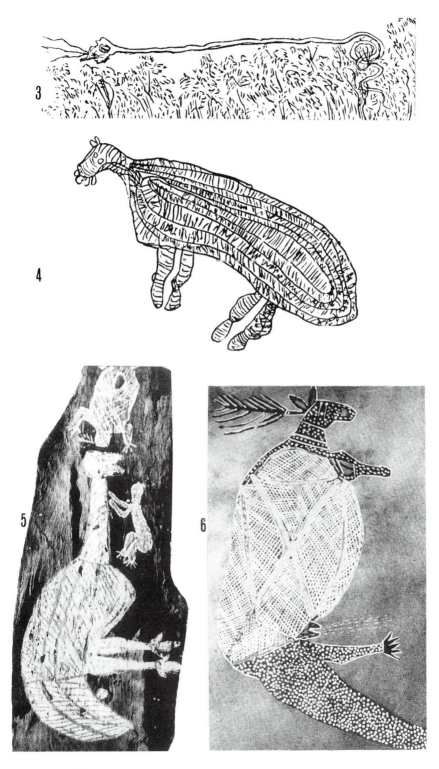

insular sites in Arnhem Land, northern Australia. At these sites the frequency and range of animals painted in caves are as follows (condensed from McCarthy 1960, table 1, omitting counts of hunting and fishing groups). The total number of motifs is 1427, comprising humans (596), mammals (412), birds (122), reptiles (106), fish (186) and invertebrates (5). Of the reptiles, lizards (33) and turtles and tortoises (61) far outnumber the serpents, including the death-adder (12). The last figure is an unimpressive 0.83% of the total at these sites, but is consistent with the central importance of the Rainbow Serpent, since the latter is represented in the guise of lizards and turtles. The visually fantastic counterparts are direct, immutable products of the mind's eye – in the Kimberley District, for example, many sites portray serpents, possibly the Rainbow Serpent itself, in the act of devouring human beings and animals. The fact remains that artistic symbols are all too often an unreliable indicator of a prehistoric society's emotional attitudes, even when the world-view of its descendants is ethnographically well documented and examined in ecological and other scientific perspectives – as indeed it has been in Australia and South Africa.

The huntsmen's slate knives in Figures 11.7 and 11.8 are from Scandinavian Stone Age sites only about 350 km south of the Arctic Circle. Their handles are shaped to represent the head of a bird and a bear, respectively, but the majority of knives in the collections of the University Museum at Trondheim, Norway, have elk-head shaped handles. As a rule the blades are bare, except for a very few on which whale or fish motifs are incised. It is therefore remarkable that the serpent, an animal quite rare at far-northerly latitudes, is symbolized on these two blades quite fortuitously – for were it not for the obvious serpent in Figure 11.7, the crudely incised double zigzag in Figure 11.8 (despite the faint bifid scratch at one end, within the zigzag) would probably have remained unidentified as a serpent with a projecting bifid tongue (cf. Gjessing 1945, pp. 267–77). Actually, ophidian traditions are hazy but fairly well attested in these northern regions. For example, the Lapps are said to detest serpents, but the stylized symbols on their ritual drums include an inconspicuous figure of the *noidekärmai*, the shaman's powerful spirit-assistant – a serpent. Not surprisingly, artefacts with serpent representations are not common in far-northerly Eurasia. What is at all extraordinary is that several of the region's varied ethnic groups still nurse cultural traditions in which this typically tropical and temperate-zone animal is invoked. Moreover, indubitable serpent effigies in carved antler are known from the Neolithic cemetery at Olenii, an island in Lake Onega, 63°N, USSR.

In the northern-Eurasian environment, with its rich, non-reptilian fauna, even the simple ophidian form is sometimes obscured by the preponderance of symbols of economically far more important animals such as cervids, birds and bears. We need a systematic understanding of all cryptic animal symbols, but the known, clear-cut examples of ophidian motifs in the petroglyphs and mobiliary art of northern peoples do reveal the hold on man's imagination by an animal that hardly menaced them. In the Kola Peninsula, USSR, well within the Arctic Circle, kinship with, and guardianship over, wild animals is personified by the antler-headed Myndash (Gribova 1975). Is the elongated stylized form at his feet (Figure 11.9) an eel, a serpent, or a nondescript artistic hybrid? It would be useful

Figures 11.7 (top) and 11.8 (bottom)   Slate knife blades with zoomorphic handles and engraved motifs, Scandinavian Stone Age (courtesy of Dr Kalle Sognnes).

to know. However, Myndash represents the animal kingdom in general – and for us this is more significant, since his economic links with game and fish are inseparable from belief in the *rå* (or similar terms). This formerly common northern and subarctic superstition was rooted in the fear that humans and beasts could be 'spirited away' or 'led astray' in the forests and 'kept' by a supernatural being. Apotropaic remedies were legion (Hultkrantz 1961).

The ecological backgrounds of the numinous beliefs of hunter–gatherers are well documented, particularly with respect to northern Eurasia and North America (Hoppál 1984, Hultkrantz 1961, 1965, Paulson 1964). The explorer Rasmussen (1931, pp. 224–7) gives details of Netsilik (far-northern Canadian) Eskimos' dependence on shamans ('whose mission it is to be protectors of mankind against all the hidden forces and dangers of life') and whose strict rules govern attitudes towards all game animals lest they be offended. The mother of all animals is a greatly feared spirit-child Nuliajuk, the mistress of the land and

Figures 11.9 and 11.10   The zooanthropomorph 'Myndash', Kola Peninsula, arctic USSR (after Gribova 1975).

sea, whose fingers gave birth to seals and all other beasts. Alaskan Eskimos, who subsist on a more varied fauna, envision a greater range of supernatural beings. Certain humans and animals have the ability, they believe, to transform themselves into other beings without losing their own *inua*, or 'soul'. This yields an unpredictable environment in which no-one can be sure of the 'true' identity of any creature and its potential to do harm – a prospect effectively nurtured by the 'greatly feared' *angalkuq*, or shaman. Actually, of all the Arctic species, only the bear is a truly aggressive adversary. It is hardly surprising that it is mythologized as a monstrous, ten-legged horror called *kokogiak*. By contrast, reptiles are practically unknown in the Alaskan fauna, yet the Eskimo nurse cultural memories of a fantastic, much-dreaded reptilian monster, the *palraiyuk* (Figures 11.11 & 12) and a caterpillar-like human giant called *ti-sikh-puk*. What is equally extraordinary, however, is that they also mythologize and (under appropriate circumstances) also fear totally innocuous animals such as seals, small mammals, birds, fish and caribou – all of which may embody evil human (or animal) *inua*. Eskimo craftsmen give visual substance to *inua* with prodigious frequency, depicting its manifestations not only on shamans' masks, but also on utilitarian objects of all kinds (Fitzhugh & Kaplan 1982, pp. 180–217, Ray 1977, pp. 20–2).

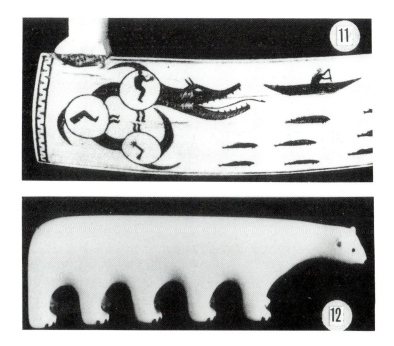

Figures 11.11 and 11.12   Alaskan and Point Barrow conceptions of *palraiyuk* and *kokogiak* (after Ray 1977).

Thus, the words 'hallucination' and 'myth' are synonymous with the awe of spirits, amounting on occasion to virtual deification. Indeed, awe is the only stuff of which religiosity is made. However, though archaeologists evaluate artefacts from many different viewpoints, they do not implicate primordial emotionality and the sociobiology of man's predilection for certain symbolic animals, regardless of their innocuity or predacity towards him. Evoked by the environment (in the widest ecological and psychobiological sense) and exacerbated by hierophants, raw (i.e. physiologically aroused) societal displays of emotion as a rule bear the stamp of adult group psychology. Yet, individually adults are liable to succumb to mental stress almost as easily as children, whom they eclipse in art and in the formalization of beliefs and rituals rooted in unrealistic fears and anxieties. It is no wonder that in the world of spirit beings the truly formidable animal species are on a par with the truly docile, and that they vie for a place in human imagination by freely assuming each other's attributes, or rather the attributes that man capriciously bestows on them.

In this scenario animals as inoffensive as land otters, pangolins and butterflies meant harm, ill-luck or death to the Alaskan Tlingit, the Burmese Chin and the Aztecs of pre-Columbian Mexico, respectively (Mundkur 1983, pp. 257f.). Cross-culturally, the choices of symbolic species have always been fortuitious, because (discounting caprice) only these three forces are at work: (a) keen awareness of the ecology and behaviour of a few species that excite a people's emotions for a variety of reasons; (b) an individual's innate sensitivities and response to stressful experiences, not necessarily involving these species; and (c) the psychological propensity to channel specific, highly personal fears and anxieties into generalized outlets. The sensitivities I have termed 'excrescential' have an important adaptive function in anticipating danger and relieving tension. This function is epitomized to an extraordinary degree by only a few potentially dangerous species. It is the reptiles, felids and raptorial birds which, by dint of 'numbers and fierceness' (to repeat Ragozin's words from my opening paragraph), have excelled as metaphors and shared their power with other species ever since they instilled 'fear and loathing' and 'the instinct of religiosity' in our primeval forebears. The serpent is but one of a very few extraordinarily powerful impellers and symbols of this urge.

Millennia after the animal motifs on stamp seals of the pre- and proto-literate periods had given way to the anthropomorphized divinities of the Sumerians, the latter's cultural heirs continued to apply animal epithets to their own divinities. In Heimpel's (1968) corpus of hymns and secular statements from Sumerian cuneiform texts, 105 species are invoked in simile and metaphor, notably in contexts of derogation, terror, threat and divine blessing. In Babylonian and Assyrian religion the pre-Sumerian term *melammu*, 'awe-inspiring supernatural radiance', characterized all divinities and eventually kings. Their omen texts and 'dream books' abound in one-line entries, each describing a well-defined event, the behaviour or feature of an animal, a specific part of its body or an astronomical event (Oppenheim 1956, 1977, pp. 16, 98). Animals lent their fearsomeness (and other qualities) impartially to the gods and demons of Mesopotamia, but no more explicitly than in other civilized societies with a script.

Long after the Pleistocene, man's emotional bond with other species persists in traditions as disparate as those of the Australian Aborigines and (for example) the pre-Israelite Jews. The latter conceived Azazel, Leviathan, Matronit, Rahab and Seraph – all monstrous zoomorphs – to befit the aniconic concept of Yahweh as a wrathful, to some even demonic, God. They were 'the creatures of Yahweh, divine in their essence', who later rebelled against him. According to rabbinical literature *yezer tov* and *yezer ra*, good and evil inclinations, are the pristine hallmarks of angels and animals, respectively, and therefore immiscible; so, out of dissatisfaction, God created man and gave him freedom to act ambivalently! Threat and retribution are implicit in the phrase 'fear of God', *yirat Elohim*, the Hebrew equivalent of 'religion'.[5] Stripped of its parochiality and moral overtones, does not that phrase more accurately describe 'religiosity' and man's inclination to imbue the supernatural with animal spirit?

Conclusions

Animals loom powerfully in mental imageries, lending themselves to simile, metaphor and reification through a range of emotional drives. Of these, fear and anxiety were (besides sexuality and aggression) the most primordial, as well as constant, factors in human evolution, with clear homologues among the anthropoids. Furthermore, human emotionality stands at the apex of a phylogenetically derived pattern of neurophysiological sensitivites and responses traceable to vertebrates with much less advanced brains. Because discrete specialized functions of the brain evolved under the crucial stimulus of predator–prey relationships, these sensitivites and responses are normal adaptive faculties that enhance survival.

In palaeoanthropological contexts this leads us to question the status of what is commonly called 'culture'. Definitions of culture are legion and usually anthropocentric. They stress man's social habits and the superiority of his intelligence, but overlook certain principles of physiological psychology that bear upon the simultaneity of organic and mental evolution of the primates as a whole. Even tool-making and speech, long considered to be solely human attainments, ought to be viewed afresh: we now know that in their natural habitat foraging chimpanzees deftly gather ground termites by manoeuvring them out of holes on to sticks of proper diameter and length, thus revealing forethought and inventiveness reminiscent of early hominid hunter–gatherers (Ch. 10, this book). If incipient speech is seen as the trait that impelled man's subsequent 'cultural' advances, then we must recognize that coeval non-human primates, too, were developing their now quite remarkable abilities of oral and gestural communication. Assuming, for the sake of argument, a continual improvement of these abilities through mutations suitably affecting the vocal chords, the lips, the brain and the survival-enhancing habits of chimpanzees, may we not envisage these highly sensitive animals acquiring increasingly efficient emotional outlets?

Presumably, emotion and mental imageries moved early human societies to respond to environmentally induced stimuli through symbolic art. However, experiments show that chimpanzees, too, respond to abstract man-made symbols when motivated, i.e. mentally comforted, by rewards. In other words, they are adept in *learning* to think symbolically and imitating other chimpanzees. Notions of 'culture', it seems, constantly necessitate refinement in the light of what anthropoids can or cannot interpret intelligently or may be able to do manually despite their handicaps.

However, our interpretation of the emotional content of prehistoric symbols is another matter. The abundance of animals around Pleistocene man's shelters seems to have caused him considerable anxiety, for arguably Palaeolithic art, which is mostly zoomorphic, everywhere signified apotropaic or other religious sentiments. There is a tendency to regard these as superstitious or hallucinatory, because of the ritual overtones or semiological ambiguities of that art, with its naturalistically portrayed animal species and fantasized animal hybrids, particularly the zooanthropomorphs. However, we know that, irrespective of provenance and epoch, *all* symbols are merely secondary developments fraught with obscure, highly variable sociocultural impetuses that frequently make interpretations of their meanings a matter of conjecture. At issue is the cross-cultural nature of *primary* motivations, not semiological explanations of any particular society's activities and symbols. In short, our focus is chiefly on the innate neurophysiological determinants of an individual's protocultural traits, and much less on predominantly socially nurtured 'cultural' traits; though admittedly, these two classes of traits lie on a continuum subsuming the strongly overt emotional displays that characterize both the human and the non-human primates.

If intelligence, imitative learning, inventiveness and emotionality are not exclusively the hallmarks of *Homo sapiens sapiens*, then what is distinctively human besides our propensity to create multifarious social systems and material objects? It is, I think, our finer emotions, for these are the fount of the various attitudes that (through language and the arts) have given shape to ethnicity and religion. At the core of those emotions, and vying with the 'thinking' frontal cortex of the brain, lurk the products of the primitive hypothalamus – our myriad animal impulses. These, as I have shown, come to the fore in diverse ways that influence mental imageries and behavioural decisions.

At the formative levels, where animal impulses prevail, conventional anthropological explanations are redundant; but so, too, for the most part, are biological explanations at the higher levels, where one's feelings are usually bent by habit or cultural precept. Fear, anxiety, dreams and the eidetic imagery of hallucinations are among the few exceptions that, ironically, inspire cultural precepts. They have direct experimentally verifiable bases in biochemistry, genetics, endocrinology and neuro-anatomy. Despite the intrusion of cultural factors, these sciences have revealed much about elementary fear, schizophrenia, the neuroses and psychoses, neuroendocrine processes during sleep, dream imageries and human behavioural modification in general, from experiments with stimulating or inhibitory drugs such as the hallucinogens, anaesthetics, anxiolytics and antidepressants that chemically resemble and mimic the brain's natural neurotransmitters.

Because basic sensory responses to environmentally induced stress are, like their underlying physiology, palpable, innate, stable, adaptively reinforced and far older than culture (however defined), they are not easily obscured by a society's traditional beliefs and practices. From my viewpoint, therefore, I see no urgent need for hypothetical units – such as sociogenes, memes, culturgens or idenes – proposed by some on the seemingly reasonable premise of a coevolution[6] of genes and human cultural attributes. Many intangible factors, ancient as well as contemporary, complicate scientific enquiry into the genome- and environment-dependent penetrance and expressivity of genes that affect the sensory systems, their mutability and mutation rates and, not least important, the little-understood relationship between mitochondrial DNA and actual evolutionary events. Biochemically active outside the nucleus in a manner slightly at variance with universal genetic (chromosomal) code theory, mt-DNA accumulates mutations faster than the nucleus, and transmits them exclusively through the maternal line. As Cann *et al.* (1987) suggest, these qualities force us to reconsider current notions of genealogical interrelationships within the genus *Homo* and the time-scale of hominid evolution itself, not to mention the transience of accidentally (or purposefully) acquired cultural refinements.

Be that as it may, scholars generally tend to focus on criteria other than fear and the ancillary emotions, choosing instead traits whose bases in testable physiological correlates can only be assumed when strong countermanding forces are also at work. This is exemplified by religion, the quintessence of primitive (and perhaps modern) human culture. Some scholars have argued that adherence to regulations governing food, marriage and other practices could have affected our ancestors' chances of survival and reproductive success. This may be true to a degree, especially in relatively recent epochs, yet most religious practices are fortuitous secondary developments that do not account for the initial, internal impetuses any more than do symbols. Indeed, their importance recedes sharply the farther back we go in the Pleistocene, when survival and reproduction were determined wholly by the biology of intuitive, i.e. acultural or at the most proto-cultural, behaviours. *Homo erectus* may or may not have been capable of rudimentary speech, but only millennia after *H. sapiens sapiens* acquired it could intelligence and the finer emotions have flourished enough to begin to mould the tension-laden labyrinths of religious thought and social rituals.

To be sure, protocultural tendencies are no less labyrinthine, but their determinants are biological and operate automatically at the fundamental levels of emotion. True human universals emerge from the mental imageries at these levels, not from the capricious finer emotions that distort the end-product we anthropocentrically call culture.

Intrinsic religiosity – a state of mind incited by belief in forces perceived as supernatural that demand placation – is embedded far less in the finer emotions than in vague and instinctively grounded fears and anxieties. Primevally, that mental state appears to have originated as a means of expressing or relieving tensions through the subconscious generalization of their specific causes. Reactions to these were apt to be intensified at the social level, and to be projected onto inanimate and animate objects that commanded attention in one way or another, eventually as numina. In the course of hominid evolution the choice of a particular animal to symbolize deep emotion was bound to be whimsical yet subject to the vicissitudes of livelihood and the composition of the local fauna, with game animals and formidable species of reptiles, raptorial birds and fierce carnivores holding an edge in the competition.

Of course, anthropocentric scholars will belittle the connection between an individual's mental tensions (particularly their involuntary determinants) and belief. In addition, they are likely to argue that symbols of social cohesion and identity flow from the human ability to reason (no matter how faultily). Yet any deeply affective belief has the potential of attaining communal recognition as a cultural tenet. Durkheim's (1915) view that this cannot be explained in terms of individual psychology is fundamentally untenable. Malinowski's psychobiological data were deficient, but he rightly held that culturally defined institutions exist because they minister to the individual's basic physiological, i.e. animal–emotional needs.

In all of these respects, intrinsic religiosity remains a part of human animality. As a universal protocultural urge it is worthy of an interdisciplinary inquiry that would take us beyond the conventional enquiry into religion as a purely sociocultural phenomenon.

Summary

That wild animals agitate the mind is apparent from the fantasized qualities attributed to them in myths and symbols. However, to deduce the origins of this discomfiture one must reckon scientifically with *intrinsic* religiosity. I define the latter as a state of mind incited by belief in forces perceived as supernatural and numinous that must be appeased. It is an innate urge embedded in fear. Because elementary fear has an adaptive function in all higher vertebrates, and also rudimentary homologues in the environmentally induced behavioural responses of animals with much simpler sensory systems, it is in man a primordial and universal, protocultural emotion. Therefore, explanations rooted in biochemical genetics, organic evolution and the neurophysiology of subconscious (and sometimes conscious) behavioural tendencies take priority, but acquire meaning only against a background of interpretations derived from sociocultural anthropology, archaeology and the history of religions. Many factors affect the behavioural psychology of individuals and groups of the higher species of non-human primates, which have much in common with our own species. This leaves little room for an understanding of intrinsic religiosity except via an exploration of the biological conditions that – mechanically, universally, and fairly predictably – determine human emotionality. By the same token, religion – the quintessence of sociocultural activity – is merely an end-product whose exceedingly protean manifestations thwart rigorous biological enquiry just as much as they prompt conventionally anthropocentric speculation.

Notes

I am indebted to Mrs Nancy Orth for translations from Russian sources.

1   Geertz (1966, pp. 10–12) discusses motivations from a social scientist's standpoint. In a later paper (Geertz 1980, pp. 167, 178) he uncritically treats sociobiology as 'a curious combination of common sense and common nonsense', but correctly concludes that 'social events do have causes and social institutions effects . . .'. Progress in any discipline depends, of course, on discriminating between the various postulated causes of phenomena within its purview, but the purely experimental sciences carry empiricism into highly technical areas rather more strictly – often beyond the purview of common sense *per se*. This is especially true of the causes of fear and ancillary emotions, the biological bases of which are not only a subject of the 'harder sciences' recommended by Geertz, but also have extraordinary relevance to, and direct applicability in, studies of humans.
2   For other treatises on sociobiology see Barlow & Silverberg (1980), Caplan (1978), Fetzer (1985), Kitcher (1985) and Montagu (1980).
3   Communication in early hominid evolution is discussed by Stephenson (1979). I have elsewhere discussed various factors linked to fear of the serpent and the cults incited by it (Mundkur 1983). For a detailed treatment of communication among primates, see Snowdon *et al.* (1983).
4   The evolution of the brain and its cognitive mechanisms are beyond the scope of this chapter. Changeux (1985, chs 8 & 9, pp. 271f.) states that ' . . . continuity of the anatomical evolution of the brain is accompanied by at least an equal continuity in

the evolution of the genome. Indeed, the genome varies much less than the brain . . . [there is] the paradox of an increase in cerebral capacity with a constant set of genes . . . . The Darwinism of synapses replaces the Darwinism of genes'. The cranial capacity of *H. erectus* was between 800 and 1200 cm^3; of *H. neanderthalensis* between 1550 and 1690 cm^3. In modern *H. sapiens* it is slightly less.

5   This information was drawn at random from Kaufmann (1969), *Encyclopaedia Judaica* and *The Jewish encyclopaedia*.

6   Strictly, coevolution is a process in which two or more species with close ecological relationships exert reciprocal selective pressures so that their evolution is inter-dependent. Advocates of 'gene-culture coevolution' are using the term in a quite different, and special, sense.

References

Adey, W. R., Kado, R. T. & Rhodes, J. M. 1963. Cortical and subcortical recordings in the chimpanzee. *Science* **41**, 932–3.

Alles, G. D. & J. M. Kitagawa 1985. The dialectic of the parts and the whole: Reflections on the past, present, future of the history of religions. In *The history of religions: retrospect and prospect*, J. M. Kitagawa (ed.), 145–81. New York: Macmillan.

Allport, G. W. 1960. *Personality and social encounter: selected essays*. Boston, Massachusetts: Beacon Press.

Archer, J. 1979. Behavioural aspects of fear. In *Fear in animals and man*, W. Sluckin (ed.), 56–85. New York: Van Nostrand.

Armon-Jones, C. 1985. Prescription, explication and the social construction of emotion. *Journal for the Theory of Social Behaviour* **15**, 1–22.

Baker, M. & R. Gorsuch 1982. Trait anxiety and intrinsic–extrinsic religiousness. *Journal for the Scientific Study of Religion* **21**, 119–22.

Barlow, G. W. & J. Silverberg (eds) 1980. *Sociobiology: beyond nature/nurture?* Washington, DC: American Association for the Advancement of Science, Selected Symposia, 35.

Bayley, N. 1968. Behavioral correlates of mental growth: birth to thirty-six years. *American Psychologist* **23**, 1–17.

Bibeau, G. 1981. Préalables à une épidémiologie anthropologique de la dépression. *Psychopathologie africaine* **17**, 96–112.

Bleek, D. F. 1933. Beliefs and customs of the /Xam Bushmen. Part 5. The rain. *Bantu Studies* **7**, 297–312.

Bleek, D. F. 1935. Beliefs and customs of the /Xam Bushmen. Part 7. Sorcerors. *Bantu Studies* **9**, 1–47.

Boulenger, J.-Ph. & T. W. Uhde 1982. Biological peripheral correlates of anxiety. *Encéphale* **8** (2 Suppl.), 119–30.

Brace, C. L. 1979. Biological parameters and Pleistocene hominid lifeways. In *Primate ecology and human origins: Ecological influences on social organization*, L. S. Bernstein & E. O. Smith (eds), 263–289. New York and London: Garland STPM Press.

Bregar, A. S. 1971. Anxiety in young children. *Young Children* **27**, 5–11.

Brown, L. B. (ed.) 1985. *Advances in the psychology of religion*. Oxford: Pergamon Press.

Budd, S. 1973. *Sociologists and religion*. London: Collier–Macmillan.

Buss, A. H., E. N. Murray & E. Buss 1968. Stimulus generalization and the fear of snakes. *Journal of Personality and Social Psychology* **1**, 134–41.

Byrnes, J. F. 1984. *The psychology of religion*. New York: The Free Press/Macmillan.

Cann R. L., M. Stoneking & A. C. Wilson 1987. Mitochondrial DNA and human evolution. *Nature* **325**, 31–6.

Cannon, W. B. 1942. 'Voodoo' death. *American Anthropologist* **44**, 169–81.

Caplan, A. L. (ed.) 1978. *The sociobiology debate: readings on ethical and scientific issues*. New York: Harper & Row.

Cardwell, J. 1980. *The social context of religiosity*. Washington, DC: University Press of America.

Changeux, J.-P. 1985. *Neuronal man: the biology of mind* (transl. by L. Gary). New York: Pantheon Books.

Chkili, T., J. Ktiouet, M. Paes & A. Messaoudi 1981. Islam, deuil et dépression. *Psychopathologie africaine* **17**, 159–62.

D'Andrade, R. G. 1973. The effect of culture on dreams. In *Dreams and dreaming*. S. G. M. Lee & A. R. Mayes (eds), 199–204. Harmondsworth: Penguin Educational.

Davidson, D. S. 1936. Aboriginal Australian and Tasmanian rock carvings and paintings. *American Philosophical Society Memoirs*, **5**.

Davidson, R. J. 1984. Cerebral asymmetry and emotion. *Psychophysiology* **21**, 564.

Dealy, R. S. 1981. Secondary depression in anxiety disorders. *Comprehensive Psychiatry* **22**, 612–18.

Debidour, V. H. 1961. *Le bestiaire sculpté du Moyen Âge en France*. Paris: Arthaud.

Du Bois, C. 1944. *The people of Alor*. Minneapolis, Minnesota: University of Minnesota Press.

Durkheim, E. 1915. *The elementary forms of the religious life: a study in religious sociology* (transl. from the French by J. W. Swain). London: Macmillan.

Ekman, P., E. Sorensen & W. Friesen 1969. Pan-cultural elements in facial displays of emotion. *Science* **164**, 86–8.

Elkin, A. P. 1977. *Aboriginal men of high degree*, 2nd edn. New York: St Martin's Press.

Eme, R. & D. Schmidt 1978. The stability of children's fears. *Child Development* **49**, 1277–9.

Evans-Pritchard, E. E. 1965. *Theories of primitive religion*. Oxford: Oxford University Press.

Ewart, J.-P. 1980. *Neuroethology*. New York: Springer-Verlag.

Farson, D. 1975. *Vampires, zombies and monster men*. London: Aldus Books.

Fetzer, J. H. (ed.) 1985. *Sociobiology and epistemology*. Dordrecht: D. Reidel.

Fitzhugh, W. W. & S. A. Kaplan 1982. *Inua: spirit world of the Bering Sea Eskimo*. Washington, DC: Smithsonian Institution.

Freud, S. 1913. *Totem and taboo: some points of agreement between the mental lives of savages and neurotics* (transl. by J. Strachey). New York: Norton.

Gale, A. & J. A. Edwards (eds) 1983. *Physiological correlates of human behaviour*, Vol. 3. London: Academic Press.

Geertz, C. 1966. Religion as a cultural system. In *Anthropological approaches to the study of religion*, M. Banton (ed.), 1–46. New York: Frederick A. Praeger.

Geertz, C. 1980. Blurred genres: the refiguration of social thought. *American Scholar* (spring issue), 165–79.

Gjessing, G. 1945. *Norges steinalder*. Oslo: Norsk Arkeologisk Selskap.

Goodnow, J. 1977. *Children drawing*. Cambridge, Massachusetts: Harvard University Press.

Gregor, T. 1981. A content analysis of Mehinaku dreams. *Ethos* **9**, 353–90.

Gribova, L. S. 1975. *Permskij zverinnyj stil*. Moscow: Nauka.

Griffith, R. M., O. Miyagi & A. Tago 1958. The universality of typical dreams. *American Anthropologist* **60**, 1173–9.

Hall, C. S. & R. Van de Castle 1966. *The content analysis of dreams*. New York: Appleton–Century–Crofts.

Harner, M. J. (ed.) 1973. *Hallucinogens and shamanism*. New York: Oxford University Press.

Hebb, D. O. 1972. *Textbook of psychology*, 3rd edn. Philadelphia, Pennsylvania: W. B. Saunders.

Heimpel, W. 1968. *Tierbilder in der sumerischen Literatur*. Studia Pohl, 2. Rome: Pontificium Institutum Biblicum.

Herrenkohl, L. R. 1982. The anxiety-prone personality: effects of prenatal stress on the infant. In *The biology of anxiety*, R. J. Mathew (ed.), 51–86. New York: Brunner/Mazel.

Hiatt, S. W., J. G. Campos & R. N. Emde 1979. Facial patterning and infant emotional expression: Happiness, surprise, and fear. *Child Development* **50**, 1020–35.

Hood, R. W. (convenor) 1985. Symposium on religious orientation typologies. *Journal for the Scientific Study of Religion* **24**, 407–42.

Hoppál, M. (ed.) 1984. *Shamanism in Eurasia*. Göttingen: Herodot.

Hoyle, G. 1984. The scope of neuroethology. *The Behavioral and Brain Sciences* **7**, 367–412.

Hultkrantz, Å. (ed.) 1961. *The supernatural owners of Nature*. Stockholm: Almqvist & Wiksell.

Hultkrantz, Å. 1965. Type of religion in Arctic hunting cultures. In *Hunting and fishing*, H. Hvarfner (ed.), 265–318. Luleå: Norbottens Museum.

Izard, C. E. 1984. The facets and interfaces of the emotions. In *Interfaces in psychology*. Vol. 1: *Developmental psychobiology and clinical neuropsychology*, R. W. Bell, J. Elias, R. L. Greene & J. H. Harvey (eds), 57–85. Lubock: Texas Tech Press.

Jersild, A. T., F. V. Markey & C. L. Jersild 1933. *Children's fears, dreams, wishes, daydreams, likes, dislikes, pleasant and unpleasant memories*. New York: Columbia University Press.

Jevning, R., A. F. Wilson & J. M. Davidson 1978. Adrenocortical activity during meditation. *Hormones and Behavior* **10**, 54–60.

Johnson, F. H. 1978. *The anatomy of hallucinations*. Chicago: Nelson–Hall.

Kalunta, A. 1981. Depressive illness: its cultural aspects. *Psychopathologie africaine* **17**, 113–26.

Kandel, E. R. 1983. From metapsychology to molecular biology: explorations into the nature of anxiety. *American Journal of Psychiatry* **140**, 1277–93.

Kaufmann, Y. 1960. *The religion of Israel from its beginnings to the Babylonian exile*. Chicago: University of Chicago Press.

Kimmins, C. W. 1973. Children's dreams. In *Dreams and dreaming*, S. G. M. Lee & A. R. Mayes (eds), 83–109. Harmondsworth: Penguin Educational.

Kirk, G. S. 1973. *Myth. Its meaning and functions in ancient and other cultures*. Cambridge: Cambridge University Press.

Kitcher, P. 1985. *Vaulting ambition. Sociobiology and the quest for human nature*. Cambridge, Massachusetts: MIT Press.

Koppitz, E. M. 1968. *Psychological evaluation of children's human figure drawings*. New York: Grune & Stratton.

Lapouse, R. & M. A. Monk. 1959. Fears and worries in a representative sample of children. *American Journal of Orthopsychiatry* **29**, 803–18.

Leach, E. R. 1982. *Social anthropology*. London: Fontana.

Lee, D. N. & H. C. Woodhouse 1970. *Art on the rocks of southern Africa*. New York: Charles Scribner's.

Leshner, A. L. 1978. *An introduction to behavioural endocrinology*. New York: Oxford University Press.

Lévy-Bruhl, L. 1966. *The 'soul' of the primitive*. London: Allen & Unwin.

Lewis-Williams, J. D. 1983. Science and rock art. *South African Archaeological Society, Goodwin Series* **4**, 3–13.

Maddock, K. 1978. Preface to *The Rainbow Serpent: a chromatic piece*, I. R. Buchler & K. Maddock (eds), The Hague: Mouton.

Marmot, M. G. 1984. The influence of psychological stresses on sudden death. In *Selected topics in preventive cardiology*, A. Raineri & J. J. Kellerman (eds), London: Plenum Press.

Marzillier, J. S., D. Carroll & J. R. Newland 1979. Self-report and physiological changes accompanying repeated imaging of a phobic scene. *Behavioural Research and Therapy* **17**, 71–77.

Mathew, R. J. (ed.) 1982. *The biology of anxiety*. New York: Brunner/Mazel.

Maurer, A. 1965. What children fear. *Journal of Genetic Psychology* **106**, 265–77.

McCarthy, F. D. 1960. The cave paintings of Groote Eylandt and Chasm Island. In *Records of the American-Australian Scientific Expedition to Arnhem Land*, C. P. Mountford (ed.), 297–444. Parkville, Victoria: Melbourne University Press.

Mehring, W. 1925. *Neubestelltes Ubenteurliches Tierhaus; eine Zoologie des Uberglaubens, der Mystik und Mythologie vom Mittelalter bis unsere Zeit*. Potsdam: Gustav Kiepenheuer.

Midgley, M. 1978. *Beast and Man: the roots of human nature*. Ithaca, New York: Cornell University Press.

Mitchell, A. R. & J. R. Gosden 1978. Evolutionary relationships between man and the great apes. *Science Progress (Oxford)* **65**, 273–93.

Mitchell, G. 1979. *Behavioral sex differences in nonhuman primates*. New York: Van Nostrand Reinhold.

Montagu, A. 1980. *Sociobiology examined*. London: Oxford University Press.

Mountford, C. P. 1978. The Rainbow Serpent myths of Australia. In *The Rainbow Serpent: a chromatic piece*, I. R. Buchler & K. Maddock (eds), 23–97. The Hague: Mouton.

Mundkur, B. 1983. *The cult of the serpent: an interdisciplinary survey of its manifestations and origins*. Albany, New York: State University of New York Press.

Noll, R. 1985. Mental imagery cultivation as a cultural phenomenon: the role of visions in shamanism. *Current Anthropology* **26**, 443–51.

O'Nell, C. W. & A. J. Rubel 1980. The development and use of a gauge to measure social stress in three Mesoamerican communities. *Ethnology* **19**, 111–27.

Opatiya (Yugoslavia) Conference 1971. *Religion et religiosité, théisme, et non croyance dans les sociétés industrielles*. Lille: Verscheure.

Oppenheim, A. L. 1956. The interpretation of dreams in the Near East. *Transactions of the American Philosophical Society* **46**(3), 179–353.

Oppenheim, A. L. 1977. *Ancient Mesopotamia: portrait of a dead civilization*. Chicago, Illinois: University of Chicago Press.

Pager, H. 1972. *Ndedema: a documentation of the paintings of the Ndedema Gorge*. Portland, Oregon: International Scholarly Book Services.

Paivio, A. & J. de Linde 1982. Imagery, memory, and the brain. *Canadian Journal of Psychology* **36**, 243–72.

Paulsen, I. 1964. The animal guardian: a critical and synthetic review. *History of Religions* **3**, 202–19.

Perris, C., M. Eisemann, L. von Knorring, L. Oreland & H. Perris 1984. Personality traits and monoamine oxidase activity in platelets in depressed patients. *Neuropsychobiology* **12**, 201–5.

Peterson, N. 1979. Aboriginal uses of Australian Solanaceae. In *The biology and taxonomy of the Solanaceae*, J. G. Hawkes, R. N. Lester & A. D. Skelding (eds), 171–189. London: The Linnean Society/Academic Press.

Phillipson, D. W. 1985. *African archaeology*. Cambridge: Cambridge University Press.

Pinkus, J. & J. Clary 1962. Fears in normal and emotionally disturbed children. *Journal of Psychological Studies* **13**, 157–64.

Plomin, R. 1983. Developmental behavioral genetics. *Child Development* **54**, 253–9.

Porteus, S. D. 1931. *The psychology of a primitive people: a study of the Australian aborigine*. New York and London: Longmans Green/Edward Arnold.

Poznanski, E. O. 1973. Children with excessive fears. *American Journal of Orthopsychiatry* **43**, 428–38.

Rachman, S. 1974. *The meanings of fear*. Harmondsworth: Penguin Educational.

Ragozin, Z. [1886] 1891. *The story of Chaldea; from the earliest times to the rise of Assyria*. New York: G. P. Putnam's.

Rasmussen, K. 1931. *The Netsilik Eskimo: social life and spiritual culture*. Copenhagen: Glyndendalske.

Ray, D. J. 1977. *Eskimo art: tradition and innovation in North Alaska*. Seattle, Washington: University of Washington Press.

Robbins, P. R. & R. Houshi 1983. Some observations on recurrent dreams. *Bulletin of the Menninger Clinic* **47**, 262–5.

Robertoux, P. 1981. L'analyse génétique des dépressions. *L'Encephale* **7**, 535–42.

Rohner, R. 1975. *They love me, they love me not: a worldwide study of the effects of parental acceptance and rejection*. New Haven, Connecticut: HRAF Press.

Rorty, A. O. (ed.) 1980. *Explaining emotions*. Berkeley, California: University of California Press.

Rosenblum, L. 1978. Affective maturation and the mother–infant relationship. In *The development of affect*, M. Lewis & L. A. Rosenblum (eds), 275–92. New York and London: Plenum Press.

Rudolph, K. 1985. The foundations of the history of religions and its future tasks. In *The history of religions: retrospect and prospect*, J. M. Kitagawa (ed.), 105–120. New York: Macmillan.

Russell, P. A. 1979. Fear-evoking stimuli. In *Fear in animals and man*, W. Sluckin (ed.), 86–124. New York: Van Nostrand Reinhold.

Scarr, S. & K. McCartney 1983. How people make their own environments. *Child Development* **54**, 424–35.

Snowdon, C. T., C. H. Brown & M. R. Petersen (eds) 1983. *Primate communication*. New York: Cambridge University Press.

Sorce, J. F., R. N. Emde, J. Campos & M. D. Klinnert 1985. Maternal emotional signaling: its effect on visual cliff behavior of 1-year-olds. *Developmental Psychology* **21**, 195–200.

Spiro, M. E. 1966. Religion: problems of definition and explanation. In *Anthropological approaches to the study of religion*, M. Banton (ed.), 85–126. New York: Frederick A. Praeger.

Spiro, M. & R. C. D'Andrade 1967. A cross-cultural study of some supernatural beliefs. In *Cross-cultural approaches*, C. S. Ford (ed.), 196–206. New Haven, Connecticut: HRAF Press.

Stephenson, P. H. 1979. A note on the dialectical evolution of human communications systems. *Journal of Human Evolution* **8**, 581–3.

Steptoe, A. 1983. Stress, helpfulness and control. The implications of laboratory studies. *Journal of Psychosomatic Research* **27**, 361–7.

Struhsaker, T. T. 1967. Auditory communication in vervet monkeys (*Cercopithecus aethiops*). In *Social communication among primates*, S. A. Altmann (ed.), 281–324. Chicago, Illinois: University of Chicago Press.

Tokarev, S. A. 1979. On religion as a social phenomenon (thoughts of an ethnographer). *Soviet Anthropology and Archaeology* **18**, 3–36.

Toynbee, A. 1956. *An historian's approach to religion*. London: Oxford University Press.

Tylor, E. B. 1871. *Primitive culture*, 2 vols. London: John Murray.

van Baal, J. 1971. *Symbols for communication*. Assen: van Gorcum.

Van de Castle, R. 1969. In *Dream psychology and the new biology of dreaming*. Springfield, Illinois: Charles C. Thomas.

van Lawick-Goodall, J. 1967. Mother-offspring relationships in chimpanzees. In *Primate ethology*, D. Morris (ed.), 287–346. London: Weidenfeld & Nicolson.

Vaughn, C. S. 1964. Behavioral evidence of dreaming in rhesus monkeys. *Physiologist* **7**, 275–82.

Vinnicombe, P. 1976. *People of the eland: rock paintings of the Drakensberg Bushmen*. Pietersmaritzburg: University of Natal Press.

Washburn, S. L. 1980. Human behavior and the behavior of other animals. In *Sociobiology examined*, A. Montagu (ed.), 254–82. New York: Oxford University Press.

Weiner, H. 1982. Psychobiology of essential hypertension. In *The biology of anxiety*, R. J. Mathew (ed.), 204–32. New York: Brunner/Mazel.

Wendt, W. E. 1974. 'Art mobilier' aus der Apollo 11–Grote in Südwest Afrika. Die ältesten datierten Kunstwerke Afrikas. *Acta Praehistorica et Archaeologica* **5**, 1–42.

Wibert, J. & K. Simoneau 1984. *Folk literature of the Gê Indians*, 2 vols. Los Angeles, California: UCLA Latin American Center Publications.

Woodhouse, H. C. 1984. On the social context of southern African rock art. *Current Anthropology* **25**, 244–8.

Woody, C. D. 1982. *Memory, learning, and higher function*. New York: Springer-Verlag.

Zeldine, G. 1977. Pensée mythique et maladie mentale: remarque ontologique. *Evolution Psychiatrique* **42**, 1143–66.

Zlotowicz, M. 1974. *Les peurs enfantines*. Paris: Presses Universitaires de France.

Zuckerman, M. & C. D. Spielberger (eds) 1976. *Emotion and anxiety. New concepts, methods and applications*. Hillsdale, New Jersey: Lawrence Erlbaum.

Further reading since original publication

Chapter 2

Clark, S. R. L. 1989. *Civil peace and sacred order*. Oxford: Clarendon.
Clark, S. R. L. 1990. *A parliament of souls*. Oxford: Clarendon.
Clark, S. R. L. 1991. *God's world and the Great Awakening*. Oxford: Clarendon.
Rodd, R. 1990. *Biology, ethics and animals*. Oxford: Clarendon.

Chapter 3

Davis, H. & D. Balfour 1992. *The inevitable bond: examining scientist–animal interactions*. Cambridge: Cambridge University Press.

Chapter 4

Horigan, S. 1988. *Nature and culture in Western discourses*. London: Routledge.
Manning, A. & J. Sherpell (eds) 1994. *Animals and human society: changing perspectives*. London: Routledge.
Noske, B. 1989. *Humans and other animals: beyond the boundaries of anthropology*. London: Pluto Press.

Chapter 5

Atran, S. 1990 *Cognitive foundations of natural history*. Cambridge: Cambridge University Press.
Berlin, B. 1992. *Ethnobiological classification*. Princeton: Princeton University Press.
Sebeok, T. A. 1991. *Semiotics in the United States*. Bloomington: Indiana University Press.
Sebeok, T. A. & J. Umiker-Sebeok 1992. *Biosemiotics (The Semiotic Web, 1991)*. Berlin: Mouton de Gruyter.

Chapter 6

Kendrick, K. 1990. Through a sheep's eye. *New Scientist* (12 May), 62–5.

Chapter 7

Carrithers, M. 1990. Why humans have cultures. *Man (New Series)* **25**, 189–206.
Ingold, T. 1989. The social and environmental relations of human beings and other animals. In *Comparative socioecology: the behavioural ecology of humans and other mammals*, V. Standen & R. A. Foley (eds), 495–512. Oxford: Blackwell Scientific.
Ingold, T. 1991. Becoming persons: consciousness and sociality in human evolution. *Cultural Dynamics* **4**, 355–78.
Ingold, T. 1994. Humanity and animality. In *Companion encyclopaedia of anthropology: humanity, culture and social life*, T. Ingold (ed.), 14–32. London: Routledge.

Chapter 8

Goodwin, B. C., A. Sibatini & G. C. Webster (eds) 1989. *Dynamic structures in biology*. Edinburgh: Edinburgh University Press.
Goodwin, B. C. & P. T. Saunders (eds) 1992. *Theoretical biology: epigenetic and evolutionary order from complex systems*. Baltimore: Johns Hopkins University Press.
Ingold, T. 1990. An anthropologist looks at biology. *Man (New Series)* **25**, 208–29.

Chapter 9

Ingold, T. 1992. Culture and the perception of the environment. In *Bush base, forest farm: culture, environment and development*, E. Croll & D. Parkin (eds), 39–56. London: Routledge.

Reed, E. S. 1991. Cognition as the co-operative appropriation of affordances. *Ecological Psychology* **3**, 135–58.

Reed, E. S. 1993. The intention to use a specific affordance: a framework for psychology. In *Development in context: acting and thinking in specific environments*, R. Wozniak & K. Fischer (eds). Hillsdale, New Jersey: Lawrence Erlbaum.

Chapter 10

Gibson, K. R. & T. Ingold (eds) 1993. *Tools, language and cognition in human evolution*. Cambridge: Cambridge University Press.

Klein, R. G. 1989. *The human career: human biological and cultural origins*. Chicago: University of Chicago Press.

Mellars, P. & C. Stringer (eds) 1989. *The human revolution: behavioural and biological perspectives in the origins of modern humans*. Edinburgh: Edinburgh University Press.

Chapter 11

Hinde, R. A. 1991. A biologist looks at anthropology. *Man (New Series)* **26**, 583–608.

Marks, I. 1987. *Fears, phobias and rituals*. Oxford: Oxford University Press.

Rozin, P. & C. Nemeroff 1990. The laws of sympathetic magic: a psychological analysis of similarity and contagion. In *Cultural psychology: essays on comparative human development*, J. W. Stigler, R. A. Shweder & G. Herdt (eds), 205–32. Cambridge: Cambridge University Press.

Willis, R. 1994. The meaning of the snake. In *Signifying animals*, R. Willis (ed.), 246–52. London: Routledge.

General

See the new journal *Society and Animals: social scientific studies of the human experience of other animals*, edited by Kenneth J. Shapiro. Two issues per year, starting with volume 1, 1993. Publisher: The White Horse Press.

Index